A Concise Introduction to Logic

Consulting Editor: VERE CHAPPELL, *University of Massachusetts*

A Concise
Introduction to Logic

IAN HACKING

Cambridge University

Random House, New York

ISBN: 0–394–31008–X

Library of Congress Catalog Card Number: 73–163199

Manufactured in the United States of America by Kingsport Press, Kingsport, Tenn.

First Edition

98765432

Preface

This book is for a first-semester college course of the sort that is recommended for students in many subjects, perhaps as part of a general education program. It teaches only the minimum that any such course must include. Students and their instructor can choose what else they want to work on. This is a modest core program to which a lot of optional extras can be attached. The core aims at acquiring both practical and theoretical knowledge:

Practical Skills

1. Sharpen usage of logical words like "all" and "if . . . then . . . ."
2. Learn to recognize arguments intended to prove conclusions from premises. Learn to distinguish premises from the conclusions.
3. Some bad arguments have false premises; in others, the conclusion does not follow from the premises. Learn the difference.
4. Learn to see the logical form of some common patterns of argument and to master a standard notation for presenting argument forms, up to the level of the predicate calculus.
5. Learn how to make counterexamples to prove invalidity and some simple tests for validity.
6. Learn to know what follows from what. This does not mean operating any particular formal system of logic, but rather, through practice, knowing which deductive steps are valid, which invalid.

Theoretical Understanding

Perhaps only one thing matters at the beginning: Start understanding what validity is. Understand that it is chiefly a matter of form, not content. Learn how, in a certain sense, the conclusion of a valid argument contains no more data than the premises. (Illustrate this by Venn diagrams.) See that in a valid argument, the conclusion is true in every possibility in which all premises are true. (Teach this with truth tables.) Diagrams and tables are not of very much practical use, but they are simple tools for explaining the very nature of logical consequence. They also serve to introduce one of the fundamental discoveries of modern logic: the distinction between classes of problems for which decision procedures exist, and classes of problems for which there is no decision procedure.

Topics Left Out

This book is the minimum. There is almost no Aristotelian analysis of the syllogism. There is no prolonged treatment of informal fallacies. There is no axiomatic method. No one semester logic course can present all three thoroughly. People disagree about which is more important. Teachers and students can make their own choice on how to supplement the core material of this text book.

Method of Presentation

This is a completely self-contained question and answer workbook. It is not a programmed text in the strict sense of that term, for it has few "branching programs" intended to help slower students or to provide short cuts for quicker ones. Only machines can adequately branch; books are helplessly linear. Attempts to avoid that fact are too cumbersome to succeed. The questions have been worked through by many groups of students. Except for the final chapters, almost all difficult questions have been deleted. The ample repetitions, and the "reinforcement" of the answer section, imitate successful machine programs.

Contents

A Concise Introduction to Logic

1 / Statements and Arguments

One aim of logic is to tell good arguments from bad ones and to discover what makes some arguments good and some arguments bad. First you should learn to recognize arguments. This chapter should help you to do so. All examples in this chapter are taken from a single editorial page of the *Chicago Tribune*, and are therefore "real."

Here are some *statements* made on the editorial page of the *Chicago Tribune*. Each is either true or false. In each case, write "T" in front of those statements you think are true, and "F" in front of those you think are false. Write "T or F" in front of those you are unsure about.

(1) T or F "It does not take many pregnancies to get a large family if twinning or having triplets is an hereditary trait."

(2) T or F "The army chooses for each man the task he can do best."

(3) T or F "Most of the scientists in the anti-ballistic missile opposition, such as Hans Bethe of Cornell, I. I. Rabi of Columbia, and Jerome Wiesner of M.I.T., are noted more for their political agitation than for their contributions to science."

(4) T or F "Proteins may be obtained from cereals, breads, milk, dairy products, fish, and meat stock soups."

(5) T or F "The last first-rate president this country had was Calvin Coolidge."

People may disagree about the truth or falsity of (1) to (5). Some will think that (3) is true, while others will be sure that it is false. At any rate it is either true or false.   This is characteristic of *statements* such as (1) to (5). They are either true or false.   In contrast, look at the question,

How many babies can a woman have?

This is neither true nor false. It may be a good question or a silly one, but it is not either true or false.   A statement is either true or false.   A question is **(6)** NEITHER TRUE NOR FALSE / EITHER TRUE OR FALSE.   From now on, when given a choice in small capital letters, *circle* the correct answer.   You can check in the answer section to see that you were right.

Here is a request, or a piece of advice:

Let the board not spend money to destroy one of the loveliest interiors we have seen and call down upon itself the name of barbarian.

Is this either true or false?   **(7)** YES / NO.   Is it a statement?   **(8)** YES / NO. A statement is **(9)** EITHER TRUE OR FALSE / NEITHER TRUE NOR FALSE.

Although every statement is either true or false, we may not know which. For example,

The United States now has 1,054 land-based missiles but only 54 of these, the liquid fuel titans, have warheads of 5+ megatons.

Hardly anyone knows whether this is true or false, but it certainly is one or the other.   So this is a **(10)** STATEMENT / QUESTION.   It is quite different, for example, from this request:

Please let the library board build elsewhere.

This is **(11)** EITHER TRUE OR FALSE / NEITHER TRUE NOR FALSE.
Write "S" in front of the statements.

(12) __S__ "Rickets is due to a deficiency of vitamin D."

(13) _____ "Look what happened!"

(14) _____ "Are there any substitutes for the meat and green vegetables that my three-year-old child will not eat?"

(15) __S__ "Whatever the court has succeeded in doing, it certainly has assured the result that lower courts will be swamped by a huge new volume of appeals that will materially add to an already encumbering backlog."

(16) _____ "Please, will all concerned citizens make their views known so that we can be guided by the wishes of the people of this city?"

Write "T" in front of the true statements and "F" in front of the false ones.

(17) _T_ There are some statements that, though true or false, we do not know to be true and do not know to be false.

(18) _F_ Some statements are neither true nor false.

(19) _T_ Every statement is either true or false, even if we do not know which it is.

(20) _F_ Every statement is either obviously true or else obviously false.

If we care about a statement, but are uncertain whether it is true or false, we can *argue* about it. We can give *reasons* for thinking that it is true or reasons for thinking that it is false. When people disagree about the truth of a statement, they argue about it. For example, an editorial in the *Chicago Tribune* says,

> The rise of unionism in public employment is a threat to the voter's choice in his own government.

If you do not believe that, you should be able to **(21)** ARGUE / FIGHT against the statement. You should be able to give **(22)** OPINIONS / REASONS for thinking that the statement is false. You should be able to produce some kind of *argument*.

How many occurrences of the letter "e" can you find in the word "argument"? **(23)** _1_. (Quite a few people spell the word with two: "arguement." That is wrong.)

Not all reasons are good ones. On the same page of the *Tribune*, H. L. Hunt recalls his statement that "he would starve if he earned less than a million dollars a week." Here is what he actually calls a "reason" for his statement:

A. Our family spends 13 times that sum—$13 million—in keeping our food, oil, ranching, real estate, and other activities as going concerns.

Do you think Mr. Hunt has given a good reason for his statement? **(24)** YES / NO. Mr. Hunt's statement that

B. He would starve if he earned less than a million dollars a week

is a certain *conclusion* that he has reached. According to him, statement A is a **(25)** REASON / BELIEF for his conclusion B. We call A the *premise* of his argument, and B the **(26)** _Conclusion_

We can divide an argument into two parts. There is the part that states the

conclusion and the part that gives the reasons. Statements giving reasons
are called **(27)** PREMISES / CONCLUSIONS. The **(28)** *PREMISES* give
reasons for the **(29)** *CONCLUSION*

Can you easily tell the conclusion of the argument from the premises?
Here are some examples to test your skill.

> Somebody has recently supported a proposed high dam for Oakley at
> Decatur as the cheapest of several alternative sources of water supply.
> A reader retorts, "The Harze engineering company of Chicago has
> studied the project and offered five alternatives which would offer the
> same benefits and cost less than the high dam. So the Oakley reservoir
> is not the best choice."

(30) Underline this reader's conclusion. The conclusion is preceded by the
little word **(31)** SO / OF / INTO / FOR. Notice that the word "so" is not
actually part of the conclusion. The conclusion is, "the Oakley reservoir is
not the best choice."   The word "so" indicates the conclusion is coming, but
is not part of the conclusion.   Here is another example.

> The longer this controversy lasts, the longer Decatur is deprived of an
> insured water supply for the future.   We can find an alternative to the
> high dam which will cost us less, satisfy our water needs, and incidentally
> preserve Allerton Park.   So we should hurry to accept the alternative.

(32)   Underline the conclusion.
(33)   Are the two other statements both premises? YES / NO.
(34)   What word precedes the conclusion? *So*   .

Another word that often points at a conclusion is "therefore."

> Recently the Blackstone Rangers gang was expelled from the Black
> Alliance, a south side community group.   The action came after the
> Black Alliance received word that property owners were being pressured
> by the gang into paying for sandblasting of buildings defaced by vandals.
> Therefore, many black citizens show that they are fed up with the
> militant groups that terrorize their community.

(35)   Underline the conclusion.
(36)   The word *THEREFORE* indicates the conclusion.
(37)   Is the word "therefore" actually part of the conclusion? YES / NO.

In the preceding examples, the conclusion came **(38)** BEFORE / AFTER the
premises. The conclusion came at the **(39)** BEGINNING / END of the argument. Some arguments are arranged in the reverse manner. Here is an
example.

The last first-rate president the country had was Calvin Coolidge, for during the five and a half years of his administration there was no subversive build-up whatever, no disastrous panic, and he reduced the small national debt of 23 million dollars by 23%.

Notice that the conclusion comes at the beginning, and it is followed by reasons for this statement. **(40)** Underline the conclusion. The word **(41)** THEREFORE / SINCE / BECAUSE / FOR stands in front of the premise of this argument. Just as words like "so" and "therefore" indicate the conclusion, so words like "for" can point to the premises.

"Because" can also be used to indicate premises:

The Russians would not have to score direct hits or even near misses to disable the electronic communications, launching, and guidance systems of our land-based missiles, because they now have 200 new SS-9 super missiles capable of carrying a 25-megaton warhead with a tremendous earth-shaking effect.

(42) Underline the conclusion. The premises are preceded by the word **(43)** _BECAUSE_. The conclusion comes at the beginning.

Since nicotinic acid dilates blood vessels and lowers the content of chloresterol, while the nicotine in tobacco does not, there is a difference between the two substances.

Here the word **(44)** FOR / BECAUSE / SINCE / THEREFORE precedes the premises. **(45)** Underline the conclusion. It comes at the **(46)** BEGINNING / END of the argument.

Some words point to the conclusion. Others indicate the premises. Write "P" in front of the premise-indicating words, and "C" in front of the conclusion-indicating words.

(47) _C_ Therefore.   (48) _P_ For.

(49) _P_ Because.   (50) _P_ Since.

(51) _C_ Thus.   (52) _C_ So.

Premises and conclusions are not always indicated in such a simplistic way. Sometimes a less common device is used, as in this example.

I can tell you that the British stand at Dunkirk was magnificent. While the evacuation was going on, my German corps was held off by a battalion of British guards. They fought us to the death with rifles against tanks. Likewise the Americans were magnificent in the South

Pacific where they were routed soon after the war started. The point I am trying to make is that the valor of troops is in no way connected with what historians call a debacle.

Here, "the point I am trying to make" is a long phrase used to indicate the **(53)** CONCLUSION / PREMISES. **(54)** Underline the conclusion.

Not every sequence of controversial statements is an argument. For example:

The balance of terror may be the salvation of the world—if we maintain the balance. We shall either do that and survive as free Americans, or, deluded by little minds unworthy of our heritage, meanly perish as a nation of sheep.

In this editorial the *Chicago Tribune* is making a controversial **(55)** STATEMENT / ARGUMENT. But it does not here offer any reasons for the statement. So there is no argument here.

Here are some more examples. Some are arguments, some are not. In each case, you are asked if the quotation constitutes an argument. When you answer "yes," underline the conclusion of the argument. Not all these examples are clear-cut. One defect of many debates is that it is hard to tell just when someone is presenting an argument and when he is merely saying what he thinks.

One might suppose that all of this could be entirely clear to any reader of the Supreme Court's opinion. But ten years of experience on the Court have taught me that the most carefully written opinions are not always the most carefully read, not even by those most directly concerned.

Is this an argument? **(56)** YES / NO.
(57) If you think the following example is an argument, underline its conclusion:

The pay of public employees these days usually reflects what the traffic will bear and what the pressure tactics of organized public employees can win from public bodies. Thus the pay frequently has nothing to do with the "merit" of the employee or his work.

Is this an argument? **(58)** YES / NO.
(59) Underline the conclusion, if there is one:

The bottomlands are not valuable, because they are flooded for brief periods during the year.

Is this an argument? **(60)** YES / NO.
(61) Underline the conclusion, if there is one:

Those of us who have visited Allerton Park realize that the bottomland forest forms an important backdrop to the statuary of the park; under the present plan, much of this forest would be replaced, not by water, but by unsightly mud flats. So it is important to keep the bottomlands as they are, and not to flood them.

Is this an argument? **(62)** YES / NO.
(63) Underline the conclusion, if there is one:

In view of the ominous implications of Secretary of Defence Melvin Laird's testimony about the Russian first-strike thermonuclear threat, the continued opposition by Senate doves and some academic scientists to the deployment of a severely limited antimissile system is incomprehensible.

Is this an argument? **(64)** YES / NO.
(65) Underline the conclusion, if there is one:

The Supreme Court in this case entered a triple barreled ruling; it held that a property owner can object to illegally overheard conversations on his premises whether or not he was present or took part in them. It held further that a defendant may examine all material obtained by illegal surveillance without preliminary screening of the material by a judge, even in cases of national security. It also held that products of illegal electronic surveillance, inadmissible against one defendant as violating his Fourth Amendment rights, may be admissible elsewhere.

Is this an argument? **(66)** YES / NO.
(67) Underline the conclusion, if there is one:

The decision must be modified to exclude foreign intelligence surveillance, for if it is not modified, the justice department might simply stop telling the courts that the transcripts of such eavesdropping even exist.

Is this an argument? **(68)** YES / NO.
(69) Underline the conclusion, if there is one:

There seems to be no limit to how many children a woman can bring forth by single births. One had 22 children in 26 years. Another woman, who married at 16, had 39 by one husband, whom she survived. Of these, 32 daughters and 7 sons, all attained adulthood. A record of some sort might be held by the Scotswoman who bore 62 children by one husband.

Is this an argument? **(70)** YES / NO.   The last example is presumably an
argument.   Those slightly incredible statistics are presumably intended to be
reasons for the conclusion, which appears at the **(71)** BEGINNING / END.
But there is a big difference between being an argument and being a good
argument.   The statistics certainly do not suffice to prove the conclusion.
Even if some woman had 62 children, there still does seem to be some limit
(say 1,000) to how many children a woman can bring forth by single births.
The last example must be an argument, but it is a very bad one. One aim of
logic is to sort out good arguments from bad ones.

2 / Criticizing Arguments

Even when you can recognize arguments it may not be easy to tell good arguments from bad ones. This chapter distinguishes two fundamentally different ways of criticizing arguments.

If someone were to say,

Please give me back my pen.

he **(1)** WOULD / WOULD NOT be making a statement. He would be **(2)** MAKING A REQUEST / GIVING AN ORDER. If he said,

Give me back my pen!

he would be **(3)** MAKING A REQUEST / GIVING AN ORDER. If someone said "Ouch!" after being hit, he would be making an exclamation or crying out in pain, but he **(4)** WOULD / WOULD NOT be making a statement. If, on the other hand, he said:

My pen fell out of my pocket and is now on the road.

he would be making a **(5)** STATEMENT / ARGUMENT / REQUEST. Statements can be either true or **(6)** _FALSE_. Questions, requests, exclamations, orders, and the like cannot be true or false, so they **(7)** ARE / ARE NOT statements.

If someone said to you as you were walking down the street,

There are a lot of policemen on the corner.

he would be making a **(8)** _STATEMENT_ His statement could be criticized on a good many grounds: It might have interrupted your train of thought and annoyed you. It might be a very boring remark, since there are always so many policemen on that corner. It might have warned someone about the police, whom you did not want to be warned. And so on. There are lots of ways to criticize the statement. But one kind of criticism is especially important. Your friend may be mistaken: Those are not policemen, but actors from the guerrilla theatre. Your friend may be lying: He wants to make you nervous, or hostile, or secure, or angry, or happy, depending on your attitude to policemen. But in reality there are no policemen there. In either case, your friend is saying something _false_. So, _one important way of criticizing a statement is to say that it is false_.

How can arguments be criticized? They can be annoying, boring, irrelevant, fatuous, and so on. But there is a fundamental way to criticize arguments. A fundamental criticism of a statement is to say that it is false. This is because a chief point of making statements is to tell something true. What is a chief point of making arguments? One main point is to convince someone, maybe yourself, that something is true. So an unconvincing argument is subject to criticism. For example, imagine that someone says:

> This child must be seen by a doctor at once.

You ask him, "why?" He replies:

> Because the child has a fever, and a temperature of 104° F, and any child with a temperature that high should be seen by a doctor immediately.

His reply is clearly a **(9)** REASON / OPINION for his first statement. He is offering an argument in which his first statement is the **(10)** CONCLUSION / PREMISE and his reply is the **(11)** CONCLUSION / PREMISE. We could schematize the argument as:

A. Any child with a fever of over 104° F should be seen by a doctor at once.
B. This child has a fever of over 104° F.
C. So, this child should be seen by a doctor at once.

Which are the premises? **(12)** A / B / C. Which is the conclusion? **(13)** A / B / C. The argument A, B, so C looks pretty convincing. Yet you might not be convinced that conclusion C is true, for you might doubt the truth of the premises. You retort:

> Oh, you're quite wrong. This kid just has a mild cold, and anyway, our thermometer is quite inaccurate. Look, according to this thermometer, even my temperature is supposed to be 103°!

With a remark like this, you are suggesting that premise **(14)** A / B̲ is false. If you really think that premise B is false, you are not likely to run for a doctor. You have not been convinced by the argument. One way an argument may fail to be convincing is that the premises do not all seem to be true. *One way to criticize an argument intended to prove some conclusion is to say that one or more of the premises is false.*

Take for example this rather trifling argument.

A. _____ Anyone who ever got to be President of the United States had rich parents.

B. _____ Lincoln was an American president.

C. _____ So, Lincoln had rich parents.

(15)   Which is the conclusion of this argument?   A / B / C̲.
(16)   Write "T" in front of the true statements, and "F" in front of the false ones.
(17)   Are any of the premises false?   YES̲ / NO.

Because the first premise is false, this argument can be criticized on the grounds that **(18)**, ALL THE PREMISES ARE FALSE / AT LEAST ONE OF THE PREMISES IS FALSE. Here is another argument of the same form:

A. _____ Anyone who ever got to be President of the United States had rich parents.

D. _____ J. F. Kennedy was an American president.

E. _____ So, J. F. Kennedy had rich parents.

(19)   Once again, write "T" in front of the true statements and "F" in front of the false ones.
(20)   Which premise is false?   A̲ / D.

This argument can be criticized on the grounds that **(21)** _Premise A is false_
Notice that in the first argument, the conclusion, Lincoln had rich parents, is **(22)** T / F̲ whereas in the second argument, the conclusion, J. F. Kennedy had rich parents, is **(23)** T̲ / F. So in the first argument, the conclusion is false, and in the second argument, the conclusion is true. Yet the two arguments are equally bad. Both begin with a premise that everybody knows is false.

Although both arguments are equally bad, the argument about **(24)** LINCOLN / KENNEDY has a true conclusion. So *bad arguments can have true conclusions.*

Some people are surprised at this. They wonder how the argument can be bad if the conclusion is true. An argument with a true conclusion is a good argument! But imagine someone who knows past American history, but is ignorant of recent events. He knows nothing about the Kennedy family fortunes. He wants to know whether J. F. K. had rich parents. He is not going to be convinced by someone who argues, "Well, all American presidents had rich parents, and, since J. F. K. was an American president, he too had rich parents." For he will protest that some presidents had poor parents, for example, Lincoln. He will say your argument is completely unconvincing, because one of the premises is false. It is a bad argument, even though the conclusion is true.

To reinforce this point, take an example you may be unfamiliar with. Julius Nyerere is the president of the East African country Tanzania. Someone tells you that Nyerere translated Shakespeare's play *Julius Caesar* into Swahili, the national language of Tanzania. You doubt whether this is true. So he argues,

A. Every person who speaks Swahili has translated *Julius Caesar* into Swahili.
B. President Julius Nyerere speaks Swahili.
C. So, Nyerere has translated *Julius Caesar* into Swahili.

Probably you do not know whether the conclusion is true or not. But the argument is unlikely to convince you. For the first premise is almost certainly **(25)** TRUE / FALSE. So the argument is **(26)** CONVINCING / UN-CONVINCING. It is a bad argument. Yet (as a matter of fact) the conclusion, C, is true.

Circle the correct answers, and fill in the blanks with either "T" or "F."

(27) The premises of an argument are ARGUMENTS / STATEMENTS.
(28) Statements are either ___TRUE___ or ___FALSE___.
(29) Hence, premises are either ___TRUE___ or ___FALSE___.
(30) One way to criticize an argument is to say that one or more of the premises is ___FALSE___.
(31) If an argument is unconvincing, the conclusion may be false. But the conclusion could even be ___TRUE___.
(32) An argument in which one of the premises looks ___FALSE___ will probably be unconvincing.
(33) To call one of the premises false, when the argument is intended to prove the conclusion, is one way of CRITICIZING / PRAISING an argument.

There are other ways of criticizing an argument. Suppose you heard this argument:

A. _T_ Some American presidents had very rich parents.

B. _T_ Richard Nixon is an American President.

C. _F_ So, Richard Nixon had very rich parents.

(34) Write "T" in front of the true statements, and "F" in front of the false ones. Are there any false premises? **(35)** YES / NO. Since none of the premises is false, we **(36)** CAN / CANNOT criticize the above argument on the ground that it has a false premise. All the same, the argument is most **(37)** CONVINCING / UNCONVINCING. It is not convincing because even though *some* U.S. presidents had rich parents, it does not follow that any particular president had rich parents. The premises of this argument are all **(38)** TRUE / FALSE, yet the conclusion **(39)** DOES / DOES NOT follow from the premises.

The last argument was unconvincing. It also had a false conclusion. Here is an example of an argument of the same form that is just as unconvincing and that has a true conclusion.

> Some people who speak Swahili have translated plays of Shakespeare into Swahili.
> President Nyerere speaks Swahili.
> So, President Nyerere has translated plays of Shakespeare into Swahili.

If you did not know that the conclusion is true, this argument **(40)** WOULD / WOULD NOT convince you of the conclusion. It would not convince you even if you accepted the premises. For the conclusion does not follow from the premises. Even if the premises are true, we **(41)** CAN / CANNOT be sure the conclusion is true, unless we know something more than the premises tell us.

Our examples suggest two different ways of criticizing an argument.

(42) An argument might be criticized if one of its premises is TRUE / FALSE.

(43) It could also be criticized on the ground that the conclusion does not FOLLOW FROM / IMPLY the premises.

(44) If an argument has at least one FALSE / TRUE premise, it may fail to be convincing.

(45) If the conclusion DOES / DOES NOT follow from the premises, it may fail to be convincing.

Here are two examples of simple though rather silly arguments.

A. Some cities whose names begin with a "C" are in Illinois.
   Chicago has a name that begins with a "C."
   So, Chicago is in Illinois.

B. All cities whose names begin with a "C" are in Illinois.
   Chicago has a name that begins with a "C."
   So, Chicago is in Illinois.

(46) Which argument can be criticized on the ground that the conclusion does not follow from the premises? **(46)** A / B.

(47) Which argument can be criticized on the ground that not all the premises are true? **(47)** A / B.

Naturally an argument could be defective in both ways. Here is an extreme example:

> Some cities whose names begin with "U" are in Illinois.
> Chicago is a city whose name begins with "U."
> So, Chicago is in Illinois.

(48) Two grounds for criticizing this ludicrous argument are:_____
A FALSE PREMISE
AND THE CONCLUSION DOESN'T FOLLOW

Note that despite the fact that the last three examples have all been **(49)** GOOD / BAD arguments, the conclusion of each of the three arguments is **(50)** TRUE / FALSE.

Although bad arguments may have false conclusions, it is also possible for a bad argument to have a **(51)** TRUE / FALSE conclusion.

> Some kinds of fruit are rich in vitamins.
> Bananas are a kind of fruit.
> So, bananas are rich in vitamins.

(52) Are all the premises true? YES / NO.
(53) Does the conclusion follow from the premises? YES / NO.
(54) Is this a convincing argument? YES / NO.

The conclusion is false.

> Every metropolis in America requires more capital to be invested in its
>   urban core.
> Chicago is an American metropolis.
> Therefore Chicago requires more capital to be invested in its urban core.

(55) Are the premises both true? YES / NO.
(56) Does the conclusion follow from the premises? YES / NO.
(57) Is the argument convincing? YES / NO.

> Lenin was a communist.
> Some communists were convicted thieves.
> Hence, Lenin was a convicted thief.

(58) Are the premises both true? YES / NO.
(59) Does the conclusion follow from the premises? YES / NO.
(60) Is the argument convincing? YES / NO.

> Louisiana is a good place for growing cotton, since Louisiana is part of
> the United States, and every part of the United States is good for
> growing cotton.

(61)   The conclusion comes at the BEGINNING / END of this argument.

(62)   Is the conclusion true?   YES / NO.

(63)   Are the premises all true?   YES / NO.

(64)   Is this argument convincing?   YES / NO.

Here are four arguments.   You may not even understand all the words used in them. Yet you should be able to tell when the conclusion follows from the premises.

✳A. __T__ All Ismailis are Muslims.
   __T__ The Aga Khan is Ismaili.
   __T__ So, the Aga Khan is a Muslim.

B. __T__ Some Ismailis are Muslims.
   __T__ The Aga Khan is Ismaili.
   __T__ So, the Aga Khan is a Muslim.

C. __F__ Some Ismailis are Christians.
   __T__ The Aga Khan is Ismaili.
   __F__ So, the Aga Khan is a Christian.

✳D. __F__ All Ismailis are Christian.
   __T__ The Aga Khan is Ismaili.
   __F__ So, the Aga Khan is a Christian.

(65) Circle the arguments in which the conclusion follows from the premises. Even if you have no idea what an Ismaili is, you should have been able to tell which of these arguments are ones with a conclusion that follows from the premises. This shows that whether the conclusion follows from the premises is not completely dependent on what the arguments are about. For you may not know quite what these arguments are about and yet know whether the conclusion follows from the premises.   *Whatever* an Ismaili is, even if the Aga Khan is Ismaili, and *some* Ismailis are Muslims, it does not follow that the Aga Khan is a Muslim.   Some Ismailis are Muslims, but, perhaps, not this particular one—the Aga Khan.

Now for some facts about religion.

The Ismailis are a sect of Muslims (just as Baptists and Roman Catholics are often described as sects of Christians).

The Aga Khan is the spiritual head of the Ismaili sect.

No Muslims, no Ismailis are Christian; the Aga Khan is not a Christian.

(66) In the light of these facts, write "T" in the parentheses in front of the true statements in arguments A to D, and write "F" in front of the false statements. The "some" statements might give you a little trouble.   All Ismailis are Muslim.   Well, is it true that some Ismailis are Muslim?   (67)

<u>YES</u> / NO. If you answered "yes," you can probably ignore the following paragraph and skip questions 68 to 72.   But if you answered "no," read the following paragraph first.

In logic, especially the logic of deductive argument, we try to be concerned with the literal truth of what is said.   We are very pedantic.   Now suppose we know nothing about the Muslim faith, and someone tells us that some Ismailis are Muslim.   We might jump to the conclusion that some Ismailis are not Muslim.   For if all Ismailis are Muslim, surely we would be told that all are Muslim, not just that some are.   If you think like this, then, since "All Ismailis are Muslim" is true, then "Some Ismailis are Muslim" must be false.   *However*, imagine further that on a trip to say East Africa (where there are a good many Ismailis) we met some Ismailis and asked them if they were Muslims.   "Of course," they reply.   Being cautious reporters, we cannot at once conclude that all Ismailis are Muslims.   We can say only, "We know for certain that some Ismailis are Muslims; we do not yet know for certain if all Ismailis are Muslim."   What we are saying is true.   It is true both that some Ismailis are Muslim, and also that (unknown to us) all Ismailis are Muslim.   In this situation, it is true that all Ismailis are Muslim. It is also **(68)** TRUE / FALSE that some Ismailis are Muslim.   Saying that some Ismailis are Muslim **(69)** DOES / DOES NOT imply that some Ismailis are not Muslim.   If we take the statement, "some Ismailis are Muslim" quite literally, it is simply **(70)** TRUE / FALSE.   Of course, there are situations where saying "Some Ismailis are Muslims" might suggest to your hearers that you are going to add, "and some Ismailis are not Muslims."   But what you suggest is not what you literally say.   All Ismailis are Muslims, because the Ismailis are a sect of Muslims.   Hence, it is **(71)** TRUE / FALSE that some Ismailis are Muslims.   For example, the first premise of argument B above is **(72)** TRUE / FALSE.

Now, if you didn't answer question 66, determine whether each statement in arguments A to D is true or false, and write "T" next to those that are true and "F" next to those that are false.

(73)   Which of the arguments can be criticized on the grounds that not all the premises are true?   A / B / C / D.

(74)   Which can be criticized on the grounds that the conclusion does not follow from the premises?   A / B / C / D.

(75)   Which of the arguments has a true conclusion?   A / B / C / D.

(76)   Which is the only argument with true premises and a conclusion that follows from the premises?   A / B / C / D.

Notice that although **(77)** ONE / TWO argument(s) in the list has (have) a true conclusion, only **(78)** ONE / TWO argument(s) has (have) all premises true and a conclusion that follows from the premises.   This reminds us that bad arguments **(79)** CAN / CANNOT have true conclusions.

In order to tell which of arguments A to D had conclusions that followed from the premises, you **(80)** DID / DID NOT need to know exactly what Ismailis are. Simply by looking at the form of arguments B and C, you could see that something was wrong. But to tell if the premises are true, you **(81)** DID / DID NOT need to know something about the Aga Khan and the Ismailis.

In order to tell when the premises are true, you **(82)** NEED / DON'T NEED information about religion. But in order to know if the conclusion follows from the premises, you **(83)** NEED / DON'T NEED information about religion.

Logic is concerned with what follows from what. Logic **(84)** IS / IS NOT concerned with details of the Muslim religion. In order to criticize C and D on the grounds that the first premise is false, we **(85)** DO / DO NOT need to know about religion. In order to criticize C and B on the grounds that the conclusion does not follow from the premises, we **(86)** DO / DO NOT need to know anything about religion. The first kind of criticism is a matter for religion. The second kind of criticism is a matter for **(87)** RELIGION / LOGIC.

In logic, an argument in which the conclusion follows from the premises is called *valid*. If an argument is valid, then the conclusion **(88)** _Follows_ from the premises. There are at least two ways of criticizing an argument. We may say that at least one of the premises is **(89)** _False_. This kind of criticism **(90)** IS / ISN'T a matter for logic. Or we may say that the conclusion does not follow from the **(91)** _Premises_. In logic, we say that an argument where the conclusion does not follow from the premises is not **(92)** _valid_. For short, we say that the argument is *invalid*. Whether an argument is valid **(93)** IS / ISN'T a matter for logic.

Here are a couple of examples:

> Venus rotates around the sun, for Venus is a planet in the solar system, and every planet in the solar system rotates around the sun.

In this example, the conclusion comes at the **(94)** BEGINNING / END of the argument. The conclusion is **(95)** T / F. Each of the premises is **(96)** T / F. Moreover, the conclusion **(97)** DOES / DOES NOT follow from the premises. In order to know that the premises are true, we need to know something about **(98)** RELIGION / ASTRONOMY. But in order to know that the conclusion follows from the premises, we **(99)** DO / DO NOT need to know any astronomy.

> Columbia University experienced student rebellions in the period 1967–1970, for every major American university experienced student rebellions in that period, and Columbia is a major American university.

Once again, the conclusion comes at the **(100)** BEGINNING / END of this argument. It is **(101)** T / F. However, one of the premises is F. Yet the conclusion follows from the premises. In order to know that not all the premises are true, you **(102)** DO / DO NOT need to know something about recent events in the academic world. But in order to know that the conclusion follows from the premises, you **(103)** COULD / COULD NOT be almost completely ignorant of recent events.   Aristotle knew nothing about Columbia or even the American continent, but so long as he was assured that the statements in the above argument made sense, he could tell you that the argument is valid. Validity is a matter for **(104)** LOGIC / RELIGION / ASTRONOMY / CURRENT EVENTS.

3 / Logical Form

We have shown that although the truth of the premises of an argument depends on what the argument is about, validity does not depend very much on subject matter. It is the form of the argument that counts. This chapter begins to explain the idea of logical form.

The premises and conclusions of arguments are **(1)** ARGUMENTS / STATEMENTS. Statements may be **(2)** TRUE OR FALSE / VALID OR INVALID. However, we do not call arguments true or false; on the contrary, we call them **(3)** TRUE OR FALSE / VALID OR INVALID. An argument is valid when the conclusion **(4)** IMPLIES / FOLLOWS FROM the premises. In logical parlance, the word "implies" is the converse of "follows from"; that is to say, if the conclusion follows from the premises, we say the premises *imply* the conclusion. Thus in a valid argument, the premises **(5)** IMPLY / FOLLOW FROM the conclusion. If an argument is invalid, the premises do not **(6)** _imply_ the conclusion. If the premises imply the conclusion, then the conclusion **(7)** _Follows From_ the premises.

Another word used here is "infer." If an argument is valid, then we can *infer* the conclusions from the premises. Thus, if the premises imply the conclusion, we can **(8)** _infer_ the conclusion from premises. If we can infer the conclusion from the premises, then the conclusion **(9)** _Follows From_ from the premises.

"Infer," "imply," and "follow from," are different verbs with different usages. Keep them distinct. Sometimes people say, "The premises infer the conclusion." That is an abuse of language. We say instead, "The premises **(10)** _imply_ the conclusion." We also say, "We can **(11)** _infer_ _____ the conclusion from the premises." While we are on this topic of correct usage, remember: The word "argument" is spelled with only one "e."

Here is a simple argument:

> Mars cannot support life as we know it, for that planet has practically
> no free oxygen, and no planet with practically no free oxygen can sup-
> port life as we know it.

The conclusion comes at the **(12)** BEGINNING / END of the argument.
Whether or not the premises are true, the conclusion of this argument does
follow from the premises.   Put an "X" in front of the following statements
that are either factually or grammatically incorrect.

(13) __X__ The conclusion of this argument is, "No planet with practically
no free oxygen can support life as we know it."

(14) __X__ Since the argument is valid, the conclusion implies the premises.

(15) _____ It is a valid argument because the premises imply the conclusion.

(16) __X__ In this argument, the premises infer the conclusion.

(17)_____ The premises imply the conclusion if and only if the conclusion
follows from the premises.

(18) _____ Since the argument is valid, we can infer the conclusion from the
premises.

(19) __X__ The conclusion infers the premises because the premises imply
the conclusion.

(20) __X__ Whether the above argument is valid depends entirely on facts
about the solar system.

(21) _____ In order to know that the above argument is valid, you do not
have to know anything about the solar system—at any rate, no
more than is needed simply to understand the statements that are
made.

So far we have not said what is necessary for an argument to be valid.
Practically everybody who speaks English (or any other language) can recognize that in some cases, premises imply conclusions.   But exactly what do
we recognize?   The basic fact about every valid argument is this: *Whenever
the premises are all true, the conclusion is true also.*   We can even say that if
the premises are all true, the conclusion *must* be true, or, the conclusion
has to be true.

In a valid argument, the truth of the premises guarantees the truth of
the conclusion.   This is why we say that the conclusion follows from the
premises.   This is also why we say that the premises **(22)** IMPLY / INFER the
conclusion.

If an argument is valid, then we can **(23)** INFER / IMPLY the conclusion
from the premises.   This means that if someone assures us the premises are

true, or if we know the premises are true, then we are justified in stating the conclusion. To infer a conclusion from premises is to state the conclusion on the basis of the premises.

There are two basic ways of criticizing an argument. We can say that not all the premises are (24) _TRUE_. We can say that the argument is not (25) _VALIS_. Arguing is a bit like traveling. A really good argument gets you somewhere. Saying that you have an argument that is valid is like saying that you have a plane ticket that is valid. Suppose you want to go from Chicago to San Francisco. If your plane ticket is invalid (it has been used already or expired last week), you are not going to get to San Francisco so easily. Also, if you are not in Chicago, but Newark, N.J., you are in trouble. Having an invalid ticket is like having an invalid argument. Being in the wrong town is like having a false premise. If an argument is valid, then the truth of the (26) PREMISES / CONCLUSION guarantees the truth of the (27) PREMISES / CONCLUSION. (This is like a valid airplane ticket: if you are in the correct city of departure, then the airline guarantees to get you to the destination indicated on the ticket.) One kind of defect is that the argument may be invalid. Another is that one or more of the premises may be (28) TRUE / FALSE. (This is like being in the wrong city. Even if you have a valid ticket from Chicago to San Francisco, the clerk in Newark is not going to be impressed.)

How can premises guarantee the truth of conclusions? Could there not be breakdowns, just as an airline is subject to snowstorms, strikes, and hijacking? The answer is, no. It will take several chapters to see why. Begin by comparing several similar valid arguments:

A. All Ismailis are Muslims.
   The Aga Khan is Ismaili.
   So, the Aga Khan is a Muslim.
B. All planets in the solar system are bodies that rotate around the sun.
   Jupiter is a planet in the solar system.
   So, Jupiter is a body that rotates around the sun.
C. All the metropolises in America are cities that require radical social improvements in their urban core.
   Chicago is an American metropolis.
   So, Chicago is a city that requires radical social improvement in its urban core.

The first argument is about (29) POLITICS / RELIGION / ASTRONOMY. B is about (30) RELIGION / ASTRONOMY / AMERICAN SOCIAL PROBLEMS. C is about (31) ASTRONOMY / AMERICAN SOCIAL PROBLEMS / GEOLOGY. Yet anyone understanding the above arguments, but otherwise knowing practically nothing about the Muslim religion, or astronomy, or America, can see at once that if the premises of the above arguments are true, then the conclusions are true, too. The premises (32) INFER / IMPLY the conclusions. Validity is a matter of **(33)** POLITICS / LOGIC / ASTRONOMY.   To reinforce this idea, consider the following example:

> All kongonis are four-legged animals.
> Sparta is a kongoni.
> So, Sparta is a four-legged animal.

Assuming that "kongoni" is a meaningful term, and that Sparta is the name of a kongoni (whatever that is), do the premises imply the conclusion?   **(34)** YES / NO.   You can **(35)** INFER / IMPLY the conclusion from the premises.

(36)   Do you know what a kongoni is?   YES / NO.
(37)   Do you know whether there is a kongoni called Sparta?   YES / NO.
(38)   Do you know whether the argument about kongonis is valid (assuming that the word "kongoni" does, after all, mean something)?   YES / NO.

A kongoni is a large deerlike animal that lives in the Savannahs of eastern Africa.   Yet whether or not you knew the recondite facts referred to in the last argument, you could see that this argument is just as valid as the arguments about the Aga Khan, Jupiter, and Chicago.

Every argument we have just examined has roughly the same *form*.   That is, each is of the form:

> All so and so's are such and such.
> This individual is a so and so.
> So, this individual is a such and such.

To judge by the last four examples, it looks as if every argument of this form may be valid.   We shall come to see that this is so, and why it is so.   The first thing to fix clearly in your mind is the form of this kind of argument.

Complete the blanks below to get arguments of the same form as those we have been looking at.

D.   All giraffes are long-necked animals.
     Thebes is a giraffe.
     So, Thebes is **(39)** _a lone neck animal_.
E.   All monkeys are **(40)** _mammals_.
     Athens is a monkey.
     So, Athens is a mammal.
F.   All **(41)** _catholic p._ are _unmarries_
     The Pope is a Catholic priest.
     So, the Pope is an unmarried man.
G.   Every philosopher who lived to be over 97 is a logician.
     (42) _Bertrand R._ is a _philosopher who live past 97_
     So, Bertrand Russell is a logician.

These arguments all have the same form. Instead of representing them using words like "so and so," we could just use blanks, as:

All ____,_____ are . . . .
_ _ _ _ _ _ _ _ _ _ is a _____.
So, _ _ _ _ _ _ _ _ _ _ is a . . . .

If you fill in the long blank (____) with "Ismailis" and the dots with "Muslims" and the dashes with "the Aga Khan," you get argument A from page 23. Which of arguments D–G do you get by filling the long blank with "monkeys," the dots with "mammals," and the dashes with "Athens"?
(43) D / _E_ / F / G.

Instead of using blanks, which are pretty cumbersome, we will represent the form of all these arguments using letters. When we look at these arguments, we see names for various individuals. For example, "the Aga Khan," "Jupiter," "Chicago," "Sparta," "the Pope," and so on. Which name of an individual occurs in argument G? **(44)** *BERTRAND RUSSELL*.
We also find various nouns or noun phrases used to name classes to which these individuals may belong; for example, "giraffe," "Muslim," "Catholic priest," "logician," "philosophers who live to be over 97." What are the nouns indicating classes in argument E? **(45)** *MAMMALS, MONKEY* -
Such nouns indicating classes are called *terms*. What are the terms in argument D? **(46)** *ANIMAL GIRAFFE* ____. *Terms* and *names* are different. "Thebes" is a name of an individual. "Giraffe" is not a name of an individual animal, but rather indicates a class of animals. So in answering 46, you should have given "giraffe" and "long-necked animal," but not "Thebes."

(47) In the following argument, *underline* the names, circle the terms.

Every (philosopher) jailed in World War I for (pacifism) was a (logician.)
Bertrand Russell is a (philosopher) jailed in World War I for (pacifism.)
So, Bertrand Russell is a (logician.)

We shall use italic capital letters to stand for terms and italic lower case letters for names. In the following list circle the letters that could stand for names. **(48)** (*a*) G / H / (*d*) F / (*c*) (*b*) P.

The form of the argument we have been examining is represented by the following scheme:

All *F* are *G*.
a is *F*.
So, *a* is *G*.

In argument D, the "*F*" corresponds to "giraffes," the "*G*" to "long-necked

animals," and the "*a*" to "Thebes."   In argument E, the "*F*" corresponds to
(49) _Monkeys_ , the "*G*" to **(50)** _Mammals_, and the "*a*" to
(51) _Athens_. · There is nothing special about these letters.   We use
a different kind of letter for names, but that is because names and terms are
different.   "Philosopher" denotes a class of individuals including Sartre and
Russell and Aristotle and Heidegger.   Name another individual in the class
of philosophers.   **(52)** _—Kant —_.   The name "Bertrand Russell" in
this context denotes a unique person, namely Bertrand Russell.

In the above argument form "All *F* are *G*, *a* is *F*, so *a* is *G*," what is the
result of replacing "*F*" by "farmers," "*G*" by "greedy," and "*a*" by "Adolph"?

(53) _All Farmers are Greedy_ .
Adolph is a Farmer .
Adolph is Greedy .

Here are several similar statements:

All giraffes are long-necked animals.
Every giraffe is a long-necked animal.
All giraffes have long necks.
Every giraffe is long-necked.
Each giraffe has a long neck.

Do these statements all mean about the same thing?   **(54)** YES / NO.   One
difference is, of course, that the first two imply that giraffes are animals; the
remaining statements do not actually say this.   But otherwise there is little
difference in meaning between these different statements.   In studying logical
form, it is convenient to refer to one standard form.   We say that the first
statement above is in *standard form*.   When the letters "*F*" and "*G*" are
meaningfully replaced by terms, the scheme,

All *F* are *G*.

gives a statement in standard form.   Which of the following are in standard
form?   Indicate by writing a check (√) in front of those in standard form.

(55) _____ All philosophers smoke pipes.

(56) _____ Every philosopher is a person who smokes a pipe.

(57) _√_ All philosophers are people who smoke pipes.

(58) _____ All cities frighten me.

(59) _____ All cities are exciting.

(60) _√_ All cities are exciting places.

(61) _√_ All cities are places that frighten me.

Example 59 is not strictly in standard form. Let us insist that the terms in standard form are nouns or noun phrases or noun clauses. The adjective "exciting" **(62)** IS / IS NOT a noun. But "exciting places" is a noun phrase. So we say that 60 is in standard form, but 59 is not.

These examples suggest that a statement not in standard form can often be paraphrased by a statement in standard form. Thus, in 55 we have the verb phrase, "smoke pipes" paraphrased in 57 by "are people who smoke pipes." Here we **(63)** DO / DO NOT get a noun phrase following the copula "are." We can usually do this by choosing some suitably general noun like "people" or "place"; if we are stuck, we can just use the word, "thing." For example, put:

All stars radiate light.

in standard form. We could use:

All stars are things that radiate light.

Now on a separate sheet of paper paraphrase each of the following into standard form:

(64) Every manager of this company is a despicable person.
(65) Sodium salts burn with a yellow flame.
(66) All the consultants are courageous.
(67) Every candidate lies.
(68) Everyone who knows him likes him.
(69) Any action as courageous as that deserves some sort of reward.
(70) Every exercise bores me.

ALL MANAGERS OF THIS company ARE DESPICABLE PEOPLE.

ALL SODIUM SALTS ARE SUBSTANCES THAT BURN WITH A YELLOW FLAME

ALL CONSULTANTS ARE COURAGES PEOPLE

ALL CANDIDATES ARE LIARS.

ALL PEOPLE WHO KNOW HIM ARE ARE PEOPLE WHO LIKE HIM.

ALL ACTIONS AS COURAGEOUS AS THAT ARE ACTIONS THAT DESERVE SOME SORT OF REWARD.

ALL EXERCISES ARE THINGS THAT BORE ME.

4 / Some Forms of Argument

This chapter will increase your familiarity with some simple forms of argument and will teach you one way of showing that an argument form is invalid.

So far we have looked at only one valid form of argument, namely:

All *F* are *G*, *a* is *F*, so *a* is *G*.

Let *F*: farmer; *G*: greedy people; *a*: Adolph. Then, replacing the letters, we get

All farmers are greedy people.
Adolph is a farmer.
So, Adolph is a greedy person.

This is called an *interpretation* of the argument form. Any assignment of terms to capital letters, and names to lower case letters, is an interpretation so long as the result is grammatically correct. Here is another interpretation of the letters: Let *F*: far away hot bodies; *G*: galaxies; *a*: Arcturus. What is the interpretation of this argument form?

(1)   All For Away Hot Bodies Are Galaxies.
      Arcturus is a Far Away Hot Body.
      So, Arcturus is a Galaxy.

Now consider the argument:

All planets of the sun are planets that are at least as big as the earth.

Mars is a planet of the sun.
So, Mars is a planet that is at least as big as the earth.

Is this of the above form?   **(2)** YES / NO.
What is the interpretation?

(3) *F*: _PLANETS OF THE SUN_

(4) *G*: _PLANETS THAT ARE AT LEAST AS..._

(5) *a*: _MARS –_

Now Mars is, in fact, smaller than earth.   Are all the premises of the above argument true?   **(6)** YES / NO.   Is the conclusion true?   **(7)** YES / NO.   Is this an example of an argument with false premises and a false conclusion? **(8)** YES / NO.   Is it an invalid argument?   **(9)** YES / NO.   Although the premises are false, they do **(10)** IMPLY / INFER the conclusion.   In contrast, look at the argument:

Some planets of the sun are at least as big as the earth.
Mars is a planet of the sun.
So, Mars is at least as big as the earth.

Are there any false premises?   **(11)** YES / NO.   Does the conclusion follow from the premises?   **(12)** YES / NO.   The argument is **(13)** VALID / INVALID. This argument **(14)** CAN / CANNOT be criticized on the ground that one or more of the premises is false, but it **(15)** CAN / CANNOT be criticized on the ground that it is invalid.   The argument could be schematized as:

Some *F* are *G*.
a is *F*.
So, *a* is *G*.

The easiest way to see that an argument form is invalid is to invent an argument of that form with true premises and a false conclusion.   An actual argument of that form, obtained by replacing the letters with terms and names, is called an **(16)** EXAMPLE / INTERPRETATION of the argument form.   If in some interpretation the premises are all true, but the conclusion is false, then the argument form is **(17)** VALID / INVALID.   This is because valid arguments are ones that can never lead from true premises to **(18)** TRUE / FALSE conclusions.

An argument form is invalid if and only if there is some interpretation in which the premises are all true and the conclusion is false.

An interpretation of an argument in which the premises are all true and the conclusion is false is called a "counterexample." If we can find a counterexample to an argument form, then the argument form is **(19)** VALID / INVALID.

Notice that not every interpretation of an invalid form has true premises and a false conclusion. Every combination is possible:

A.   One or more false premises, true conclusion.
B.   One or more false premises, false conclusion.
C.   All true premises, true conclusion.
D.   All true premises, false conclusion.

Which of the four combinations provides a counterexample? **(20)** A / B / C / D. We should have before us an example of each of the four combinations in the form:

Some *F* are *G*.
a is *F*.
So, *a* is *G*.

Here is an example for combination A.

A.   One or more false premises, true conclusion.

Let:

F: women
G: men
a: Hugh Hefner (the owner of *Playboy*)

Interpretation:

Some women are men.
Hugh Hefner is a woman.
So, Hugh Hefner is a man.

Now make up your own examples for combinations B and C. Be sure that you have examples where the truth or falsehood of the statements is obvious to anyone. Don't make your examples too personal. For example, don't give an example like, "Some of my shoes are brown. Argus is a shoe of mine. So Argus is brown." I happen to know that none of my shoes is brown, that Argus is the name of my friend's dog, and that Argus is brown. So I happen to know that both premises are false and the conclusion is true. But hardly anyone else does, so this is a terrible example. The example about *Playboy* is sufficiently a matter of common knowledge that almost everyone will know at once which statements are true and which are false.   Now give your examples for B and C.

(21) B. _Some men are women_.
Hugh Hefner is a man.
So, Hugh Hefner is a woman.

(22) C. _Some men are people_.
Hugh Hefner is a man.
So, Hugh Hefner is a person.

Finally, we take case D, which gives a(n) **(23)** INTERPRETATION / COUNTER-EXAMPLE because it is the combination with true premises and a false conclusion.

Let *F*: large cities; *G*: cities where shooting seldom occurs; *a*: Chicago. Using this interpretation for the letters, the interpreted argument is:

(24) Some _large cities_ are _cities . . . ._
Chicago is a _large city_.
So, _Chicago_ is a _city . . . . ._

The premises are both true.   Chicago certainly is a large city, and there are cities that are large, but where shootings seldom occur.   The city of London is an example.   The conclusion is **(25)** TRUE / FALSE.   (The newspaper this morning reported 51 separate "shooting incidents" in Chicago during a "quiet" weekend. London has about that many a year.)   Thus this interpretation provides a **(26)** PROOF / COUNTEREXAMPLE for the argument form "Some *F* are *G*; *a* is *F*, so *a* is *G*."

In the case of a valid argument form, we cannot have true premises with a false conclusion.   That is just what validity means: true premises can never lead to false conclusions.   Give examples of interpretations of the argument form:

All *F* are *G*.
a is *F*.
So *a* is *G*.

which consist of:

A.   One or more false premises, true conclusion.
(27) _All cows are grass eaters._
(Marys little lamb) Frank is a cow
(marys little lamb)Frank is a grasseater

B.   One or more false premises, false conclusion.
(28) _All cats are dogs_
Felix is a cat
So, Felix is a dog

C. All true premises, true conclusion.

(29) *Au MILLIONAIRES ARE RICH* .
H. HUGHES IS A MILLIONAIRE .
H. HUGHES IS RICH . .

Write "T" in front of the true statements and "F" in front of the false ones.

(30) *F* An argument is valid when the conclusion is true and the premises are true.

(31) *T* A valid argument has a true conclusion when the premises are all true.

(32) *T* A counterexample to an argument form is an interpretation in which the premises are all true and the conclusion is false.

(33) *T* There could not be a valid argument with true premises and a false conclusion.

(34) *T* There can be invalid arguments with true premises and a true conclusion.

(35) *F* It is impossible for a valid argument to have a false conclusion.

(36) *T* Any interpretation of a valid argument form is a valid argument.

(37) *F* Every valid argument has true premises.

(38) *T* If you can find a counterexample to an argument form, you know that it is invalid.

(39) *F* If you try to find a counterexample to an argument form, but do not succeed, then you know the argument form is valid.

The last two questions illustrate an important difference between proving validity and proving invalidity. An invalid argument form can be shown to be invalid by citing a single counterexample. That is enough to show you that arguments of this form can lead you from (40) TRUTH / FALSEHOOD to (41) TRUTH / FALSEHOOD. However, failing to find counterexamples does not prove validity. No amount of citing favorable examples—true premises, true conclusion—will ever prove that an argument form is valid. Other techniques are needed. We shall develop these techniques in later chapters.

Contrast these two argument forms:

A. All *F* are *G*.   B. All *F* are *G*.
    a is *F*.   *a* is *G*.
    So, *a* is *G*.   So, *a* is *F*.

What is the difference between these two argument forms?

(42) *F & G ARE INTERCHANGED IN THE TWO PREMISE & THE CONCLUSION -*

Which is the valid form? (43) *A*.

The argument form B is invalid. Here is a counterexample: Let *F*: Wall street stockbrokers; *G*: people with offices in New York; *a*: U Thant (the Secretary General of the U.N.). Using this interpretation for the letters, the interpretation of the argument on the right is:

(44) All *WALL STREET BROKERS* are *PEOPLE WITH OFFICES ...*
U. THANT is a *PERSON WITH AN OFFICE ..*
So, *U. THANT* is a *STOCK BROCKER*.

In this interpretation, the premises are both (45) TRUE / FALSE. The conclusion is (46) TRUE / FALSE. Hence, we have not just an interpretation, but a (47) PROOF / COUNTEREXAMPLE / IMPLICATION. Now make up your own counterexample to this argument form. Make the premises pretty obviously and publicly (48) TRUE / FALSE, and the conclusion pretty obviously and publicly (49) TRUE / FALSE.

(50) *All TEACHERS ARE PAID WELL*
R. NIXON IS PAID WELL
So, R. NIXON IS A TEACHER -

Sometimes a counterexample helps you see just what is wrong with a dubious argument. For example, suppose you hear someone argue,

All the anarchists in Cleveland are members of the *ad hoc* committee on urban reform. J. B. Baxter is a member of that committee. So, J. B. Baxter is an anarchist.

If you are not reading attentively, this could sound like a valid argument. But on closer inspection, you see that this is an example of the argument form, "All *F* are *G*, *a* is *G*, so, *a* is *F*." The interpretation is got by taking,

(51) *F: ANARCHISTS IN CLEVELAND*
(52) *G: MEMBERS OF THE AD. HOC. Com ...*
(53) *a: J. B. BAXTER -*

So the argument about Mr. Baxter is invalid. You might convince someone of this by producing this schematic form and pointing out that it is obviously invalid. But often we are more informal, at least in ordinary conversation. You could say, "That is a crazy argument. It is like saying,

'All draft card burners are Americans: President Nixon is an American. So, President Nixon is a draft card burner.' There is no difference at all in the way you're arguing." Here, someone is producing an argument of the same form, but which obviously is invalid. Thus concrete examples often bring home the fact that an argument is invalid in a more vivid way than abstract schemes. The abstract schemes, however, capture exactly what is common to the two invalid arguments, namely the form of the arguments.

(54) Circle the invalid argument forms.

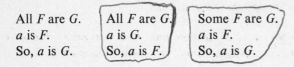

All *F* are *G*.
a is *F*.
So, *a* is *G*.

All *F* are *G*.
a is *G*.
So, *a* is *F*.

Some *F* are *G*.
a is *F*.
So, *a* is *G*.

Both of the invalid forms are often used in fallacious "guilt by association." Thus in the argument about Mr. Baxter, someone thought he was an anarchist because he had joined an organization joined by all anarchists. This is an example of an invalid argument of the form on the **(55)** LEFT / RIGHT / MIDDLE above.

The form on the right can also be used in guilt by association. Perhaps the following is an example:

> The best compliment Apollo 10 has received so far has come from the Russian newspapers, which suggest that the moon program has become a plaything for the American power structure and that it really isn't going to achieve very much.

Perhaps this quotation from the *Chicago Tribune* (May 27, 1969) is not intended to be a serious argument. If it is, it probably has some unstated first premise like:

A. Some statements made in Russian newspapers are false and are asserted only for reasons of propaganda.

Then we have the stated next premise:

B. The statement, that the moon program has become a plaything for the American power structure and that it really isn't going to achieve very much, is a statement made in Russian newspapers.

Then we get the conclusion:

C. The statement in question (about the moon program being a plaything for the American power structure, etc.) is false and asserted only for reasons of propaganda.

The argument, A, B, so C is an invalid argument of the form Some *F* are *G*, *a* is *F*, so *a* is *G*, with,

B (56) F: _Statements made in Russian New..._

A (57) G: _Statements that are false. .. Propagand_

C (58) a: _The statement in question-_

We had to make up the premise A because the *Tribune* did not tell us what premise it has in mind.   Perhaps someone believes,

D.   All statements made in Russian newspapers that concern the United States are false and are asserted only for propaganda reasons.

The argument D, B, so C is (59) <u>VALID</u> / INVALID.   The argument form is:

(60) ___ _All F are G_ ___
___ _a is F_ ___
___ _a is C_ ___

Now we have a valid argument form all right, but there are two ways of criticizing an argument.   We can say that the conclusion does not (61) _Follow From_ the premises, so the argument is (62) _invalid_. We can also criticize the argument on the grounds that not all the premises are (63) _true_ .   Now statement D above is certainly false: it is just not true that every statement made in a Russian newspaper about the United States is a lie.   On the other hand, statement A is true.   How would you criticize the argument, A, B, so C?

(64) _invalid argument -_

How would you criticize the argument D, B, so C?

(65) _Premise D is false_

Now let us stand back and reconsider the remarks quoted in the *Tribune*. The controversial proposition is:

E.   The moon program has become a plaything for the American power structure, and it really isn't going to achieve very much from a scientific point of view.

This is debatable; that is, arguments can be produced pro and con.   Perhaps if we know enough about both the moon program and the American power structure, we can discover true premises and construct valid arguments that will definitely settle the question.   But one thing is clear: The fact that E was stated in a Russian (or any other) newspaper does not establish that E is false. Anyone who thinks the opposite is using either an unstated false premise or an invalid argument (or both).

Many books on elementary logic have long chapters on *fallacies*. They distinguish many different ways in which arguments can go wrong. This is often interesting, and looking at a lot of different examples can make you better at detecting bad arguments. However, there are only two fundamental ways in which an argument intended to prove a conclusion by deduction can fail. The premises may not all be **(66)** _TRUE_____ or the argument may be **(67)** _INVALID_.

Sometimes these two fundamental ways can be combined in a particularly dangerous way. Some word may be used in two different senses. For example,

F.   All laws that are operative are enforced by some authority.
G.   Newton's laws of motion are operative.
H.   So, Newton's laws of motion are enforced by some authority.

If we let *F*: laws that are operative; *G*: laws that are enforced by some authority; *a*: Newton's laws of motion, the form of the above argument appears to be:

(68)
$$\frac{\begin{array}{l} All\ F\ are\ G \\ a\ is\ F \end{array}}{a\ is\ G}$$

In that event, the argument is **(69)** VALID / INVALID. However, then the first premise is false. For if "law" is used in a way which includes natural laws like Newton's laws of motion, then F just isn't true (or if it is true, because there is some divine law enforcement officer making sure the world works right, then it needs a lot of argument to prove *that*). However, there is another sense of "law" which means a rule in a legal code. In that sense, premise F is true, but the argument form is: Let *F*: laws that are part of a legal code and operative; *G*: laws that are enforced by some authority; *H*: laws, including natural laws, that are operative; *a*: Newton's laws of motion. The argument form is:

   All *F* are *G*.
   a is *H*.
   So, *a* is *G*.

Is this argument form valid? **(70)** YES / NO. Make up a counterexample. Let

(71)   *F*: _BUNNIES (PLAYBOY)_
         G: _WOMEN_____.
         H: _MAN_____.
         a: _HUGH HEFNER_____

Your counterexample:

(72)

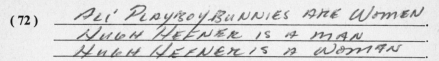

So there are two ways to construe the argument, F, G, so H.   In the first way of understanding the word "law," we got an argument in which the premises are probably **(73)** TRUE / FALSE and the argument is **(74)** VALID / INVALID.   In the second way, treating the word "law" in two senses, the premises are probably **(75)** TRUE / FALSE and the argument is **(76)** VALID / INVALID.   This is called *equivocation.*   To equivocate is to use words in different senses in the course of an argument.   In this case, we are tricked into thinking an argument is valid, with true premises, because in one sense of the word "law" the premises are probably true whereas in another sense the argument is valid.   But there is no sense in which the premises are probably true and the argument is valid.

5 / Drawing Statements (I)

This chapter tells how to make diagrams of the information contained in statements that are in standard form. These diagrams help one to see when different sounding statements express the same information. They will also be used in later chapters as part of a device for testing validity.

A counterexample to an argument form is an **(1)** INTERPRETATION / PROOF in which the premises are all **(2)** TRUE / FALSE, and the conclusion is **(3)** TRUE / FALSE. If we can find a counterexample, we know that the argument form is **(4)** VALID / INVALID. If we cannot hit on a counterexample, are we entitled to believe the argument form is valid? **(5)** YES / NO. Because an argument form can be invalid even though we are not smart enough to think of a counterexample, it would be good to have a definite and conclusive way of testing for validity. One way will be developed in the next few chapters. A first step toward mastering this skill is learning how to diagram the information contained in statements in standard form.

Take for example the statement:

All farmers are greedy.

This statement is almost certainly **(6)** TRUE / FALSE. But whether it is true or false **(7)** IS / IS NOT a matter for logic. So it does not matter to us whether we take true or false statements for our examples.

We can draw a picture of what this statement says. Suppose we rounded up all the farmers in the world and put them in a big round fence. Then we could represent what we have done as follows:

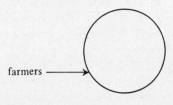

38

Likewise, if we rounded up all the greedy people in the world, we could draw this picture of what we have done:

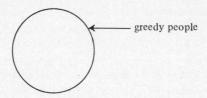

On the other hand, if we round up the farmers and then the greedy people, we will get a picture like this:

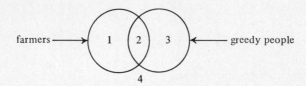

The fences will overlap. Notice there are four regions created by these fences, if we include the region outside any fence.

What is in these numbered regions? In region 1, we have the farmers who are not greedy people. What is in region 2? Region 2 is in both the farmer circle and the greedy circle. So the people in region 2 must be both **(8)** _Farmers_ and **(9)** _Greedy_. Who is in region 3? **(10)** _Greedy Non Farmers_. In region 4, we have the left-overs: all the things that are neither **(11)** _Farmers_ ~~nor~~ **(12)** _Greedy_.

You should think of the picture we have just drawn as representing our state of knowledge when we know nothing at all about the relation between farmers and greediness. We have drawn two fences. If there are absolutely no farmers in the world, then regions 1 and 2 will be empty. If there are absolutely no greedy people in the world, then regions **(13)** _2_ and **(14)** _3_ will be empty. If there are farmers, but none of them is greedy, region 2— the region for farmers who are greedy—will be **(15)** FULL / EMPTY. If there are greedy people, but none of them are farmers, once again, region **(16)** _2_ will be empty. If all farmers are greedy, region number 1 will be empty; all the farmers will be pushed into the greedy circle. If all greedy people are farmers, all the greedy people get pushed into the farmers' circle, and region number **(17)** _3_ is empty. On the other hand, if no greedy people are farmers, the region common to both greedy people and farmers is empty, that is, region **(18)** _2_ is empty.

We have just listed a lot of different possibilities; all farmers greedy, no farmers greedy, and so on. If we do not know which possibility in fact is true, then we are in a state of **(19)** COMPLETE / NO information about the relation between farmers and greediness. The picture we drew represents this state of **(20)** *No* information. But suppose we are now told that

A.   All farmers are greedy.

This tells us that all the farmers are in the greedy circle. This tells us that region number **(21)** *1* is empty. We represent this by the simple device of *scratching out* region 1, which statement A tells us is empty. So our previously uninformative diagram gets to look like this:

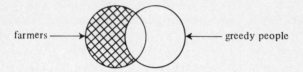

If, on the other hand, we were not told A but *instead* were told:

B.   All greedy people are farmers.

we would know that region number **(22)** *3* is empty and so would proceed to scratch out region 3. Do it.

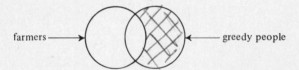

If we were told both A and B, we would have **(23)** MORE / LESS information than if we were told just A or just B alone. Hence, we have to draw more information than in our two previous pictures, or rather, we must combine the pictures. If all farmers are greedy, and all greedy people are farmers, our world must look like this:

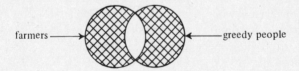

Suppose now that we were told something different from either A or B. We are told that,

C.   No greedy people are farmers.

Then there cannot be anybody in the region common to farmers and greedy

people.   This means that region number **(24)** _2_ has to be scratched out.
This is the lens-shaped region in the middle.   Scratch it out.

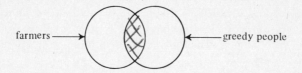

You have just represented the statement **(25)** A. ALL GREEDY PEOPLE ARE
FARMERS / C. <u>NO GREEDY PEOPLE ARE FARMERS</u>.

Notice that in each case we start with a diagram that conveys **(26)** <u>NO</u>/
SOME information and that represents the possibilities before we know anything.   Every statement rules out some possibilities.   We can regard a
statement as a piece of information, and the diagram is a picture of this
(27) _information_.   When we get two statements, then we have to
represent the **(28)** _information_ given by each statement.

Sometimes different sounding statements turn out to convey exactly the
same information.   Compare:

C.   No greedy people are farmers.
D.   No farmers are greedy people.

These two certainly look different, but they are actually equivalent.   Draw a
diagram of D.   The statement tells us that there is nothing in common to the
farmer circle and the greedy people circle.   So region number **(29)** _2_
must be scratched out.   This is the region in the middle.   Scratch it out:

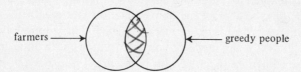

This is the diagram for D.   Now look back at the last diagram you drew.
Are they the same?   **(30)** <u>YES</u> / NO.   The last diagram was the diagram
for **(31)** A / B / <u>C</u>.   Thus the diagrams for C and D are **(32)** THE SAME /
DIFFERENT.   This shows that C and D convey the same **(33)** _information_
Two statements conveying the same information in this sense are called
logically equivalent.   Thus, our diagrams show us that C and D are **(34)**
logically equivalent In general, two statements with identical diagrams are called **(35)** _logically equivalent_ When we
say that the diagrams are the same, we mean that the circles indicate the same
properties (like farmers and greedy people) and that the same portions are
marked on the same circles.

+ + + + + +

If this is the only method of diagraming you have ever seen, skip the next paragraphs, and pick up at the next row of plus signs (+ + +).

You may have encountered another method of diagraming, and this might lead to some confusion. In the other method, we indicate that all farmers are greedy people by putting a small circle for farmers inside a big circle for greedy people. Thus, one class is quite literally contained in the

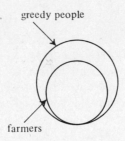

greedy people

farmers

other, as shown here. This perhaps seems simpler to you than the method we have been using. First of all notice that there is no real difference between the resulting diagrams. The above picture shows the farmer area entirely inside the greedy people area. But if you look back at the very first diagram we drew, the one with an area scratched out, you'll see exactly the same thing. *All that is left of* the farmer circle is in the greedy people circle. But, you will ask, surely it is simpler to do the latter diagram? For the purpose of diagraming just one statement, yes. But the circles-within-circles method is much less versatile and is less easily adapted to testing the validity of all the different kinds of arguments we shall examine. Moreover, it is less well adapted for situations when more information is provided. For example, suppose you draw the above diagram and are then told that, in addition, all greedy people are farmers. Then you have to redraw the whole diagram. But with our method, you just scratch out a little more of the diagram (remember the diagram with both areas 1 and 3 scratched out: this represented "all farmers are greedy people and all greedy people are farmers"). A final virtue of our method is that it enables us in part to explain the concept of validity in a way that is impossible with the circles-inside-circles method; the explanation will wait a few chapters, but for the present, try to draw diagrams in the way explained in this book.

+ + + + + +

(36) Circle the statement that this diagram represents:

famous people ———→ 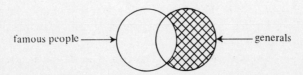 ←——— generals

E. Some famous people are generals.
F. All famous people are generals.
(G.) All generals are famous people.
H. No generals are famous people.

Match these pictures with the statements that follow:

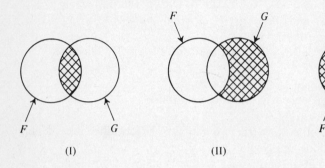

(I)   (II)   (III)

"F" and "G" stand for terms beginning with those letters.

(37) _____ No generous people are famous.

(38) _____ All generals are famous people.

(39) _____ All future events are ghastly to think about.

(40) _____ No ghosts are female.

(41) _____ All films about the Roman Empire are gory.

(42) _____ All giraffes are fleet-footed.

(43) _____ Every generalization about people is far-fetched.

(44) _____ None of the fascists I have met is good company.

(45) _____ Anything good to eat that you can think of is to be found in that delicatessen.

(46) _____ Not a single giant is friendly to small children.

Now consider the statement:

Only fresh meat is good for lions in zoos to eat.

This too can be diagramed in the above way.   The statement is of the form:

Only F is G.

We are saying that the only place G is found is in the F circle.   So we scratch out that part of the *G* circle outside the *F* circle. This is diagram II. To take our concrete example, we are saying that the only area allowed for things that are good for caged lions to eat is in the fresh meat area. So we scratch out that part of the **(47)** FRESH MEAT / GOOD TO EAT area outside of the **(48)** FRESH MEAT / GOOD TO EAT area.

Notice that "Only *F* are *G*" is diagramed by **(49)** I / II / III. This is also the diagram that matches **(50)** ALL *F* ARE *G* / NO *F* ARE *G* / ALL *G* ARE *F*. Thus "Only *F* are *G*" and "All *G* are *F*" are **(51)** COUNTEREXAMPLES / LOGICALLY EQUIVALENT / TRUE / VALID.

Be careful about "only." Contrast the two following statements:

I.   Only gullible people are faithful husbands.
J.   The only gullible people are faithful husbands.

You might think the little word "the" could not make any difference. But in fact it turns everything upside down. We begin by diagraming I. Only gullible people are faithful husbands: so there cannot be any faithful husbands who are not gullible. We diagram this as:

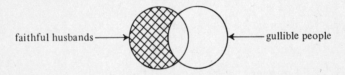

faithful husbands ———→   ←——— gullible people

This is logically equivalent to **(52)** ALL FAITHFUL HUSBANDS ARE GULLIBLE PEOPLE / ALL GULLIBLE PEOPLE ARE FAITHFUL HUSBANDS.

Now look at J. The only gullible people are faithful husbands. So there cannot be any gullible people who are not faithful husbands. We therefore cross out the area of gullible people who are not faithful husbands:

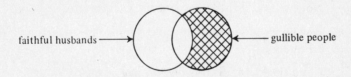

faithful husbands ———→   ←——— gullible people

This is logically equivalent to **(53)** ALL FAITHFUL HUSBANDS ARE GULLIBLE PEOPLE / ALL GULLIBLE PEOPLE ARE FAITHFUL HUSBANDS.

Our diagrams teach us that:

"All F are G" and *"Only G are F"* are logically equivalent.
"All F are G" and *"The only F are G"* are logically equivalent.

Each of the statements in the left-hand column is logically equivalent to *two* statements in the (a)–(f) column. Match the logically equivalent schemes and leave no blanks.

(54) __C__ __b__ All F are G. (a) Only F are G.

(55) __a__ __d__ All G are F. (b) Only G are F.
(c) The only F are G.

(56) __e__ __f__ No F are G. (d) The only G are F.
(e) No F are G.

(57) __e__ __f__ No G are F. (f) No G are F.

Still other logical equivalences can be found. For example:

M. All films about the Roman empire are gruesome.
N. No films about the Roman empire are not gruesome.

Perhaps you can see at once that statements M and N convey about the same facts. If in doubt, you can draw diagrams to be sure. Thus, let us diagram N. It is of the form "No F are not G." That means there can be nothing in the F area that is not in the G area. So all the area of F that is outside G must be scratched out. **(58)** Do it.

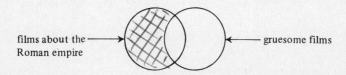

films about the ⟶ ⟵ gruesome films
Roman empire

This is the same diagram as for **(59)** ALL F ARE G / NO F ARE G / ALL G ARE F.

We conclude that:

"*All F are G*" and "*No F are not G*" *are logically equivalent.*

Thus, for example:

No children are undeserving.

is logically equivalent to:

(60) All children are DESERVING.

This is because the prefix "un-" has the force of "not" or "non-". The statement:

No members of this church are noncommunicants.

is logically equivalent to:

(61) All _MEMBERS OF THIS CHURCH_ are _COMMUNICANTS._

Another negative prefix is "in-". The statement

No good leaders are indecisive.

is logically equivalent to:

(62) All _GOOD LEADERS_ are _DECISIVE_.

A statement of the form "All *F* are *G*" is called an A statement where the "A" just stands for "all." Thus the statement:

All opium derivatives are habit-forming.

is an **(63)** A / B / E / I / O / U statement. The statement:

No opium derivatives are legally sold without prescription.

(64) IS / IS NOT an A statement.

Write out logically equivalent A statements for the following statements:

The only people he trusts are under 30.
(65) _ALL PEOPLE HE TRUSTS ARE UNDER 30_.
Only children of missionaries are eligible for this scholarship.
(66) _ALL PEOPLE ELIGIBLE " ARE CHILDREN OF MISSIONARIES_
No master of yoga is unrelaxed.
(67) _ALL MASTERS OF YOGA ARE RELAXED_.
Every child who is rejected by its mother develops neurotic traits during adolescence.
(68) _ALL CHILDREN REJECTED ... ARE CHILDREN..._
The only vehicles allowed on this path are bicycles.
(69) _ALL VEHICLES ALLOWED ON THIS PATH ARE BIKES_.
Bicycles are the only vehicles allowed on this path.
(70) _ALL VEHICLES ALLOWED ON THIS PATH ARE BIKES_
Only bicycles are allowed on this path.
(71) _ALL VEHICLES ALLOWED ON THIS PATH ARE BIKES_.

No rock band is inaudible.

(72) *All Rock Bands are Audible.*

We conclude this chapter with a final logical equivalence. Suppose several people have been making speeches. It is said that:

All Joseph's speeches are audible.

This is equivalent to saying:

All inaudible speeches are not Joseph's speeches.

We can check this by drawing a diagram. On the left we have Joseph's speeches, and on the right, audible speeches. If all inaudible (not audible) speeches are not Joseph's, then in the area of Joseph's speeches, we shall find only (at most) audible speeches. So we have to scratch out the area for Joseph's speeches outside the circle of audible speeches. **(73)** Do it.

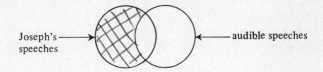

This is the same as the diagram for **(74)** ALL JOSEPH'S SPEECHES ARE INAUDIBLE / ALL JOSEPH'S SPEECHES ARE AUDIBLE / ALL AUDIBLE SPEECHES ARE JOSEPH'S SPEECHES.

We conclude that, in general,

"All F are G" and "All non-G are non-F" are logically equivalent.

Are "All F are G" and "All G are F" logically equivalent? **(75)** YES / NO. They certainly aren't the same: "All men are people" is true, but "All people are men" is something different; it is **(76)** TRUE / FALSE. Be careful not to confuse the logical equivalence in italics above with a mistaken confusion between "All F are G" and "All G are F."

Write in A form, with no negatives:

All irresponsible people are untrustworthy people.

(77) *All ~~Responsible People~~ are Trustworthy People.*

Responsible People

Answer "T" or "F."

(78) __*F*__ "Only *F* are *G*" means the same as "The only *F* are *G*."

(79) __*T*__ "Only *F* are *G*" is logically equivalent to "The only *G* are *F*."

(80) __*F*__ "All *F* are *G*" is logically equivalent to "All *G* are *F*."

(81) __*F*__ "All non-*F* are non-*G*" is logically equivalent to "All *F* are *G*."

6 / Drawing Statements (II)

The last chapter showed how to draw "all" statements and variations on them.   This chapter teaches how to draw statements of the form "Some *F* are *G*" and completes the preparation for a method of testing for validity.

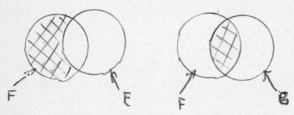

Draw a diagram, on your own paper, for each of the following statements.

(1)   All frankfurters are good to eat.
(2)   No farmers are generals.

In each case, you began with two overlapping circles representing a state of **(3)** MUCH / NO information.   Then you took the information given by the statement and drew it on to the empty diagram.   In the case of both 1 and 2, you **(4)** CROSSED OUT / ERASED part of the diagram.   This is because both 1 and 2 tell us that certain regions on the diagram are **(5)** EMPTY / FULL. Statement 1 tells us that the region of frankfurters that are not good to eat is **(6)** EMPTY / FULL.   Diagram 2 tells us that the region of farmers who are generals is **(7)** _EMPTY_ .
Now consider the statement:

Some fake Rembrandts are genuinely beautiful.

This is entirely the opposite of a statement such as 2.   Statement 2 is of the form **(8)** NO *F* ARE *G* / SOME *F* ARE *G* / ALL *F* ARE *G*.   The statement about Rembrandts would be schematized: **(9)** NO *F* ARE *G* / SOME *F* ARE *G*.   "No *F* are *G*" tells us there is **(10)** NOTHING / SOMETHING common to *F* and *G*. But "Some *F* are *G*" tells us there is **(11)** NOTHING / SOMETHING common to *F* and *G*.   Hence, the two will have to be diagramed in **(12)** THE SAME /

DIFFERENT ways. We diagram "No *F* are *G*" by scratching out that part of
the diagram common to *F* and **(13)** _G_. We diagram "Some *F* are *G*" by
putting something in the area common to *F* and *G*. Thus, starting with the
blank diagram on the left, which represents a state of no **(14)** *INFORMATION*
we diagram "Some *F* are *G*" by putting a short *bar* into the area common to
(15) _F_ and **(16)** _G_ :

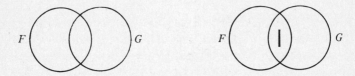

The diagram on the right is also the diagram of "Some *G* are *F*," because
"Some *G* are *F*," like "Some *F* are *G*," tells us there is something common to
F and **(17)** _G_.   So the two statements are logically **(18)** _EQUIVALENT_ ,
But consider:

Some fish are not golden creatures.

Letting "*F*" stand for "fish" and "*G*" for "golden," this statement **(19)**
IS / IS NOT of the form "Some *F* are *G*."   On the contrary, it is of the form
"Some *F* are not *G*."   It tells us that some fish are not in the golden circle.
Hence, it will be diagramed as:

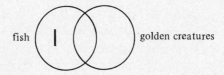

The statement:

Some good examples are not fatuous examples.

could be schematized as **(20)** NO *F* ARE *G* / SOME *G* ARE *F* / SOME *G* ARE NOT *F*.
Hence it is to be schematized by **(21)** SCRATCHING OUT / PUTTING A BAR IN
the area of *G* but not *F*.   **(22)** Do it.

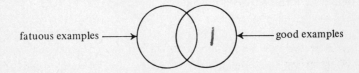

You will have put a bar in the right hand "half-moon" shaped area. You
can think of these bars as actually representing some thing. Some fish are

not golden creatures: if you look at the diagram, you can see a fish that is not a golden creature.   It is represented by that bar on the left.

These diagrams make clearer the way in which we understand the word "some."   Occasionally, if you hear someone say, for example, "Some students will be failed from the engineering school this year," you suppose that he means, "Some *but of course not all* students will be failed from the engineering school this year."   So you think "some" implies "not all." This is, however, misleading.   If I am going through the files of the engineering school, and start reading about the students in alphabetical order, and find that Mr. Aardvark, Mr. Abson, and Mr. Acno are going to be failed, and then you come in and ask me, "What have you found out so far?" I can correctly say **(23)** SOME STUDENTS WILL FAIL / NO STUDENTS WILL FAIL. Since I have only read about three students so far (there are about 180 in the files) am I entitled to say, "Not all the students will fail"?   **(24)** YES / NO. Thus there **(25)** ARE / ARE NOT situations where I can say something of the form "Some F are G" without implying "Not all F are G."

"Some F are G" does *not* mean "Some but not all F are G."

If you are speaking literally, and want to say "Some but not all of the students will fail," say it.   Don't just say "Some students will fail."

If someone says:

Some fake Rembrandts are genuinely beautiful.

we would probably take him to mean that several of the forgeries are good to look at.   If he knew of only one fake Rembrandt that he admired, we should expect him to say

At least one fake Rembrandt is genuinely beautiful.

We shall be less subtle.   We shall diagram both statements in exactly the same way.   We will not distinguish the information given by "some" statements from that given by "at least one" statements.   Both will be diagramed by **(26)** SCRATCHING OUT / PUTTING A BAR IN some chosen area.

We have various ways of conveying the same idea.   Here is a list of statements.   All but two mean approximately the same.   *Cross out* the two odd men out.

(27)   Some cars have defective brakes.
(28)   At least one car has defective brakes.
(29)   There exist cars with defective brakes.
(30)   Some things with defective brakes are cars.
(31)   ~~Some cars do not have defective brakes.~~
(32)   At least one of the things with defective brakes is a car.

+(33) Something is a car with defective brakes.

+(34) ~~Everything with defective brakes is a car.~~

—(35) One or more cars has defective brakes.

(36) One or more of the things with defective brakes is a car.

(37) Something with defective brakes is a car.

—(38) There are cars with defective brakes.

(39) There exist things with defective brakes that are cars.

(40) Diagram statement 39:

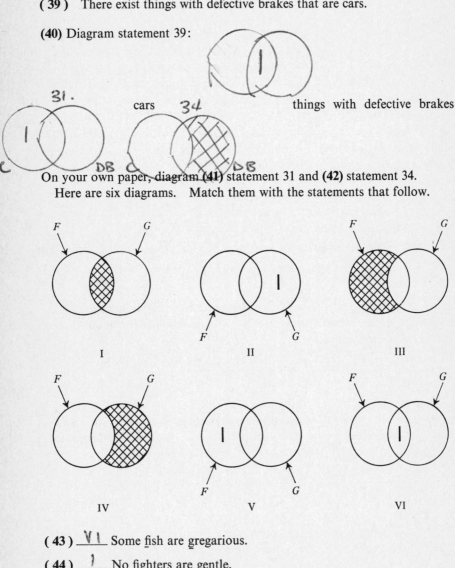

cars   things with defective brakes

On your own paper, diagram **(41)** statement 31 and **(42)** statement 34.

Here are six diagrams.   Match them with the statements that follow.

(43) _VI_ Some fish are gregarious.

(44) _I_ No fighters are gentle.

(45) _IV_ All giraffes are four-legged.

(46) _V_ Some fantastic hallucinogens are not good for you.

(47) _VI_ Some gentle people are furious when provoked.

(48) _V_ Some facades of the older buildings are not going to be repaired.

(49) _III_ Only gravel is used for fill.

(50) _IV_ Every gallant soldier is fooled by the military-industrial complex.

(51) _V_ There are frank discussions that are not going to be published.

(52) _III_ The only fools in the room are gamblers.

(53) _II_ There are giants that are not found on this continent.

(54) _IV_ Only fools are gamblers.

(55) _II_ Some gambler is no fool.

For convenience we have been using a lot of examples with terms that begin with "f" and "g" but this is inessential. Also, it is irrelevant (except for ease of reference) whether the *F* or the *G* circle is on the right. For example, take the statement:

Some teachers are uncooperative.

This could be represented by two of the following diagrams. Which?
(56) I / II / III / IV.

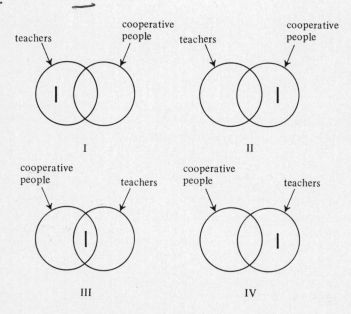

What statement does diagram II represent?
(57) _SOME COOPERATIVE PEOPLE ARE NOT TEACHERS_

What statement does diagram III represent?

(58) *Some teachers are cooperative people*

Diagrams I and IV look different until you realize that IV is just I turned back to front. **(59)** On a separate sheet of paper draw a diagram of statement 57, represented by diagram II, except put "teachers" on the right and "co-operative people" on the left.

A blank diagram of two intersecting circles represents a state of **(60)** LOTS OF / NO information. When we draw on a statement, we are representing the information conveyed by the statement. If we are told something more, by a further statement, it should be possible to represent the further **(61)** *information* conveyed by the second statement. For example, suppose we are told, in this order, that:

> No farmers are generals.
> Some farmers are not generals.

Then our increasing information is represented by this sequence of diagrams. We start knowing nothing. We learn the first fact, represented on the second diagram; then we learn the second fact; and both facts are represented on the third diagram.

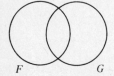 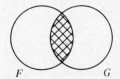 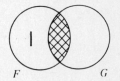

F   G   F   G   F   G

Now, on your own paper, put this pair of statements on a single diagram:

(62) Some gentlemen are frivolous people.
Some frivolous people are not gentlemen.

Diagram:

(63) All giants are fortunate beings.
Some fortunate beings are not giants.

What about this pair:

> Some females are ghosts.
> No ghosts are female.

We can diagram either statement, as shown on page 55 by the two diagrams on the left. But if we try to combine them, we get the mess on the right:

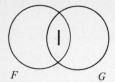 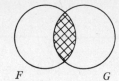 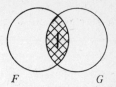

The diagram on the right does not make sense. For the bar in the central area indicates that there **(64)** IS / IS NOT something in that area. The scratching out shows that there is **(65)** SOMETHING / NOTHING in that area. We can't have it both ways. Thus the two statements:

> Some females are ghosts.
> No ghosts are female.

(66) CAN / CANNOT be represented on the same diagram. This is reasonable. The two statements are *inconsistent*. They say opposite things. One says there are female ghosts, and the other denies it. These statements **(67)** CAN / CANNOT both be true. They are not consistent. When two statements are not consistent, they are **(68)** _INCONSISTENT_.

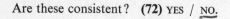

> *If two statements can be diagramed on the same diagram, they are consistent.*

Test the following pairs for consistency. Draw diagrams on your own paper.

(69) All mice are timid animals.
Some timid animals are mice.

Are these consistent? **(70)** YES / NO.

(71) No monsters are found in the lake.
Some of the things found in the lake are monsters.

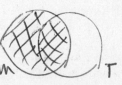

Are these consistent? **(72)** YES / NO.

(73) All mice are timid animals.
No mice are timid animals.

Are these consistent? **(74)** YES / NO.

Your last result may surprise you. The two statements certainly look inconsistent. Yet we can diagram them:

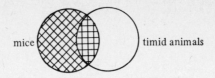

We can diagram the two statements, but the result is crossing out the entire circle for (75) MICE / TIMID ANIMALS. Thus the two statements taken together imply that (76) THERE ARE NO MICE / THERE ARE PLENTY OF MICE. The reason we think that 73 is an inconsistent pair, is that we know there are mice.   But in fact the two statements in 73, namely:

>   All mice are timid animals.
>   No mice are timid animals.

are really consistent because they (77) CAN / CANNOT be put on the same diagram.   However, the following three statements really are inconsistent:

>   All mice are timid animals.
>   No mice are timid animals.
>   There are mice.

Diagram the following pair:

>   All unicorns are one-horned animals.
>   No one-horned animals are unicorns.

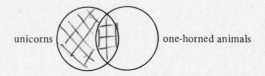

Here you have scratched out the circle for (78) UNICORNS / ONE-HORNED ANIMALS.   That is not too surprising.   This means that there are (79) SOME / NOT ANY unicorns.   And there are not any.

Similarly, it will be possible to diagram,

>   Every baby gorilla is an animal that clings to its mother for almost
>   exactly 14 months before leaving her.
>   No animals cling to their mother for almost exactly 14 months before
>   leaving her.

But this can be diagramed only at the expense of scratching out the whole baby gorilla circle.   Since gorillas are rapidly becoming extinct, it is not surprising that the last pair of statements should be consistent.

In our usage, a pair of statements schematized:

All *F* are *G*.
No *F* are *G*.

is **(80)** CONSISTENT / INCONSISTENT. However, these two statements together make the **(81)** *F* / *G* circle scratched out.

The fact that these two statements are consistent shows that in our usage, "All *F* are *G*" does *not* imply that some *F* are *G*. For of course,

Some *F* are *G*.
and No *F* are *G*.

are **(82)** CONSISTENT / INCONSISTENT.

In our usage, to say that all gorillas are fat **(83)** IS / IS NOT to imply that some gorillas are fat, or that there are some gorillas. This is a very strict usage: very often, if someone said that all gorillas are fat, we would suppose that he thought there were some gorillas. But we will not jump to that conclusion. In our usage, "All *F* are *G*" **(84)** DOES / DOES NOT imply that there are any *F*, or that some *F* are *G*.

Aristotle developed a system of logic in which the Greek word roughly meaning "all" implied the Greek word roughly meaning "some." This book is written in English, and we will not translate his custom. But a system of logic in which the word "all" has so-called "existential import" can be very interesting and is developed in many other logic books.

7 / Venn Diagrams

This chapter shows how the diagrams you have learned to draw can be used to test arguments for validity.

It is now time to combine the discussion of validity in Chapters 1 to 4 and the diagrams of Chapters 5 and 6.   First, it is worth reviewing the early material.

A statement can be criticized on the grounds that it is **(1)** <u>FALSE</u> / INVALID. Arguments, on the other hand, are not called true or false, but valid or **(2)** _INVALID_ .   An argument can be criticized on the grounds that one or more of the premises is **(3)** TRUE / <u>FALSE</u>.   Such criticisms are in general not a matter for logic.   An argument can also be criticized on the ground that it is **(4)** VALID / <u>INVALID</u>.   Whether an argument is valid **(5)** <u>IS</u> / IS NOT a matter for logic.

An argument is valid when the conclusion **(6)** _Follows_ from the premises.   If an argument is valid and the premises are all true, then the conclusion must be **(7)** <u>TRUE</u> / FALSE.

  (8) Can a valid argument have false premises? <u>YES</u> / NO.
  (9) Can a valid argument have a false conclusion? <u>YES</u> / NO.
  (10) Can an invalid argument have true premises? <u>YES</u> / NO.
  (11) Can an invalid argument have a true conclusion? YES / NO.
  (12) Can an invalid argument have all premises true and the conclusion true too? YES / <u>NO</u>.
  (13) Can a valid argument have false premises and a true conclusion? <u>YES</u> / NO.
  (14) Can a valid argument have true premises and a false conclusion? YES / <u>NO</u>.

An argument form is invalid if there is an **(15)** EXAMPLE / <u>INTERPRETATION</u> of the argument form in which the **(16)** <u>PREMISES</u> / CONCLUSION are (is) true and the **(17)** PREMISES / <u>CONCLUSION</u> is false. Such an interpretation are (is) called a **(18)** VALIDITY / VERIFICATION / <u>COUNTEREXAMPLE</u> / DIAGRAM. If you can find a counterexample to an argument, you know that the argument form is **(19)** VALID / <u>INVALID</u>. If you are unable to find a counterexample, can you conclude that the argument form is valid? **(20)** YES / <u>NO</u>.

(21) Circle the invalid argument forms:

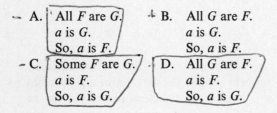

A. All *F* are *G.*
   a is *G.*
   So, *a* is *F.*

B. All *G* are *F.*
   a is *G.*
   So, *a* is *F.*

C. Some *F* are *G.*
   a is *F.*
   So, *a* is *G.*

D. All *G* are *F.*
   a is *F.*
   So, *a* is *G.*

We have learned how to diagram single statements and how to diagram two statements when both statements use the same terms. All the statements we have looked at are statements such as:

All farmers are greedy people.

which have **(22)** ONE / <u>TWO</u> / THREE terms, namely **(23)** *Farmers* and **(24)** *Greeny People*. Suppose we want to diagram that statement, and diagram in addition the statement that:

All greedy people are hungry people.

In this statement there are **(25)** ONE / <u>TWO</u> / THREE terms, namely **(26)** *Greeny People* and **(27)** *Hungry People*. In the pair of statements "All farmers are greedy people" and "All greedy people are hungry people," we find a total of **(28)** ONE / TWO / <u>THREE</u> / FOUR terms, namely **(29)** *Farmers*, **(30)** *Greeny People*, and **(31)** *Hungry People*.

When we diagramed a statement with two terms, we had to draw **(32)** ONE / <u>TWO</u> / THREE circles. Now if we wish to diagram a pair of statements with a total of three terms, we will need **(33)** ONE / TWO / <u>THREE</u> / FOUR circles.

Our first step is to draw a blank diagram. A blank diagram represents a state of no **(34)** *Information*. On the left we show the blank diagram for *F* and *G*; on the right, we see how to extend it to three terms.

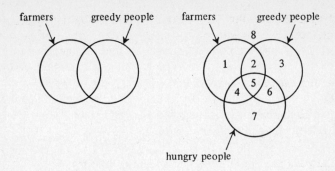

In the three-circle diagram, there are a total of **(35)** FOUR / SIX / <u>EIGHT</u> / TEN / THREE areas, counting the area outside the diagram. In the two-circle diagram, there are **(36)** TWO / THREE / <u>FOUR</u> / SEVEN / EIGHT areas, counting the area outside the diagram. Thus the three-term diagram has **(37)** JUST AS MANY / <u>TWICE AS MANY</u> areas as the two-term diagram. On the following blank diagram on the right, *print in the numbers, exactly as they have been printed in on the above three-term diagram.*

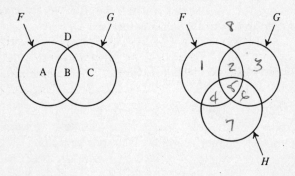

It is not an accident that there are twice as many areas in the three-term diagram as in the two-term diagram. For every area in the two-term diagram has been split in two. For example, area A is split into areas 1 and 4. Areas 6 and 3 make up area **(38)** A / B / <u>C</u> / D on the two-term diagram. What is area B split into? Circle two of these! **(39)** 1 / 2 / 3 / 4 / 5 / 6 / 7 / 8. Note that areas 7 and 8 are outside the *F* and *G* circles. Hence, between them they make up area **(40)** A / B / C / <u>D</u>.

Now what does each area denote? Area B is the area of farmers who are greedy people. Area A is the area of farmers who are not **(41)** _____ *GREEDY PEOPLE* _____. Area C is the area of **(42)** *GREEDY NON-FARMERS*

Area 1 is inside the farmers circle, but outside the greedy people circle and outside the hungry people circle. So it is the area of farmers who are not greedy and who are not **(43)** *HUNGRY*.

Area 2 is **(44)** <u>INSIDE</u> / OUTSIDE the farmers circle, **(45)** <u>INSIDE</u> / OUTSIDE

the greedy people circle, and **(46)** INSIDE / OUTSIDE the hungry people circle.
So it is the area for farmers who are **(47)** _GREEDY_ but not **(48)**
HUNGRY-

Now match area numbers opposite the following descriptions.

(49) _5_ Farmers who are greedy and hungry.

(50) _2_ Farmers who are greedy but not hungry.

(51) _4_ Farmers who are not greedy but are hungry.

(52) _1_ Farmers who are neither greedy nor hungry.

(53) _6_ Greedy, hungry people who are not farmers.

(54) _3_ Greedy people who are not hungry nor farmers.

(55) _7_ Hungry people who are not greedy nor farmers.

(56) _8_ Things which are not farmers, not greedy, and not hungry.

In diagraming three terms, it is important to allow for every possible
combination. This has been done in the above list, so our diagram, though
blank, allows for any possibility. With three terms you need eight areas to
allow for every possibility. Hence, a correct diagram has **(57)** _EIGHT_
areas, including the area outside all the circles. Other than this, it does not
particularly matter what shape our diagrams are. Here are several diagrams. Cross out all those that are incorrect.

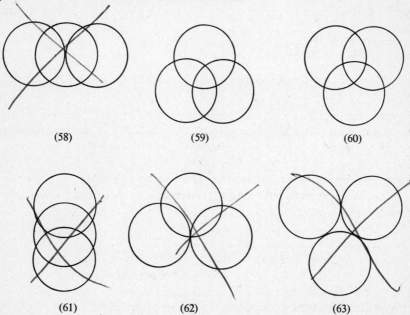

(58)   (59)   (60)

(61)   (62)   (63)

Note that having eight regions is not, in itself, enough, for 61 has eight regions, but does not allow all possibilities.

(64) Represent on the following diagram the statement:

All farmers are greedy people.

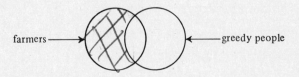

farmers ⟶ ⟵ greedy people

This will be represented on the three-term diagram in exactly the same way:

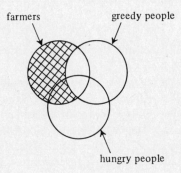

farmers   greedy people

hungry people

Notice that we have scratched out exactly the same area as on the two-term diagram.

(65) On the next diagram, represent the statement:

All greedy people are hungry.

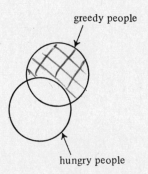

greedy people

hungry people

You will have scratched out the upper right-hand half-moon. **(66)** Now scratch out exactly the same half-moon on the three-term diagram.

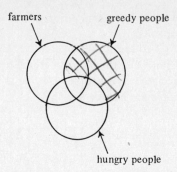

Here are two *incorrect* diagrams of "All farmers are greedy." In the left-hand one, too little has been scratched out. **(67)** Scratch out the rest.
On the right-hand diagram, too much has been scratched out.

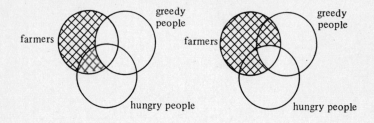

Next we have three diagrams. Diagram III is the result of combining

    All greedy people are hungry.
and All farmers are greedy people.

Which is the diagram for "All greedy people are hungry"? **(68)** I / II.
Which is the diagram for "All farmers are greedy people"? **(69)** I / II.

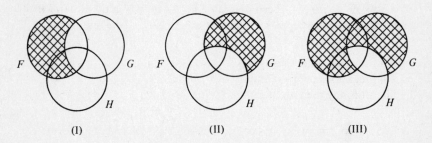

On your own paper, diagram the following pairs of statements. For ease of checking the answers, keep the above pattern, with the *F* circle on the upper left, the *G* circle on the upper right, and the *H* circle in the middle below.

(70) All friends are generous.
No friends are horrible.
(71) All heart transplants so far are failures in the long run.
Nothing that is a failure in the long run is guaranteed eventual success.
(72) All funny men are gregarious people.
All gregarious people are harmless.

Your diagram of 72 will look like this:

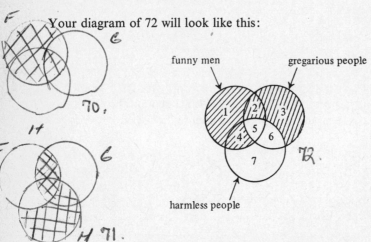

Which areas have been scratched out? **(73)** 1 / 2 / 3 / 4 / 5 / 6 / 7.
The pair of statements in 72 tell us that these four areas are **(74)** EMPTY / FULL.
Now consider a third statement:

All funny men are harmless.

According to this, the areas of funny men outside the harmless circle are **(75)**
FULL / EMPTY. These are areas **(76)** _1_ and **(77)** _2_. These areas
have **(78)** ALREADY / NOT YET been scratched out by the pair of statements
72. Hence, the information conveyed by "All funny men are harmless" has
(79) ALREADY / NOT YET been diagramed. There is a good reason for this.
The third statement follows from the first two. That is, the argument:

All funny men are gregarious.
All gregarious people are harmless people.
So, all funny men are harmless people.

is a **(80)** VALID / INVALID argument. In general, the argument form:

All *F* are *G*.
All *G* are *H*.
So, all *F* are *H*.

is **(81)** <u>VALID</u> / INVALID.
   Now go back to 71:

   All heart transplants so far are failures in the long run.
   Nothing that is a failure in the long run is guaranteed eventual success.

Your diagram for 71 should look like this.

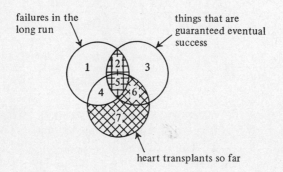

failures in the
long run

things that are
guaranteed eventual
success

heart transplants so far

(82)   Which areas have been scratched out? 1 / 2 / 3 / 4 / 5 / 6 / 7.
(83)   Area 2 is the area for *FAILURES OF GUARANTEED Success*
(84)   Area 5 is the area for *FAILURES, GUARANTEEDS, H. TRANS.*
(85)   Area 6 is the area for *H. TRANSPLANTS GUARANTEEDS.*
(86)   Area 7 is the area for *HEART TRANSPLANT SO FAR*

Every one of these areas has already been scratched out.   Diagram 71 tells
us that these four areas are **(87)** FULL / <u>EMPTY</u>.   Now consider the third
statement:

   No heart transplants so far are guaranteed eventual success.

This statement tells us that areas **(88)** *5* and **(89)** *6* are also empty.
However, these areas have **(90)** <u>ALREADY</u> / NOT YET been scratched out.
Since they have already been scratched out, the third diagram has already
been put on the above diagram.   This is because the third statement follows
from the statements of 71.   The argument form:

   All *H* are *F*.
   No *F* are *G*.
   So, no *H* are *G*.

is **(91)** <u>VALID</u> / INVALID.
   We have just looked at two valid argument forms.   Here is an invalid
argument:

   All female foxes are gentle to their children.
   All harmless animals are gentle to their children.
   So, all female foxes are harmless animals.

(92) Represent the *first two* statements on the following diagram:

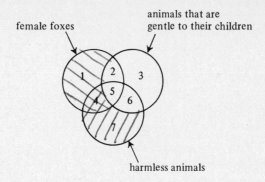

The conclusion, "All female foxes are harmless animals," tells us that areas number **(93)** ~~1~~ and **(94)** ~~2~~ must be scratched out. Have they been? **(95)** YES / <u>NO.</u> The first premise told us to scratch out areas number 1 and 4. The second premise told us to scratch out areas number 4 and 7. So, all in all, areas **(96)** 1 / 2 / 3 / <u>4</u> / 5 / 6 / <u>7</u> got scratched out. However, the conclusion requires that areas number 1 and 2 be scratched out. Area 1 has been scratched out, but not area **(97)** <u>2</u> Hence, the conclusion is not automatically diagramed when the premises are diagramed. Hence, the above argument is **(98)** VALID / <u>INVALID.</u>

An argument is valid if the conclusion is true on the diagram of the premises; that is, the argument is valid when the conclusion is diagramed as soon as the premises have been diagramed.

Now draw diagrams on your own paper to test for the validity of the following argument forms:

(99) All *F* are *G.*
VALID No *H* are *G.*
So, no *H* are *F.*

(100) No *F* are *G.*
INVALID No *G* are *H.*
So, no *F* are *H.*

(101) All *F* are *G.*
VALID No *G* are *H.*
So, no *F* are *H.*

(102) All *F* are *H.*
VALID All *H* are *G.*
So, all *F* are *G.*

(**103**) No *H* are *G*.
All *F* are *G*.
So, no *H* are *F*.

VALID

(**104**) All *H* are *G*.
All *F* are *G*.
So, all *F* are *H*.

INVALID

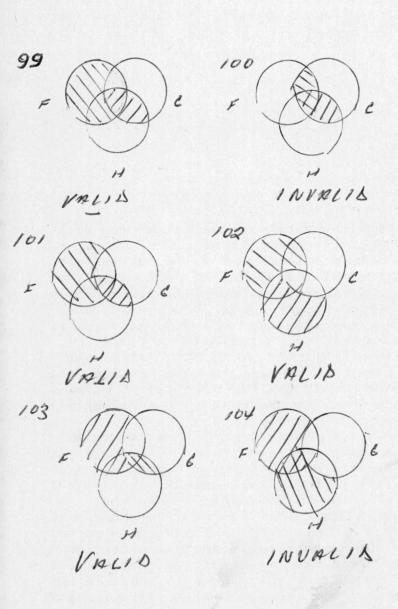

99

F   *C*

H

VALID

100

F   *C*

H

INVALID

101

F   *G*

H

VALID

102

F   *C*

H

VALID

103

F   *G*

H

VALID

104

F   *G*

H

INVALID

8 / Valid Syllogisms

This chapter uses diagrams to explain what validity means and completes the method of testing validity given in the last chapter.

In the last chapter we were chiefly concerned with arguments containing **(1)** TWO / THREE terms, usually denoted by the letters "*F*," "*G*," and "*H*." The premises and conclusion have all been of the sort that can be put into one of the standard forms: "All *F* are *G*," "No *F* are *G*," "Some *F* are *G*," and "Some *F* are not *G*." Arguments with two premises of this form and a conclusion of this form are called "syllogisms." These were first studied by Aristotle (384–322 B.C.) whose work in logic was far more original and important than anything done in the field until the late nineteenth century. The method of testing by drawing diagrams, however, was developed by John Venn, a logician who published this method in 1880. Hence, these diagrams are called Venn **(2)** _DIAGRAMS_ It is possible, and instructive, to study the syllogism along the lines laid down by Aristotle, but that is not the procedure followed in this book.

If the conclusion of a syllogism is diagramed as soon as the premises are diagramed, the argument is **(3)** VALID / INVALID. If the conclusion is not completely diagramed as soon as the premises are diagramed, the argument is **(4)** VALID / INVALID. In diagraming an argument, we start with a **(5)** BLANK / FULL diagram. The blank diagram represents a state of **(6)** COMPLETE / NO information. When we diagram the first premise, we put on the diagram all the **(7)** INFORMATION / TRUTH given by the first statement. After we have diagramed both premises, we have set out on the diagram all the **(8)** _INFORMATION_ contained in the first two premises. If the argument is valid, the conclusion is diagramed as soon as both **(9)** _PREMISES_ have been diagramed. So, if the argument is valid, the information contained

68

in the conclusion has already been put on the diagram.   Thus, the conclusion conveys **(10)** MORE / NO MORE information than the premises.   In some sense, the information contained in the conclusion is already **(11)** CONTAINED IN / EXPLAINED BY the premises.   This is why it is sometimes said that in a valid argument, the conclusion is contained in the premises.

If an argument is valid, the conclusion must be **(12)** TRUE / FALSE when all the premises are **(13)** TRUE / FALSE.   Our diagrams show us how it is possible for there to be such a thing as a valid argument.   For there can be pairs of statements that already contain the information contained in the third statement.   When this happens, the argument is **(14)** VALID / INVALID. Such an argument can never go from true premises to a **(15)** _False_ conclusion.   It can never go from truth to falsehood because in the sense explained by the diagrams the conclusion is already **(16)** CONTAINED IN / CHOSEN BY the premises.   Since the conclusion is already **(17)** _Contained_ the premises, it is automatically true when all the premises are **(18)** _True_

In the sense explained by the diagrams, the conclusion of a valid argument conveys no more **(19)** EXAMPLES / INFORMATION than the premises.   Of course, the conclusion of an argument might still be surprising, for we may not see that the conclusion follows from the premises until we are actually presented with the argument.   So we may find the conclusion informative even though we knew the premises beforehand.   Nevertheless, the information contained in the premises conveys the information in the conclusion, even though we may take some time to see this.

Recall our method of counterexamples for showing that an argument form is invalid.   A counterexample is an **(20)** INTERPRETATION / DIAGRAM of the argument form in which the premises are all patently **(21)** TRUE / FALSE whereas the conclusion is **(22)** TRUE / FALSE.

Diagrams are related to counterexamples in the following way.   If we diagram some argument form and find that the conclusion is not yet diagramed, we know the argument form is **(23)** VALID / INVALID.   The conclusion **(24)** IS / IS NOT contained in the premises.   Hence, it is possible for the conclusion to be false even though the premises are all true.   Hence, a **(25)** COUNTEREXAMPLE / VALIDITY is possible.   Here is a concrete example:

> All *F* are *G*.
> All *H* are *G*.
> So, all *H* are *F*.

(26) Diagram the premises of the above argument on this diagram.

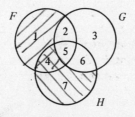

Is the conclusion diagramed? **(27)** YES / _NO_.

To diagram "All *H* are *F*," you would have to scratch out areas **(28)** _6_ and **(29)** _7_. Of these two, area **(30)** _7_ has been scratched out thanks to the second premise. But area **(31)** _6_ has not yet been scratched out. This shows how to get a counterexample to the above argument. We want an example where area 6 is definitely not scratched out, but where the premises are all true. This must be an example where the premises are all true, and, in addition, something is in *G*, in *H*, but not in *F* (that is, area 6).

Let *F*: women; *G*: human beings; and *H*: men. Notice that there are things that are in *G* (human beings), in *H* (men) but not in *F* (women). Under this interpretation, are the first two premises true? **(32)** _YES_ / NO. Is the conclusion true? **(33)** YES / _NO_. Hence, this interpretation provides a **(34)** _COUNTEREX_, which shows that the argument form is **(35)** _INVALID_.

If a syllogism is invalid, the information conveyed by the **(36)** _CONCLUSION_ is not diagramed even when all the information conveyed by the **(37)** _PREMISES_ has been diagramed. Hence, even if the information stated by the premises is correct, some of the information stated by the conclusion could be **(38)** INTERPRETED / _INCORRECT_. That is to say, the premises could all be **(39)** _TRUE_ / FALSE whereas the conclusion is **(40)** TRUE / _FALSE_. This is why the method of Venn diagrams enables us to tell when syllogisms are valid. If the conclusion is not diagramed as soon as the premises are diagramed, we see that it is possible for the conclusion to be false even though the premises are all true. Hence, the argument must be **(41)** VALID / _INVALID_.

If we find a counterexample to some argument form, we know that the argument form is **(42)** _INVALID_. But if we are unable to discover a counterexample, can we be certain that the argument is valid? **(43)** YES / _NO_. Thus the method of counterexamples cannot decide for us, in every case, whether a syllogism is valid. However, Venn diagrams can decide for us, in every case, whether a syllogism is valid. Venn diagrams provide what is called a "decision procedure" for validity of syllogisms. A decision **(44)** _PROCEDURE is_ a routine procedure by which you can calculate whether something has a certain property, in this case, whether a syllogism is valid. We have seen that counterexamples do not provide a **(45)** _DECISION PROCEDURE_ for validity. Venn diagrams, on the other hand, do provide a **(46)** _DECISION PROCEDURE_.

Aristotle also had a decision procedure for syllogisms. There are just four standard forms of statements used in syllogisms, namely:

(47) _All F are G_ .

(48) _Some F are G_ .

(49) _No F are G_ .

(50) _Some F are not G_ .

Aristotle wrote out every possible combination of these statement schemes to get an exhaustive list of every possible form of syllogism. Then he divided his list in two parts: one was a list of valid syllogisms and the other, a list of invalid syllogisms. After this, he had a decision procedure for validity. You can take an argument, note the form of the argument, and then see which list it is in. Many traditional logic books still follow this course (they even have a name for every possible kind of syllogism). We are not doing that here because Venn diagrams provide an easier decision procedure and, more important, they illustrate why some arguments are valid and some are invalid. An argument is invalid when the conclusion conveys **(51)** AS MUCH AS / MORE THAN / LESS THAN the premises. It is invalid because if it conveys more information than the premises, the information conveyed by the premises could be correct whereas the further information conveyed by the conclusion could be **(52)** CORRECT / INCORRECT. But we also see from Venn diagrams that some conclusions convey no more information than the premises. The information conveyed by the conclusion is drawn as soon as the information conveyed by the premises is drawn. Such an argument is **(53)** VALID / INVALID.

Write "T" in front of the true statements and "F" in front of the false ones:

(54) _F_ In a valid argument, the premises convey no more information than the conclusion.

(55) _T_ Aristotle had a decision procedure for the validity of syllogisms.

(56) _T_ If there exist counterexamples to some argument form, the conclusion will not be diagramed as soon as the premises are diagramed.

(57) _F_ No valid argument could have a false conclusion.

(58) _F_ The method of counterexamples provides a decision procedure for validity of the syllogism.

(59) _T_ The conclusion of one argument could be the premise of another argument.

We have not yet explained how to use Venn diagrams for "some" statements. First, review your use of the bar. Here are several diagrams; match them with the statements that follow on page 72.

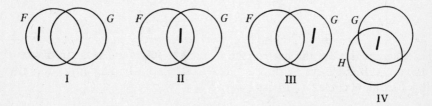

I II III IV

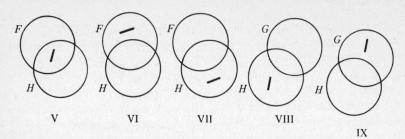

(60) __V__ Some harmless people are fighters.

(61) __ll__ Some gorillas are female.

(62) __lll__ Some gorillas are not female.

(63) __l__ Some females are not gorillas.

(64) __Vlll__ Some hairy animals are not gorillas.

(65) __V__ Some fallacious proofs are horrible mistakes.

(66) __Vlll__ Some hashish is not good for you.

(67) __lV__ There is at least one hateful general.

A "some" or a "some not" statement is diagramed in exactly the same way on a three-term diagram with three circles. Here is a diagram for "Some F are G":

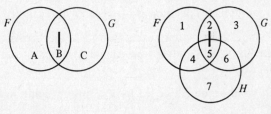

Notice that we have drawn the bar *across* the H circle. Here are two *incorrect* diagrams of "Some F are G."

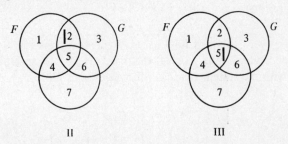

In diagram II, does the bar cut the H circle? **(68)** YES / NO. In diagram III, is the H circle cut by the bar? **(69)** YES / NO. In diagram I, does the bar cut the H circle? **(70)** YES / NO.

In diagram I, the bar has the following meaning: there is something in area B, that is, the area made up of 2 and 5. Area B is the area for things that are both *F* and **(71)** _*G*_. Area 2 is the area for things that are *F*, *G*, and not *H*. Area 5 is the area for things that are **(72)** _*F*_, **(73)** _*G*_, and **(74)** _*H*_.

Diagram II says that there is something in area 2 alone. Area 2 is the area for things that are *F*, *G*, and not *H*. But our statement was of the form, "Some *F* are *G*." It does *not* tell us whether anything is not *H*. Hence, diagram II represents more information than is given by the statement "Some *F* are *G*." Thus diagram II is a **(75)** RIGHT / ~~WRONG~~ picture of that statement. Diagram II represents the following: "Some things are *F*, *G*, but not *H*."

Diagram III tells us that there is something in area **(76)** _5_ alone. This area is the area for things that are **(77)** _*F*_, **(78)** _*G*_, and **(79)** _*H*_. But our statement to be diagramed was **(80)** _Some F are G_ It does not tell us whether anything is *H*. So diagram III represents **(81)** ~~MORE~~ / LESS information than this statement. Hence, it **(82)** IS / IS NOT an accurate diagram of this statement. Diagram III is an accurate representation of a different statement form, namely, **(83)** _Some F are G + H._

(84) Now put "Some *F* are *G*" in the correct way on this diagram:

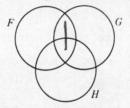

Does your bar cut the *H* circle? **(85)** YES / NO. Is part of your bar in area 2 and part in area 5? **(86)** YES / NO.

A bar between two areas, like areas 2 and 5 in the above diagram, means that there is something in one or the other area. It does not mean there is definitely something in both areas.

Notice how "Some *F* are not *G*" will be diagramed:

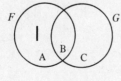   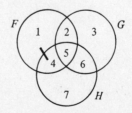

Once again, the bar (87) <u>CUTS</u> / DOES NOT CUT the H circle. This diagram means that there is something in area (88) __/__ or (89) __4__.

Does it mean that there is something in area 1 and something in area 4? (90) YES / NO. It means that there is something in area A, perhaps in the 1 part of A, perhaps in the 4 part, but we don't know which. That is why the bar cuts across the (91) __H__ circle.

Match these diagrams with the statements below:

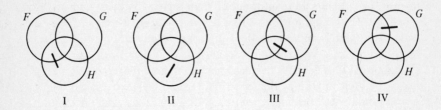

(92) __IV__ Some godfathers are not husbands.

(93) __I__ Some husbands are not godfathers.

(94) __II__ Some husbands are not godfathers and are not even friendly.

(95) __III__ Some godfathers are husbands.

(96) __I__ Some horses are not good at running.

(97) __II__ Some hunting hounds are not foxes and are not goats.

(98) __III__ There are hostile geese.

(99) __I__ There are hostile things other than geese.

Remember, a bar indicates that there is *something* in an area whereas scratching out an area means there is *nothing* in the area. Notice what happens when we diagram two statements such as:

All *F* are *G*.
Some *F* are *H*.

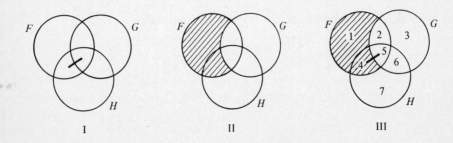

Which is the diagram of "All *F* are *G*"? **(100)** I / II / III. Which is the diagram of "Some *F* are *H*"? **(101)** I / II / III. In diagram III we see both statements. Notice that part, but only part, of the bar has been scratched out. The bar lies in areas number **(102)** _4_ and **(103)** _5_. But area number **(104)** _4_ has been scratched out. The bar is in areas 4 and 5; this means that there is something in **(105)** BOTH 4 AND 5 / EITHER 4 OR 5. But area 4 has been scratched out. This means **(106)** THERE IS SOMETHING IN 4 / THERE IS NOTHING IN 4.

So we know there is something either in 4 or 5, and we know it is not in 4. So it must be in 5. So according to the above diagram III there is definitely something in **(107)** _5_.

Notice that diagram I does *not* say there is something definitely in 5. It only says there is something either in **(108)** _4_ or in **(109)** _5_. Only when we put diagrams I and II together to get III, do we get something definitely in **(110)** _5_.

Now consider the argument form:

VALID

All *F* are *G*.
Some *F* are *H*.
So, some *G* are *H*.

Is the conclusion true in diagram III? Yes, because the conclusion says there is something to be found in the area common to *G* and *H*. This area is numbered **(111)** _5_ and **(112)** _6_ on III. On this diagram, the premises assure that there is definitely something in area **(113)** _5_. This is in both *G* and *H* so the conclusion, some *G* are *H*, is made true. The information conveyed by the conclusion is already conveyed by the premises. (In fact the premises tell us more than the conclusion: the conclusion just says there is something in 5 or 6; the premises tell us that something is definitely in 5. But this still makes the conclusion true.) The argument just examined must be **(114)** VALID / INVALID.

Now we look at the invalid argument form:

INVALID
All *F* are *G*.
Some *G* are *H*.
So, some *F* are *H*.

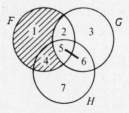

We have drawn the premises on the right. The conclusion requires that there is something in either area **(115)** _4_ or **(116)** _5_. Of these two, we see that one has already been scratched out. Which? **(117)** _4_. So if the conclusion is true, there must be something in area 5. The bar tells us there

is something either in 5 or 6.   Does it tell us there is definitely something in
5? **(118)** YES / NO. Hence, the conclusion is not automatically diagramed.   Hence, this argument form is **(119)** VALID / INVALID.

Now we work two more examples:

VALID
No *G* are *H*.
Some *F* are *G*.
So, some *F* are not *H*.

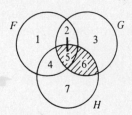

The conclusion requires that something is in area **(120)** _1_ or **(121)** _2_.
The bar is put into areas **(122)** _2_ and **(123)** _5_. However, of these
two, the area **(124)** _5_ is scratched out.   The only bit of the bar left is in
area **(125)** _2_. Thus, there is definitely something in area 2, and hence,
something in either 1 or 2.   So the conclusion is true on the diagram of the
premises.   Hence, the argument is **(126)** _VALID_.

INVALID
No *F* are *G*.
Some *H* are not *F*.
So, some *H* are not *G*.

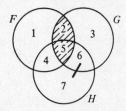

The conclusion requires that there be something definitely in the areas
(127) _4_ or **(128)** _7_. But the bar tells us only that there is something
in areas **(129)** _6_ or **(130)** _7_. It does not tell us that there is definitely
something in 7.   Hence, the conclusion **(131)** IS / IS NOT made true on the
above diagram.   Hence, the argument is **(132)** _INVALID_

Test the following argument forms for validity by drawing diagrams on
your own paper.

(133)   All *F* are *G*.
Some *G* are *H*.
So, some *F* are *H*.

(134)   All *F* are *H*.
VALID   No *G* are *H*.
So, no *F* are *G*.

(135)   Some *F* are *G*.
Some *G* are *H*.
So, some *F* are *H*.

(**136**) Some *F* are *G*.
Some *H* are *G*.
So, some *F* are *H*.

(**137**) All *F* are *G*.
Some *G* are not *H*.
So, some *F* are not *H*.

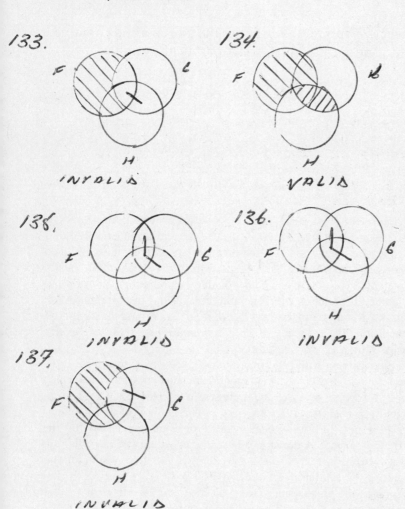

9 / Review with Applications

This chapter is a summary of the results and methods obtained so far, and it applies them to some practical examples.

Statements are true or **(1)** _FALSE_ , whereas arguments are said to be **(2)** _VALID_ or **(3)** _INVALID_. A valid argument **(4)** <u>CAN</u> / CANNOT have a false conclusion. If the premises are all true, however, then the conclusion must be **(5)** _TRUE_ , too. In the case of an invalid argument, we can have any of the four possible combinations of truth and falsehood, namely: premises all true and conclusion true, premises all **(6)** ~~TRUE/FALSE~~ and conclusion **(7)** ~~TRUE/FALSE~~ premises not all true and conclusion **(8)** ~~FALSE~~, and premises not all **(9)** _TRUE_ and conclusion **(10)** _FALSE_ .

If we find an argument with true premises and a false conclusion, we know that it is **(11)** VALID / <u>INVALID</u>. A counterexample to an argument form is an **(12)** _INTERPRETATION_ in which the premises are all **(13)** _TRUE_ and the conclusion is **(14)** _FALSE_ . The method of finding counterexamples **(15)** DOES / <u>DOES NOT</u> provide a decision procedure for the validity of the syllogism. A decision procedure for validity of the syllogism is provided by **(16)** _VENN DIAGRAMS_ In a Venn diagram of the syllogism, the syllogism is valid if the **(17)** _CONCLUSION_ is diagramed as soon as the premises are **(18)** _DIAGRAMED_ In such a situation, all the information conveyed by the conclusion is **(19)** EXEMPLIFIED BY / <u>CONTAINED</u> IN the information conveyed by the **(20)** _PREMISES_. Hence, if the information conveyed by the premises is correct, the information conveyed by the conclusion will also be **(21)** _CORRECT_, for the conclusion is in this sense contained in the premises.

Remember that although "The only *F* are *G*" is logically equivalent to "All *F* are *G*," the statement form "Only *F* are *G*" is logically equivalent to **(22)** ALL *F* ARE *G* / <u>ALL *G* ARE *F*</u>.

Here are some statements in standard form. Match them with logically equivalent statements below.

(23) _c_ Not a single dangerous thing is an airplane.

(24) _b_ There are dangerous airplanes.

(25) _e_ The only dangerous things there are, are airplanes.

(26) _d_ Airplanes are dangerous.

(27) _c_ There aren't any dangerous airplanes.

(28) _a e_ All things that are not dangerous are not airplanes.

(29) _a_ Every airplane is dangerous.

(30) _a_ Only dangerous things are airplanes.

(31) _a_ The only airplanes in existence are dangerous.

(32) _b_ At least one airplane is dangerous.

(a) All airplanes are dangerous things.

(b) Some airplanes are dangerous things.

(c) No airplanes are dangerous things.

(d) Some airplanes are not dangerous things.

(e) All dangerous things are airplanes.

(f) Some dangerous things are not airplanes.

Here are some examples of syllogisms. In each case, represent on your own paper the standard form of the argument, and then draw a diagram to test for validity. Say whether the argument is valid or not. If it is invalid, think up a counterexample to the argument form.

There is no need to use "*F*," "*G*," and "*H*" to stand for the terms. It is easier to see what you are doing, if you take the first letter of the term to denote it. Be careful to distinguish the premises from the conclusion of the argument. Remember that generally speaking, the words "so," "thus," "therefore," "hence," indicate that a (33) PREMISE / CONCLUSION is coming whereas "since," "for," and often "because" indicate reasons or premises.

(34) No (people who are allowed draft deferment) are (college dropouts,) because all (medical students) are allowed draft deferment,) and no (medical students) are (college drop-outs.)

(35) Since only people who believe in God are Christians, some people who refuse to bear arms are not Christians, for some people who refuse to bear arms do not believe in God.

(36) All graduate students must take a preliminary examination. This is because all graduate students must prove they are capable of independent study, and anyone who must prove he is capable of independent study must take a preliminary examination.

(37) Some of the best teachers do not have a PhD. Since some people who lack a PhD are denied promotion, some of the best teachers are denied promotion.

(38) None of these medicines is effective against viral diseases, for no antibiotics are effective against viral diseases, and some of these medicines are antibiotics

34.

P   C

m

— INVALIS —

35

VALIA —

36.

6   P

C

— VALIA —

37.

T

PH. D.

D.

— INVALIA —

38. M

E

A.

INVALID —

38. No Moles are female. Some Humans are females. No Humans are males.

Counter Exs.
34. All Men are Humans
No Men are Women
No Humans are Women

38. Some women are not pregnant
Some People who are not pregnant are men.
So Some women are men.

10 / Compound Statements

This chapter begins the study of a new kind of argument. We begin by learning how to schematize arguments of this kind and in later chapters develop more tests of validity.

The only words that *occur essentially* in syllogisms in standard form are little logical words like "all," "some," "no," and "not," together with the copula "is" or "are." But these are not the only logical words. Look at these two simple arguments.

A. Either this newspaper is lying, or one and a half million people were murdered in Viet Nam immediately after the nationalist forces defeated the French. Nothing like that many people were killed. <u>So, this newspaper is lying</u>.

B. If this newspaper is reporting accurately, then one and a half million people were slaughtered in Viet Nam immediately after the French were defeated by the nationalist forces. This newspaper is reporting accurately. <u>So, that many people were slaughtered at that time.</u>

Here are two shorter arguments that appear to be of the same forms:

C. Either Joseph is at home or in his office.
Joseph is not in his office.
<u>So, Joseph is at home.</u>

D. If Lydia is playing softball, then she is in Lincoln Park.
Lydia is playing softball.
<u>So, Lydia is in Lincoln Park.</u>

(1) Underline the conclusions of arguments C and D, then underline the

conclusions of arguments A and B. In argument **(2)** C / D the first
premise is of the form "either . . . or . . . ." But in argument **(3)** C / D the
first premise is of the form, "if . . . then . . . ."

(4)   Which of A or B has an "if, then" premise?   A / B.
(5)   Which has an "either, or" premise?   A / B.
(6)   Do you think argument C is valid?   YES / NO.
(7)   Do you think argument D is valid?   YES / NO.
(8)   Do you think argument A is valid?   YES / NO.
(9)   Do you think argument B is valid?   YES / NO.

Most people would say that all four arguments are valid. But the theory of
the syllogism is of no use to us here. We need a new technique for studying
validity.

On first sight, some people may feel that both C and D are valid, but that
at least one of A and B is invalid. This is probably because the conclusions
of A and B appear incompatible (assuming that in both paragraphs we are
talking about the same newspaper article). But remember there are two
ways of criticizing an argument. We may criticize it on the grounds that
not **(10)** *All the premises* are true. We may also criticize it on the grounds
that the argument is **(11)** *invalid*, that is to say, the conclusion does
not follow from the premises.

At least one of A and B is open to criticism. For the premises of A are
inconsistent with the premises of B. Hence, at least one set of premises
must be **(12)** FALSE / INVALID. Hence, at least one of the arguments could
be criticized on the grounds that not all the premises are **(13)** *True*.
But this is **(14)** THE SAME AS / DIFFERENT FROM criticizing the argument on
the ground that it is invalid. Both A and B are valid arguments; however,
at least one has false premises.

Now consider two statements such as:

E.   The students were allowed to remain in the administration building.
F.   The police were called and forced the students out.

E and F are examples of **(15)** STATEMENTS / ARGUMENTS. We can *connect*
these statements in various ways to form *compound* statements. Thus:

G.   Either the students were allowed to remain in the administration
building, or the police were called and forced the students out.

Statement G says **(16)** THE SAME AS / SOMETHING DIFFERENT FROM statements
E and F.

The *compound* statement G is built up from the *component* statements E
and F using the *connective* "either, or."

(17) Which is the compound statement? E / F / <u>G.</u>

(18) What is the connective? *Either ... or ...*

(19) Which are the components? <u>E</u> / <u>F</u> / G.

Here is another compound statement:

> The ministers were obviously wary about the North Atlantic Alliance taking on the task of creating better human environments (and) some ministers feared that Mr. Nixon's other two ideas might undercut the Permanent Council.

Here the little word "and" connects two statements. **(20)** Circle this connective, and underline the two components. The statement as a whole is a **(21)** <u>COMPOUND</u> / COMPONENT / CONNECTIVE statement.

If my soldiers began to think, then every soldier would quit my army.

This statement by Frederick the Great is a **(22)** COMPONENT / <u>COMPOUND</u> statement. The connective used here is "if, then." Notice that the connective is not part of the components. Rather, it connects the components.

(23) Write a check in front of the components:

_____ (a) If my soldiers began to think.

✓_____ (b) My soldiers began to think.

_____ (c) Every soldier would quit thinking.

✓_____ (d) Every soldier would quit my army.

_____ (e) Then every soldier would quit my army.

_____ (f) If my soldiers began to think, then every soldier would quit my army.

In each of the following examples, circle the main connective and underline the components.

(24) <u>The communique reflects some of the President's thoughts on NATO's future</u> (but) <u>it does not immediately accept any of his three ideas for additional alliance machinery.</u>

(25) (<u>If</u> <u>the faculty refuses to speak out plainly on this issue of the original humiliation of the university,</u> (then) <u>it will be forever unable to defend the principle of the peaceful settlement of disputes.</u>

(26) <u>Our lives will be terminated by attack from outside</u> (or) <u>by revolution from within.</u>

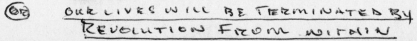

⊙⊙ OUR LIVES WILL BE TERMINATED BY REVOLUTION FROM WITHIN

In example 26 you might think that "revolution from within," is a component statement. But this phrase **(27)** IS / <u>IS NOT</u> a statement at all. Rather 26 is a shortened form of the equivalent statement:

(26*)   <u>Our lives will be terminated by attack from outside</u> or <u>our lives will be terminated by revolution from within.</u>

Instead of underlining the component statements in the elliptical 26, underline them in the more complete 26*.

In the following example, the connective is "neither, nor."

Neither Moscow nor the world can really expect the NATO countries to act as if these brutal repressions had never occurred.

(28) Which are the complete components? Check them on this list.

_____ (a)   Moscow can really expect the NATO countries to act as if these brutal repressions had never occurred.

_____ (b)   Moscow.

_____ (c)   Nor the world can really expect the NATO countries to act as if these brutal repressions had never occurred.

_____ (d)   These brutal repressions had never occurred.

_____ (e)   The world.

_____ (f)   The world cannot really expect the NATO countries to act as if these brutal repressions had never occurred.

_____ (g)   The world can really expect the NATO countries to act as if these brutal repressions had never occurred.

In the following examples, circle the connectives. Underline the complete components if you can, but if they have been telescoped, as in 26, write out the complete components.

(29)   <u>The Army has an overriding concern for the preservation of discipline,</u> but <u>the employment of McCarthy-type tactics will command no respect.</u>

(30)   <u>The blacks in this country have many grievances that are not removed by peaceful debate,</u> and <u>even at Columbia there were appalling stupidities that no amount of polite discourse seemed to change.</u>

(31) Only if the government is responsive to citizen protest will such discussions have any effect.

SUCH DISCUSSIONS WILL HAVE ANY EFFECT

(Remember, everything you call a component must be a statement capable of standing on its own.)

(32) For decades men have used the oceans and the navigable waters as free dumping grounds.

FOR DECADES MEN HAVE USED THE NAVIGABLE WATERS AS FREE DUMPING GROUNDS

(33) The bill makes the owner or operator liable for up to $10 million.

THE BILL MAKES THE OPERATOR LIABLE FOR UP TO $10 MILLION ~~bill~~

Fill in the following blanks with your choice of the words *connective, compound, component,* and *statement*: A **(34)** *CONNECTIVE* is a word or phrase, or possibly several words occurring at different places in a sentence that is used to build up a **(35)** *COMPOUND* statement from some **(36)** *COMPONENT* statements. A component is itself a **(37)** *STATEMENT,* although in forming the **(38)** *COMPOUND* using the connective, one or more **(39)** *COMPONENT* statements may be telescoped or otherwise altered in accordance with grammatical rules that make our speech briefer. Thus, for example, in the statement "only if I go will she go," the first component occurs straightforwardly. It is, "I go." But the second **(40)** *COMPONENT,* namely, "she will go," is written backwards in the construction where "only if" is the **(41)** *CONNECTIVE.* We cannot call the turn of words, "will she go," a **(42)** *COMPONENT* simply because it is not even a **(43)** *STATEMENT*

Connectives are used to form new statements from old. So is the word "not." Take for example the statement:

> In scientific research a straight line is not necessarily the shortest distance between two points.

This statement is the *denial* of the following statement:

> In scientific research a straight line is necessarily the shortest distance between two points.

What is the difference between the two statements? **(44)** *THEY'RE OPPOSITES AS ONE HAS "NOT" + ONE DOESN'T*

There are several ways to express a denial. Thus for example if someone says:

A. Joseph is at home.

we can retort:

B.   Joseph is not at home.

or:

C.   It is not true that Joseph is at home.

Both B and C are built up from A.   Both are **(45)** DENINALS / RESTATEMENTS
of A.   We shall say that B and C are both **(46)** COMPONENT / COMPOUND
statements built up from the single component A.
   Here is another example of a denial.

D.   The imposition of Neanderthal disciplinary practices is not going to
     command the respect of the educated young men needed to man a
     modern army.

What is the statement that it is denying?   **(47)** *THE IMPOSITION O*
NEANDERTHAL DISCIPLINARY PRACTICES
IS GOING TO COMMAND . . . .

D is a **(48)** COMPOUND / CONNECTIVE statement that is the denial of the
component statement you wrote out in answer to 47.   Although the word
"not" isn't strictly a connective, for it does not connect two or more things,
it is convenient to include it in our list of connectives.   Thus from now on,
when we speak of connectives, we **(49)** SHALL / SHALL NOT mean to include
the word "not."   In our usage, is "it is not true that" counted as a connective?   **(50)** YES / NO.
   Be careful about "not."   Not every occurrence of this word is a connective.   For example, consider the statement:

E.   Some people are not at home.

This is *not* the denial of,

F.   Some people are at home.

The denial of "some people are at home," would be

G.   It is not true that some people are at home.

Notice that E and G do not mean the same.   For according to **(51)** E / G,
absolutely nobody is at home.   But according to **(52)** E / G, although
some people are not at home, there might be other people who are at home.
   We shall call "not" a connective only when it is used to form the denial
of a statement.   In the above example, the denial of F is **(53)** E / G.   On
the other hand, E **(54)** IS / ISN'T the denial of F.

Here are two pairs of statements. In one pair, the second statement is the denial of the first. In the other pair, the second statement is *not* the denial of the first. Find out which is which.

A. There are military programs that have been subjected to a tough survey of their strategic necessity since World War II.
B. There are military programs that have not been subjected to a tough survey of their strategic necessity since World War II.

(55) Is B the denial of A? YES / <u>NO</u>.

C. Strictly on the question of academic merit, an ROTC course is worthy of full academic credit towards a college degree.
D. Strictly on the question of academic merit, an ROTC course is not worthy of full academic credit towards a college degree.

(56) Is D the denial of C? <u>YES</u> / NO.

(57) What is the denial of A? *IT IS NOT TRUE THAT THERE ARE MILITARY PROGRAMS — THAT HAVE BEEN SUBJECTED . . .*

Notice that we can combine connectives to build up even more complex statements. For example, consider these two statements:

A. Their communique reflects some of President Nixon's thoughts on NATO's future.
B. Their communique immediately accepts President Nixon's three ideas.

We can form the denial of B to get:

C. Their communique does not immediately accept President Nixon's three ideas.

Then this can be combined with A to get, in idiomatic English:

D. Their communique reflects some of President Nixon's thoughts on NATO's future, but it does not immediately accept his three ideas.

We say that A and B are the *base components* of D. Components that are not built up from simpler components by the use of connectives are called

(58) *BASE COMPONENTS.*

In the following examples, indicate the base components and the connectives:

(59) The army has an overriding concern for the preservation of discipline, but the imposition of Neanderthal disciplinary procedures is not going

to command the respect of the educated young men needed to man
a modern army.
Connectives: _BUT , NOT -_
Base components: _THE ARM ... DISCIPLEN
THE IMPOSITION ... IS GOING TO ... ARMY._

(60) It is not true that he can complain of lack of freedom or abuse of
administrative authority at Harvard.
Connectives: _IT IS NOT TRUE THAT , OR -_
Base components: _HE ... FREEDOM OR ADMINISTRATION
HE ... OF ABUSE ... HARVARD._

(61) Every organic species naturally procreates its kind at so high a rate
that, if most of its members were not destroyed, the earth would soon
be covered by the progeny of a single pair.
Connectives: _IF , NOT_
Base components: _EVERY ... THAT THE EARTH ... PAIR
MOST OF ITS MEMBERS WERE DESTROYED._

(62) Even slow breeding man has doubled in twenty-five years and, at this
rate, in less than a 1,000 years there would literally not be standing
room for his progeny.
Connectives: _AND , NOT, EVEN , LITERALLY_
Base components: _SLOW BREEDING ... 25 YEARS
AT THIS RATE IN LESS THAN A 1,000
YEARS THERE WOULD BE STANDING
ROOM FOR ITS PROGENY._

11 / "And," "Or," and "Not"

This chapter presents some logical properties of three of the connectives noticed in the last chapter.

Almost anyone can see at once that the following argument is valid:

> Joseph is at home or in his office.
> Joseph is not at home.
> So, Joseph is in his office.

The first premise uses the connective **(1)** _____ *o re* _____. The two base components are **(2)** _J. is at Home_ and **(3)** _J is in itis office_ _____. The second premise uses the connective **(4)** _not_ _____. The base component of the second premise is **(5)** _J. is at Home_.

If you wanted to know where Lydia is, and someone told you:

> Lydia is playing softball in Lincoln Park, or she is resting at home. But she is not resting at home.

what would you infer about Lydia? She is **(6)** IN LINCOLN PARK / AT HOME. That is, the two stated premises lead us to the conclusion:

> Lydia is playing softball in Lincoln Park.

The argument about Lydia has a form that is **(7)** THE SAME AS / DIFFERENT FROM the argument about Joseph. Let us use capital letters like "*P*" and

89

"*Q*" to stand for statements.   Then the form of the two arguments would be schematized as:

> *P* or *Q*.
> Not *P*.
> So, *Q*.

Let *P*: He will spend five years in jail; *Q*: He will pay a $10,000 fine.   Then write out an argument of the above form:

(8) *HE WILL SPEND FIVE YEAR IN JAIL OR HE WILL...在*
    HE WILL NOT SPEND FIVE YEAR IN JAIL
So, HE WILL PAY A $10,000 FINE .

The key words of this new argument form are **(9)** OR / IF, THEN / BOTH / NOT / SOME.   So we single out "not" and "or" for a new study.   Take any statement, say:

A.   Dr. Jensen was primarily concerned with a study of genes.

The denial of this could be expressed:

B.   Dr. Jensen was not primarily concerned with a study of genes.

Now if A is true, the denial of A, namely B, is **(10)** TRUE / FALSE.   If A is false, then B is **(11)** TRUE / FALSE.

We call "true" and "false" *truth values* of statements.   If a statement is true, we say its truth value is T for "true"; if a statement is false, we say its **(12)** *TRUTH VALUE* is F for "false."

If the truth value of A is T, then the truth value of its denial B is **(13)** *F*.
If the truth value of A is F, then the truth value of its denial B is **(14)** *T*.
Thus the truth value of a denial of a statement is always **(15)** THE SAME AS / OPPOSITE TO the truth value of the original statement.

This fact can be represented in a table called a *truth table*.

P	Not *P*
T	F
F	T

Read this table in the obvious way.   In the first horizontal row of truth values, we see "T" under "*P*" and **(16)** "*F*" under "Not *P*."   This means that when "*P*" is T, then "Not *P*" is **(17)** *F*.

The bottom row of the truth table tells us that when "*P*" is F, then "Not *P*" is **(18)** *T*.

If the truth value of "*P*" is T, what is the truth value of "Not *P*"? **(19)** *F*. If the truth value of "Not *P*" is F, what is the truth value of "*P*"? **(20)** *T*.

In symbolic logic, it is usual to abbreviate even the little word "not." We do this by writing a *bar* in front of the letter standing for a statement. So instead of "not *P*" we write:

$$-P$$

What is the abbreviation for "not *Q*"? **(21)** *Q* / −*P* / −*Q* / *Q*−.
(22) Complete the following truth table for −*P*:

P	−*P*
T	F
F	T

In the argument form:

P or *Q*
Not *P*.
So, *Q*.

the other connective besides "not" was **(23)** ___or___. It is not quite so easy to draw a truth table for "or." The trouble is that the word "or" is slightly ambiguous. Consider the statement:

Students will be admitted to the freshman year if they have high school grades in the top 30 percent or if they have passed the university entrance examination.

Circle the "or" in this statement. According to this statement, would a student be admitted if his high school grades were in the top 30 percent? **(24)** YES / NO. According to this statement, would a student be admitted if he passed the university entrance examinations? **(25)** YES / NO. Would you expect a student to be admitted if he *both* was in the top 30 percent at high school *and* passed the university entrance examination? **(26)** YES / NO.

Most people answer "yes" to the last question. They take the college admissions policy as meaning students will be admitted:

if they are in the top 30 percent at high school,
or if they pass the entrance exams,
or both.

But now consider the statement,

Adam wants coffee or tea.

Do you suppose that Adam wants *both* coffee and tea? **(27)** YES / NO.
Most people would expect Adam to be pleased if he got coffee or pleased if
he got tea, but surprised, perhaps revolted, if he got both.   Thus the statement about college admission policy seems to mean, in schematic form:

P or Q or both.

But the statement about Adam's beverage seems to mean **(28)** P OR Q OR
BOTH / P OR Q BUT NOT BOTH.
There are even clearer examples of P or Q but not both.   If a schoolboy is
trying to get out of some homework and miss a day at school because of his
grandmother's funeral, his teacher might say:

You will be allowed to miss a day of school *or* you will be excused
homework.

Has the boy been authorized to miss school *and* avoid his homework?
(29) YES / NO.   Most people, including the teacher, would say he has been
allowed to do one or the other, but not both.
Thus, there appear to be **(30)** ONE / TWO / THREE sense(s) of "or" illus-
trated by these examples.   In one, "P or Q" means "P or Q or both," in
the other, it means **(31)** *P or Q but not both*.
The sense of "or" where "P or Q" means "P or Q or both," **(32)** INCLUDES /
EXCLUDES the case of "both."   Hence, it is called the *inclusive* sense of "or."
The sense of "or" where "P or Q" means "P or Q but not both," **(33)**
INCLUDES / EXCLUDES the case of "both."   Hence, it is called the **(34)**
INCLUSIVE / EXCLUSIVE sense of "or."
Inclusive uses of "or" preponderate.   Hence, we shall adopt the conven-
tion that, unless there is good reason to the contrary, "or" will be read in the
inclusive sense.   Thus we are going to understand "or" to mean **(35)** P OR Q
OR BOTH / P OR Q BUT NOT BOTH.
The Romans actually had two different words for our single "or."   They
used the word "aut" for the exclusive sense.   They used the word "vel" for
the inclusive sense.   Thus in Latin, the word "vel" means **(36)** P OR Q BUT
NOT BOTH / P OR Q OR BOTH.   Because of this, we take the letter "v," the
first letter of the Latin word **(37)** *vel*, to stand for the inclusive sense of
"or."   Thus

$$P \lor Q$$

stands for **(38)** P OR Q OR BOTH / P OR Q BUT NOT BOTH.   In our notation,
the bar, written "−," stands for **(39)** AND / OR / NOT.   The letter "v"

looks like a **(40)** FLAG / HORSE / <u>WEDGE</u> / HORSESHOE. Hence, we call it the *wedge*. The wedge stands for the **(41)** <u>INCLUSIVE SENSE OF "OR"</u> / EXCLUSIVE SENSE OF "OR."

Consider the statement:

Joseph is a swimmer or a runner.

What is the connective? **(42)** _____ *or* _____. What are the base components, in full? **(43)** _Joseph is a swimmer — Joseph is a runner —_____.

(44) Is this statement true if Joseph is a swimmer? <u>YES</u> / NO.
(45) Is this statement true if Joseph is a runner? <u>YES</u> / NO.
(46) Is this statement true if Joseph is such a good athlete that he is both a swimmer and a runner? <u>YES</u> / NO.
(47) Is this statement true if Joseph is not a swimmer, and not a runner, but a cripple? YES / <u>NO.</u>

If you read the "or" as instructed, in the **(48)** <u>INCLUSIVE</u> / EXCLUSIVE sense, you will have answered "yes" to 44, 45, 46, and "no" to 47. Thus these four questions illustrate **(49)** ONE / TWO / THREE / <u>FOUR</u> / FIVE different possibilities. In the first three, the statement:

Joseph is a swimmer or a runner.

is **(50)** <u>TRUE</u> / FALSE. The statement is false only when **(51)** EITHER / <u>BOTH</u> alternatives are false, that is when Joseph is both not a runner and not a swimmer.

(52) Is P or Q true if P is true? <u>YES</u> / NO.
(53) Is P or Q true if Q is true? <u>YES</u> / NO.
(54) Is P or Q true if both P and Q are T? <u>YES</u> / NO.
(55) Is P or Q true if both P and Q are false? YES / <u>NO.</u>

$P \vee Q$ is F if and only if both P and Q are F.

These facts are represented in the following table:

P	Q	$P \vee Q$
T	T	T
T	F	T
F	T	T
F	F	F

There is only one possible combination of truth values for P and Q in which $P \lor Q$ takes the value F. This is when P is **(56)** _F_ and Q is **(57)** _F_. This is indicated by the FIRST / SECOND / THIRD / <u>FOURTH</u> row on the truth table.

If $P \lor Q$ takes the value F, then P takes the value **(59)** _F_ and Q takes the value **(60)** _F_.

According to the first row on this table, if P is T and Q is **(61)** _T_, then $P \lor Q$ is **(62)** _T_.

According to the second row, when P is **(63)** _T_ and Q is **(64)** _F_, then $P \lor Q$ is **(65)** _T_.

According to the third row, when P is **(66)** _F_ and Q is **(67)** _T_, then $P \lor Q$ is **(68)** _T_.

According to the fourth and last row, when P is **(69)** _F_ and Q is **(70)** _F_, then $P \lor Q$ is **(71)** _F_. This is the **(72)** FOURTH / <u>ONLY</u> situation where $P \lor Q$ is F.

Some people like to think of the rows in truth tables as representing different possibilities. To take a concrete example, let:

P: The builders will use reinforced concrete.

Q: The building will collapse during the earthquake.

Then $P \lor Q$ is the statement, written in full: **(73)** _THE BUILDERS WILL USE REINFORCED CONCRETE OR THE BUILDING WILL COLLAPSE DURING THE EARTHQUAKE._

The first row in the truth table represents the possibility that both P and Q are true. The builders use reinforced concrete, but even so, it collapses during the earthquake. That is one (remote) possibility.

The second row represents another possibility, namely, the possibility that P is T and Q is F. This is the possibility that the builders use reinforced concrete, and the building **(74)** DOES / <u>DOES NOT</u> fall down, during the next earthquake.

The third row represents a third **(75)** _possibility_ namely the possibility that P is **(76)** _F_ and Q is **(77)** _T_. This is the possibility that the builders **(78)** DO / <u>DO NOT</u> use reinforced concrete, and the building **(79)** DOES / <u>DOES NOT</u> collapse, during the next earthquake.

The fourth row represents a fourth and last possibility, namely the **(80)** _possibility_ that P is **(81)** _F_ and Q is **(82)** _F_, too. This is the lucky chance that the building is not built with reinforced concrete, but still, it **(83)** DOES / <u>DOES NOT</u> collapse during the earthquake.

Which is the only possibility in which the statement:

The builders will use reinforced concrete or the building will collapse during the earthquake.

is false? **(84)** 1 / 2 / 3 / <u>4</u>.

Finally we look at the connective "and." Here is an example of the use of this connective:

Joseph has a good job (and) a pretty wife.

Circle the "and." What are the base components, written out in full? (85) _JOSEPH HAS A GOOD JOB -_
JOSEPH HAS A PRETTY WIFE.
Would this statement be true if Joseph has a poorly paid job in uncomfortable surroundings doing boring work with no chance of advancement? **(86)** YES / NO. Would it be true if Joseph has an ugly wife? **(87)** YES / NO.

Would it be right to say that the statement is true if and only if Joseph *both* has a good job *and* a pretty wife? **(88)** YES / NO.

In general, a statement of the form *P* and *Q* is true if and only if both *P* and *Q* are true. If one or the other is F, then the whole statement is **(89)** T / F.

Complete the following truth table for "and."

	P	*Q*	*P & Q*
1	T	T	T
2	T	F	F
3	F	T	F
4	F	F	F

You will have *P & Q* T in row **(90)** 1 / 2 / 3 / 4 only. In every other row the value of the compound statement will be **(91)** T / F. Notice that we abbreviate the word "and" with the familiar sign "&." This sign is called the *ampersand.* Thus, the wedge stands for **(92)** _OR_, the bar for **(93)** _NOT_, and the ampersand for **(94)** _AND_.

Once again we can think of the table as showing various possibilities. If we know nothing about Joseph's job or wife, it is possible that he has a good job and a pretty wife. This possibility indicated by row **(95)** 1 / 2 / 3 / 4 on the table. This is the possibility that the compound statement:

Joseph has a good job and a pretty wife.

is **(96)** T / F. It is the **(97)** ONLY / SECOND possibility in which this compound statement is T.

The second row is for the possibility where Joseph has a good job but an ugly wife (or he's a bachelor). That is, *P* is **(98)** T and *Q* is **(99)** F. *P & Q* is **(100)** F.

The third row is the case where *P* is **(101)** F, *Q* is **(102)** T, and *P & Q* is **(103)** F. In plain English, this is the case when Joseph **(104)** DOES / DOES NOT have a good job, but he **(105)** DOES / DOES NOT have a pretty wife. In this situation, the compound statement is false.

Note the difference between the wedge and the ampersand: There is only

one row where the $P \lor Q$ is (106) _F_ and only one row where $P \& Q$ is
(107) _T_. $P \lor Q$ is F if and only if both P and Q are (108) _F_;
$P \& Q$ is T if and only if both P and Q are (109) _T_. There is a sort of
symmetry here that we will use later, but do not confuse the wedge and the
ampersand.

Draw up a table for all three connectives. In filling in the column under
$P \lor Q$, it saves time to put a single F in the only row where $P \lor Q$ is F,
namely the row where P is (110) _F_ and Q is (111) _F_. Then fill in all
the other rows unthinkingly with T.

Similarly, in filling under $P \& Q$, first find the row where $P \& Q$ is T,
namely the row where P and Q are both (112) _T_. Then fill in the other
spaces unthinkingly with (113) T /_F_.

(114)

P	Q	$P \lor Q$	$P \& Q$	$-P$	$-Q$
T	T	T	T	F	F
T	F	T	F	F	T
F	T	T	F	T	F
F	F	F	F	T	T

A final word of caution. We noticed two senses of the word "or." We
have spoken as if "and" always meant the same thing. But sometimes it is
used to mean "and then." Here is an example:

Lydia got married and had a baby.
Lydia had a baby and got married.

A lot of people would say these two statements meant pretty different things.
We shall tend to ignore this use of "and" meaning "and then."

In a statement of the form "P or Q," "P" and "Q" are different *alternatives*
and a statement with a central wedge is called an *alternation*. A statement of
the form "P and Q" joins or conjoins "P" and "Q," and so is called a
conjunction. The components are called *conjuncts*. Circle the conjunction
and underline the alternation:

(115) He is rich or strong. — ALTERNATION -
(116) He is rich and strong. — CONJUNCTION .

Complete this table:

(117)

P	Q	$P \lor Q$	$Q \lor P$	$P \& Q$	$Q \& P$
T	T	T	T	T	T
T	F	T	T	F	F
F	T	T	T	F	F
F	F	F	F	F	F

Is the column under "$P \lor Q$" any different from the column under "$Q \lor P$"? **(118)** YES / NO. Thus the order of the alternatives around a wedge **(119)** DOES / DOES NOT matter to the truth value.

Is the column under "$P \& Q$" any different from the column under "$Q \& P$"? **(120)** YES / NO. Thus the order of the conjuncts around an ampersand **(121)** DOES / DOES NOT matter to the truth value.

As the example of Lydia's baby shows, the order of the conjuncts around "and" can matter in English. To this extent, our notation is an idealization on English. Also, the order of the alternatives around "or" can matter in English as shown by the following contrast:

> They will use reinforced concrete or the building will collapse.
> The building will collapse or they will use reinforced concrete.

The former makes more sense than the latter, because the first alternative suggests a way of preventing the second alternative from being true; you cannot say the same thing of the second statement. We shall, however, disregard these important nuances of English in our notation.

The idea of alternation can be expressed in English by "or" and by "either, or." So we represent "P or Q" and "Either P or Q" using the wedge in the same way, as **(122)** $P \lor Q$.

Consider the statement:

> They used reinforced concrete but the building fell down.

Here the connective is **(123)** *But* . In the following statement:

> They used reinforced concrete and the building fell down.

the connective is **(124)** *and* . The two statements have slightly different nuances: the first expresses surprise that the building fell down after reinforced concrete had been used. But the truth values of the statements are surely **(125)** THE SAME / DIFFERENT. So we paraphrase both "but" and "and" using the **(126)** WEDGE / AMPERSAND.

12 / Truth Tables

This chapter shows how to use truth tables to test some arguments for validity.

The previous chapter opened with this valid argument:

> Joseph is at home or in his office.
> Joseph is not at home.
> So, Joseph is in his office.

Letting P: Joseph is at home; Q: Joseph is in his office, write out the form of this argument, using the wedge and the bar:

(1)

$$P \lor Q$$
$$- P$$
$$Q$$

We expect this to be a valid argument form. That is, every interpretation of the letters "P" and "Q" should give a (2) _VALID_ / INVALID argument. In a valid argument, when the premises are all true, the conclusion must be (3) ___TRUE___, too. If it is possible for the premises to be T and the conclusion to be F, then the argument is (4) VALID / _INVALID_. Venn diagrams provided a (5) COUNTEREXAMPLE / _DECISION PROCEDURE_ for validity of the syllogism. That is, they give a mechanical test of whether any syllogistic form of argument is valid. It turns out that truth tables provide a decision procedure for validity of arguments like the one cited above.

Using Venn diagrams, we drew diagrams for the premises and looked to

98

see if the conclusion was true on the diagrams of the premises. Now we draw truth tables:

		First Premise	Second Premise	Conclusion
P	Q	P ∨ Q	−P	Q
T	T	T	F	T
T	F	T	F	F
F	T	T	T	T
F	F	F	T	F

We ask, is it possible for the premises to be true and the conclusion false? Our table shows every different possible combination of truth values for P and Q. Each row in the truth table represents some possibility or other. For example, the first row represents the possibility that P is T and Q is T. In the interpretation where P: Joseph is at home; Q: Joseph is in his office, this is the possibility that Joseph is both at home and in his office (his office is in his own home).

The second row represents the possibility that P is T and Q is F. What would this be, in our interpretation?

(6) _JOSEPH IS AT HOME AND NOT IN HIS OFFICE_

The third row represents the (7) _Possibility_ that P is (8) _F_ and Q is (9) _T_. What would this be, in our interpretation? _HE IS_

(10) _JOSEPH IS NOT AT HOME AND IN HIS OFFICE_

What possibility is represented by the fourth row? P is (11) _F_ and Q is (12) _F_. What is this possibility in our interpretation?

(13) _JOSEPH IS NOT AT HOME AND HE IS NOT IN HIS OFFICE._

In the first possibility, P is T and Q is T. What is the truth value of the first premise, $P \vee Q$? (14) _T_. What is the truth value of the second premise, $−P$? (15) _F_. In this situation, are both premises true? (16) YES / <u>NO</u>. Are both premises true in the second row? (17) YES / <u>NO</u>. Are both premises true in the third row? (18) <u>YES</u> / NO. Are both premises true in the fourth row? (19) YES / <u>NO</u>. Thus there is only one row where both premises take the value T. This is the (20) _THIRD_ row, where P is (21) _F_ and Q is T. Is the conclusion T in the third row? (22) <u>YES</u> / NO.

Is the following observation correct? (23) <u>YES</u> / NO.

The conclusion is T in every row where all the premises are T.

This observation is correct because there is (are) (24) <u>ONE</u> / TWO / THREE / FOUR row(s) where all the premises are T. In this row (row 3) the conclusion is (25) _T_.

The observation could be phrased differently:

⇢ *In every possibility where all the premises are T, the conclusion is also T.*

Is the following yet another restatement of this fact? **(26)** YES / NO.

⇢ *There is no possibility of the premises all being true while the conclusion is false.*

Now an argument is valid if it is not possible for all the premises to be **(27)** _T_ while the conclusion is **(28)** _F_. Thus the truth table shows us that the argument is **(29)** VALID / INVALID.

An argument is invalid if there is any row in the truth table where all premises are T and the conclusion is F.

An argument is valid if the conclusion is T at every row where the premises are all T.

We have just shown that the argument form:

P or Q.
Not P.
So, Q.

is valid. Complete the following truth table to see if the argument form P or Q, − Q, so P is valid:

(30)

P	Q	P ∨ Q	− Q	P
T	T	T	F	T
T	F	T	T	T
F	T	T	F	F
F	F	F	T	F

Is it valid? **(31)** YES / NO.

In contrast, consider the similar looking argument forms

P ∨ Q.
P.
So, Q.

and

$P \lor Q$.
Q.
So P.

The truth table for the first is worked out on the left.

	P	Q	$P \lor Q$	P	Q	$P \lor Q$	Q	P
1	T	T	T	T	T	*T*	*T*	*T*
2	T	F	T	T	F	*T*	*F*	*T*
3	F	T	T	F	T	*T*	*T*	*F*
4	F	F	F	F	F	*F*	*F*	*F*

For the first argument form, there are two rows in the truth table in which both premises are true. Which are the rows in question? **(32)** 1 / 2 / 3 / 4. In the first row, both premises are T, and the conclusion is T. Does this show the argument form is valid? **(33)** YES / NO. In the second row, both premises are T and the conclusion is F. Does this show the argument form is invalid? **(34)** YES / NO.

Thus the truth table established that the first argument form is invalid. Now draw a truth table for the other argument form, using the spaces allotted on the right. Is the second argument form valid? **(35)** YES / NO.

These examples suggest the following *rule of inference*:

"$P \lor Q$, $-P$, so Q" is valid.
"$P \lor Q$, $-Q$, so P" is valid.

We often want to write things like ". . ., so ___ is valid." We do this by writing the sign "⊢" between premise and conclusion. We write:

$$P \lor Q, -P \vdash Q.$$

This means, "the argument form '$P \lor Q$, $-P$, so Q' is valid." What does this mean: "$P \lor Q$, $-Q \vdash P$"? **(36)** _$P \lor Q$, $-Q$ so P is valid._

(37) Is it true that $P \lor Q$, $-Q \vdash P$?   YES / NO.
(38) Is it true that $P \lor Q$, $-P \vdash Q$?   YES / NO.
(39) Is it true that $P \lor Q$, $P \vdash Q$?   YES / NO.
(40) Is it true that $P \lor Q$, $Q \vdash P$?   YES / NO.

Draw a truth table to find out whether $P \lor Q, Q \vdash -P$:

(41)

P	Q	$P \lor Q$	Q	$-P$
T	T	_T_	_T_	_F_
T	F	_T_	_F_	_F_
F	T	_T_	_T_	_T_
F	F	_F_	_F_	_T_

(42) Is it true that $P \lor Q, Q \vdash -P$? _NO_ It is not true that $P \lor Q, Q \vdash -P$.
This means (check A or B): **(43)** A. The argument form "$P \lor Q, Q$, so $-P$"
is valid. / _B._ The argument form "$P \lor Q, Q$, so $-P$" is not valid. It is not
true that $P \lor Q, P \vdash -Q$. What does this mean? **(44)** _THE_
ARGUMENT FORM $P \lor Q, P \vdash -Q$ IS NOT VALID

So far we have drawn tables for statements using just one connective. But
suppose we are asked whether:

CONNECTIVES $(-P \lor Q), P \vdash Q.$

Then we have one statement with two connectives. **(45)** Circle the statement
and each connective within it.

We shall read $-P \lor Q$ by taking the wedge to be the central connective,
connecting two alternatives, namely $-P$ and Q. What are the alternatives
in "$P \lor Q$"? **(46)** _P_ and **(47)** _Q_. What are the alternatives in
"$-P \lor -Q$"? **(48)** _-P_ and **(49)** _-Q_. What are the conjuncts in
"$-P \& -Q$"? **(50)** _-P_ and **(51)** _-Q_.

In drawing a table for a scheme such as $-P \lor Q$ where there are two connectives, it is best to proceed systematically. The two alternatives are
(52) _-P_ and **(53)** _Q_. So the truth value for the whole compound is
derived from the value of these two alternatives. But the truth value of $-P$
is itself determined by the truth table for P. So we draw the following table.
If you have any trouble completing it, read the instructions below.

	P	Q	$-P$	$-P \lor Q$
1	T	T	_F_	_T_
2	T	F	_F_	_F_
3	F	T	_T_	_T_
4	F	F	_T_	_T_

In the last column you should get TFTT. If you have no trouble getting
this, omit the following paragraph. Otherwise, read on.

The column for $-P$ is just the opposite of the column for P, that is, FFTT.
Fill it in. We can fill in the column for $-P \lor Q$ as follows. We know that

an alternation takes the value F if and only if **(54)** BOTH ALTERNATIVES ARE FALSE / ONE ALTERNATIVE IS FALSE. The alternatives of $-P \lor Q$ are $-P$ and Q. In the first row, the alternative $-P$ is **(55)** T / _F._ In the first row, the alternative Q is **(56)** T / F. Are both alternatives false in the first row? **(57)** YES / NO. Hence, the value of $-P \lor Q$ in the row is **(58)** T / F. Fill it in. You can proceed in the same way for every row, getting TFTT in the final column. But there is a shortcut. An alternation is F if and only if **(59)** _BOTH ALTERNATIVES ARE F_ Thus we will enter an F in the column under an alternation only for those rows in which both alternatives are false. The alternatives are **(60)** $-P$ and **(61)** Q. So run two fingers down the columns for $-P$ and Q. Every time you run into a row with both alternatives being F, enter an F under the alternation. Try it. Which is the first row you hit with both alternatives F? **(62)** 1 / _2_ / 3 / 4. Are there any more such rows? **(63)** YES / NO. Thus you know that the alternation takes F in the second row only. At every other row it must be T. Now see if the following assertions are correct:

(64)　$-P \lor Q, P \vdash Q.$ 　 = VALID

(65)　$P \lor -Q, -Q \vdash P.$ 　=INVALID

(66)　$-P \lor -Q, Q \vdash -P.$ 　= VALID

		(64)			(65)				(66)		
				Premise		Premise	Conclusion			Premise	Conclusion
		Premise	Premise	Conclusion	Premise				Premise		
P	Q	$-P$	$-P \lor Q$	P	Q	$-Q$	$P \lor -Q$	P	$-P$	$-Q$	$-P \lor -Q$	Q	$-P$
T	T	F	T	T	T	F	T	T	F	F	F	T	F
T	F	F	F	T	F	T	T	T	F	T	T	F	F
F	T	T	T	F	T	F	F	F	T	F	T	T	T
F	F	T	T	F	F	T	T	F	T	T	T	F	T

Circle the correct assertions: (64) / 65 / (66)

Is it true that $P \vdash --P$ and $--P \vdash P$? **(67)** YES. Check by completing this table:

P	$-P$	$--P$
T	F	T
F	T	F

Is there any difference between the column under P and the column under $--P$? **(68)** YES / NO. The truth values of P and $-P$ are always **(69)** THE

SAME / DIFFERENT. But the truth values of P and $--P$ are always **(70)** THE SAME / DIFFERENT. Because they are equivalent in this way, P and $--P$ are called *logically equivalent*.

Now suppose we have some statement, P. The denial of P is written by writing a **(71)** BAR / WEDGE in front, resulting in: **(72)** $-P.$ The denial $-P$ is in turn derived by writing a bar in front, resulting in **(73)** $--P$ However, this is logically equivalent to P. So, we shall loosen our use of the word "denial." We will say that $-P$ is the denial of P, and that either $--P$ or P is a denial of $-P$.

(74) Is Q a denial of $--Q$? YES / NO.

(75) Is $-Q$ a denial of Q? YES / NO.

(76) Is Q a denial of $-P$? YES / NO.

(77) Is Q a denial of $-Q$? YES / NO.

Examples such as 64 and 66 show us we can state a quite general rule of inference:

From any alternation, plus a denial of one alternative, we can infer the other alternative.

Which of the following are examples of this rule? Check the correct statements, cross out the incorrect ones.

(78) _____ $-P, \quad P \vee -Q \vdash Q.$

(79) _____ $-P, \quad Q \vee P \vdash Q.$

(80) _____ $P, \quad -P \vee Q \vdash Q.$

(81) _____ $-P, -Q \vee P \vdash -Q.$

(82) _____ $-Q, -Q \vee -P \vdash P.$

(83) _____ $-Q, \quad Q \vee -P \vdash P.$

Complete the blanks in the following:

(84) $P, -P \vee Q \vdash Q.$

(85) $-Q \vee P, -P \vdash -Q$

(86) $Q \vee P, -P \vdash Q.$

(87) $P \vee Q -P \vdash Q.$

Which of the following are correct?

(88) ✔ $--P \vdash P$.

(89) ✔ $-P \vdash ----P$.

(90) ✔ $-P \vdash ------P$.

(91) _____ $---P \vdash P$.

(92) _____ $--P \vdash -P$.

(93) ✔ $----P \vdash ---P$.

We conclude with a few more rules of inference. Suppose you bet that the racehorse Alphabet Soup will come in first or second in the next race. You will collect if it comes in first. Will you collect if it comes in second? **(94)** YES / NO. Thus, if the horse comes in first, it will come in first or second. And if it comes in second, it will come in first or second. So you would expect the following to be true:

$$P \vdash P \vee Q \qquad \text{and} \qquad Q \vdash P \vee Q$$

On the other hand, from the statement that the horse came in either first or second, you **(95)** CAN / CANNOT infer that it came in first, so the argument form "$P \vee Q$, so P" is **(96)** VALID / INVALID. On your own paper, draw truth tables to check that:

(97) $Q \vdash P \vee Q$.

(98) The argument form "$P \vee Q$, so Q" is invalid.

On the other hand, if the horse came in third in the first race and last in the fifth, you can infer that the horse came in last in the fifth. But from the fact that it came in last in the fifth, you cannot conclude that it came in last in the fifth and third in the first. Check the correct statements and cross out the incorrect one:

~~(99)~~ _____ $P \vdash P \& Q$.

(100) ✔ $P \& Q \vdash P$.

(101) ✔ $P \& Q \vdash Q$.

Notice that the order of conjuncts in a conjunction and the order of alternatives in an alternation do not matter to the truth value. **(102)** Draw truth tables to check that $P \vee Q$ and $Q \vee P$ are logically equivalent.

Finally, we say that one statement is *stronger* than another if it says more. Thus, P is stronger than Q if P implies Q but Q does not imply P. If P is stronger than Q, is the argument "P, so Q" valid? **(103)** YES / NO. If P is stronger than Q, is it true that $Q \vdash P$? **(104)** YES / NO. **(105)** Draw truth tables to show that $P \& Q$ is stronger than $P \vee Q$. Is it true that $P \& Q$ is stronger than $Q \vee P$? **(106)** YES / NO.

Check the correct assertions, and cross out the incorrect ones:

(107) _____ A conjunction is F if and only if both conjuncts are F.

(108) _____ An alternation is F if and only if one alternative is F.

(109) _✓_ An alternation is F if and only if both alternatives are F.

(110) _✓_ P and $--P$ are logically equivalent.

(111) _✓_ $-P$ and $---P$ are logically equivalent.

(112) _____ $P \vee Q \vdash P$.

(113) _____ $P \vdash P \& Q$.

(114) _✓_ $P \vdash P \vee Q$.

(115) _✓_ $P \vee Q \vdash Q \vee P$.

(116) _✓_ $Q, -Q \vee P \vdash P$.

(117) _✓_ $P \vdash P \vee -Q$.

(118) _____ $-P, Q \vee P \vdash -Q$.

(119) _____ $-P, Q \vee -P \vdash Q$.

(120) _✓_ $Q \& P \vdash P \vee Q$.

(121) _✓_ $P \vee Q$ and $Q \vee P$ are logically equivalent.

(122) _✓_ $P \& Q$ and $Q \& P$ are logically equivalent.

(123) _____ The alternatives of $-P \vee -Q$ are P and Q.

(124) _✓_ The base components of $-P \vee -Q$ are P and Q.

(125) _✓_ The alternatives of $-P \vee -Q$ are $-P$ and $-Q$.

(126) _____ "$P \vdash Q$" means "P, so Q."

13 / De Morgan's Laws

This chapter shows how to build more complex truth tables and applies this to developing some important logical equivalences.

The alternatives of $-P \vee Q$ are **(1)** _$-P$_ and **(2)** _q_ . The conjuncts of $P \& - Q$ are **(3)** _P_ and **(4)** _$-q$_. The bar in front of the P applies only to P. $-P$ is the denial of **(5)** $P \vee Q$ / _P._ If we wish to form the denial of $P \vee Q$ we do it by bracketing "$P \vee Q$" and then writing a bar in front: $-(P \vee Q)$. What is the denial of $P \& Q$? **(6)** _$-(p \& q)$_

We have less formal ways of bracketing in ordinary speech. Compare these two statements:

A. He is a swimmer and not a runner.
B. He is not both a swimmer and a runner.

These two mean **(7)** THE SAME / _SOMETHING DIFFERENT._

Let P: He is a swimmer; Q: He is a runner. Now, paraphrase symbolically statements A and B:

(8) A. _$P \& - q$_.

(9) B. _$- (p \& q)$_

If he is not both a swimmer and a runner, notice that he could be a runner, so long as he is not a swimmer. Could he be a swimmer, if he was not a

107

runner? **(10)** YES / NO. Could he be both a swimmer and a runner?
(11) YES / NO. Could he be neither a swimmer nor a runner? **(12)** YES / NO.

To draw a truth table of $-(P \& Q)$, it is best to proceed step by step.
First work out the table for $(P \& Q)$, then for the denial. So draw up a
table like this and complete the blank spaces:

(13)

P	Q	P & Q	−(P & Q)
T	T	T	F
T	F	F	T
F	T	F	T
F	F	F	T

To see that $-(P \& Q)$ and $P \& -Q$ are not equivalent, draw up a truth
table for the latter:

P	Q	−Q	P & −Q
T	T	F	F
T	F	T	T
F	T	F	F
F	F	F	F

The conjuncts of $P \& -Q$ are **(14)** _P_ and **(15)** _−Q_. Note that Q is not
a conjunct; the conjunct required is $-Q$. Hence, we draw a column for
the conjunct $-Q$. A conjunction is T if and only if both conjuncts are
(16) _T_. So we run down the columns for the conjuncts, namely for
(17) _P_ and **(18)** _−Q_, until we find rows with both conjuncts T; then we
enter **(19)** _T_ in the same row for the conjunction $P \& -Q$. Complete
the table by filling in all remaining rows for the conjunction with an **(20)** _F_.
Now compare tables. Is the column under $-(P \& Q)$ in the previous table
the same as the column under $P \& -Q$ here? **(21)** YES / NO. So the two
forms of statement **(22)** ARE / ARE NOT equivalent.

Would you expect $-(P \& Q)$ to have the same truth table as $-P \& Q$?
(23) YES / NO. Do brackets matter? **(24)** YES / NO.

Evidently bracketing helps to avoid ambiguity. The difference between
$-(P \& Q)$ and $-P \& Q$ corresponds to the difference between:

He is not both a swimmer and a runner.

and

He is not a swimmer, and he is a runner.

Let P: He is an athlete; Q: He is a scholar.   Match:

(25) _d_ $-(P \& Q)$.

(26) _e_ $-P \& -Q$.

(27) _c_ $P \& -Q$.

(28) _f_ $-(-P \& Q)$.

(29) _b_ $-P \& Q$.

(30) _h_ $-(-P \& -Q)$.

(31) _g_ $-(P \& -Q)$.

(32) _a_ $P \& Q$.

(a)   He is an athlete and a scholar.
(b)   He is not an athlete, but he is a scholar.
(c)   He is an athlete, but he is not a scholar.
(d)   He is not both an athlete and a scholar.
(e)   He is not an athlete, and he is not a scholar.
(f)   He is not both not an athlete and a scholar.
(g)   He is not both an athlete and not a scholar.
(h)   He is not both not an athlete and not a scholar.

To see that none of the expressions 25–32 are logically equivalent, construct the following table:

(33)

				32	29	27	26
P	Q	$-P$	$-Q$	$P \& Q$	$-P \& Q$	$P \& -Q$	$-P \& -Q$
T	T	F	F	T	F	F	F
T	F	F	T	F	F	T	F
F	T	T	F	F	T	F	F
F	F	T	T	F	F	F	T

	25	28	31	30
	$-(P \& Q)$	$-(-P \& Q)$	$-(P \& -Q)$	$-(-P \& -Q)$
	F	T	T	T
	T	T	F	T
	T	F	T	T
	T	T	i	F

Notice that the table is arranged in a systematic way.   To work out $P \& Q$, run your finger down the P and Q columns and every time you find both components T, enter **(34)** _T_ in the $P \& Q$ column.   Enter F for every row you have not filled in with T.

To work out $-P \& Q$ run down the $-P$ and Q columns.   Every time you find both components T, enter **(35)** _T_ in the corresponding row in the $-P \& Q$ column; fill in the remaining rows with **(36)** _F_.

Carry on in this way.   To fill in the $-(P \& Q)$ column, write down the exact opposite of the $P \& Q$ column; to fill in the $-(-P \& -Q)$ column, write down the exact opposite of the **(37)** _$-P \& -Q$_ column.

Do any of expressions 25–32 have the same truth values in every row? **(38)** YES / <u>NO</u>.

There are great symmetries between the wedge and the ampersand, for most of the points made in expressions 8–38 are repeated for the wedge. To begin with, note the difference between:

A. He is either a swimmer or not a runner.

and

B. He is not either a swimmer or a runner.

Which of these would normally be expressed by

"He is neither a swimmer nor a runner"? **(39)** A / <u>B.</u>

Letting P: He is an athlete; Q: He is a scholar, match:

(40) _m_ $-(P \vee Q)$.

(41) _l_ $-P \vee -Q$.

(42) _k_ $P \vee -Q$.

(43) _o_ $-(-P \vee Q)$.

(44) _j_ $-P \vee Q$.

(45) _p_ $-(-P \vee -Q)$.

(46) _n_ $-(P \vee -Q)$.

(47) _i_ $P \vee Q$.

(i) He is either an athlete or a scholar.

(j) Either he is not an athlete, or he is a scholar.

(k) Either he is an athlete, or he is not a scholar.

(l) Either he is not an athlete, or he is not a scholar.

(m) He is neither an athlete nor a scholar.

(n) He is neither an athlete nor not a scholar.

(o) He is neither not an athlete nor a scholar.

(p) He is neither not an athlete nor not a scholar.

The symmetries between the wedge and the ampersand go very deep. First, recall the idea of logical equivalence. In terms of truth tables, we explain it as follows: two statements are logically equivalent if it is impossible for them to differ in truth value. Thus, if P and Q are logically equivalent, then whenever P is T, Q is **(48)** _T_. Whenever P is F, Q is **(49)** _F_. Whenever Q is T, P is **(50)** _T_. Whenever Q is F, P is **(51)** _F_. If at each row in the truth table two statements have the same truth value, then the statements are logically **(52)** _Equivalent_. If there is some row where they differ in truth value, then they are not **(53)** _logically equivalent_. If two statements are logically equivalent, could they both take the value F is in some row? **(54)** <u>YES</u> / NO. Are P and $--P$ logically equivalent?

(55) YES / NO.   Are $P \vee Q$ and $Q \vee P$? **(56)** YES / NO.   Now draw truth tables on your own paper to compare 25 and 41: $-(P \,\&\, Q)$ and $-P \vee -Q$. Are they logically equivalent? **(57)** YES / NO.

(58) On your own paper draw a truth table to show that 26 $-P \,\&\, -Q$ and 40 $-(P \vee Q)$ are logically equivalent.

(59) Then show that 27 $P \,\&\, -Q$ and 43 $-(-P \vee Q)$ are logically equivalent.

A pattern begins to emerge.   We have the following logical equivalences:

$$-P \vee -Q = -(P \,\&\, Q)$$
$$-P \,\&\, -Q = -(P \vee Q)$$
$$P \,\&\, -Q = -(-P \vee Q)$$

The underlying general rule was noticed long ago, certainly by the fourteenth century A.D., but is usually called after Augustus De Morgan who set out the rule very clearly in the middle of the last century.

To change a conjunction to an alternation:
1.   *Replace the ampersand by a wedge.*
2.   *Write a bar in front of each conjunct.*
3.   *Write a bar in front of the whole compound that results.*
4.   *Delete double bars, because $--P$ and P are equivalent.*

To change an alternation to a conjunction:
1.   *Replace the wedge by the ampersand.*
2.   *Write a bar in front of each alternative.*
3.   *Write a bar in front of the resulting compound.*
4.   *Delete double bars.*

These rules for obtaining equivalences are called "De Morgan's laws."

EXAMPLE $-P \vee -Q$.

1.   Replace the wedge by an ampersand: $-P \,\&\, -Q$.
2.   Write a bar in front of each alternative: $--P \,\&\, --Q$.   *Remember*: the alternatives are themselves $-P$ and $-Q$, so we get $--P$ and $--Q$ at this stage.
3.   Write a bar in front of the resulting compound: $-(--P \,\&\, --Q)$.
4.   Delete double bars: $-(P \,\&\, Q)$.

Here we have passed from expression 41 to the logically equivalent 25.

EXAMPLE $P \ \& \ Q$.

1. Replace the ampersand by the wedge. $P \vee Q$.
2. Write bars in front of the conjuncts: $-P \vee -Q$.
3. Write a bar in front of the compound. $-(-P \vee -Q)$.
4. Delete double bars.   There are none.

EXAMPLE $-(P \ \& \ Q)$.

The conjunction here is $(P \ \& \ Q)$. By the last example, this is logically equivalent to (60) $-(-P \vee -Q)$. So $(P \ \& \ Q)$ with a bar in front is logically equivalent to $-(-P \vee -Q)$ with a bar in front. This is $--(-P \vee -Q)$. Delete double bars. We get $(-P \vee -Q)$. Thus we have passed from 25 to the logically equivalent 41. Now do your own examples.

Start with $-P \ \& \ Q$. The conjuncts are (61) _____ $-P$ _____ and
(62) _____ Q _____ .

1. Change ampersand to wedge.   (63) _____ $-P \vee Q$
2. Write bars in front of the conjuncts: (64) _____ $--P \vee -Q$
3. Write a bar in front of the compound: (65) _____ $-(--P \vee -Q)$
4. Delete double bars: (66) _____ $-(P \vee -q)$

So we have passed from the statement $-P \ \& \ Q$ to the logically equivalent
(67) _____ $-(-P \vee -Q)$
Start with $-(-P \ \& \ Q)$. From (67), we know the conjunction $-P \ \& \ Q$
is logically equivalent to (68) _____ $-(-P \vee -Q)$. So $-(-P \ \& \ Q)$ is logically
equivalent to $--(P \vee -Q)$. Delete double bars: (69) _____ $P \vee -Q$ _____ .
Start with $P \vee -Q$. The alternatives are: (70) _____ P and (71) $-Q$.

1, 2. Change wedge to ampersand and write bars in front of alternatives:
(72) _____ $-P \ \& \ --Q$
3.   Write a bar in front of the compound: (73) _____ $-(-P \ \& \ --Q)$ _____ .
4.   Delete double bars: (74) _____ $-(-P \ \& \ Q)$

So we have passed from (75) _____ $P \vee -q$ _____ to the logically equivalent
(76) _____ $-(-P \ \& \ q)$
Start with $-(P \vee -Q)$. From (76), we know that $P \vee -Q$ is logically
equivalent to (77) _____ $-(-P \ \& \ q)$. So $-(P \vee -Q)$ is logically equivalent
to (78) $--(-P \ \& \ --q)$. Delete double bars: (79) _____ $-P \ \& \ q$ _____ . So
we have passed from (80) _____ $-(P \vee -Q)$ to the logically equivalent
(81) _____ $-P \ \& \ Q$.

It turns out that every item in the list 25–32 on page 109 is logically equivalent to exactly one item on the list 40–47 on page 110. Match them up, using your own paper to make the transformations where necessary.

(82) _26_ 40. $-(P \lor Q)$ 25. $-(P \& Q)$

(83) _25_ 41. $-P \lor -Q$ 26. $-P \& -Q$

(84) _28_ 42. $P \lor -Q$ 27. $P \& -Q$

(85) _27_ 43. $-(-P \lor Q)$ 28. $-(-P \& Q)$

(86) _31_ 44. $-P \lor Q$ 29. $- P \& Q$

(87) _32_ 45. $-(-P \lor -Q)$ 30. $-(-P \& -Q)$

(88) _21_ 46. $-(P \lor -Q)$ 31. $-(P \& -Q)$

(89) _30_ 47. $P \lor Q$ 32. $P \& Q$

Two statement schemes having identical truth values at each row in the truth table are called logically (90) _EQUIVALENT_ If there is some row in the truth table where the schemes differ in truth value, then they are not (91) _LOGICALLY EQUIVALENT_

(92) Draw truth tables on your own paper to check that (29) and (46) are logically equivalent.

If you want practice in drawing truth tables, you should check that each of the matched pairs above is a logical equivalence. First check with the answer section to see that you have matched correctly. Then draw truth tables for the matched items. Go on doing this until you have no trouble obtaining identical columns of truth values for matched items.

Here are some rather complicated assertions in plain English. In each case, paraphrase into our notation, then apply De Morgan's laws, then translate back into English to get a simpler statement. Thus one merit of De Morgan's laws is that they let us change statements that are hard to understand into statements that are easy to grasp.

It is not true both that he didn't fail the examination and that he was detested by his teacher.

Let F: He did fail the examination; D: He was detested by his teacher.

(93) Paraphrase: _$-(-F \& D)$_

(94) Result of applying De Morgan's laws: _$F \lor -D$_

(95) Translation back into English: _HE EITHER DID FAIL THE EXAM OR HE WAS NOT DETESTED._

It is altogether false that he is both irresponsible and untrustworthy.

Let R: He is responsible; T: He is trustworthy.

(96) Paraphrase: $-(-R \mathrel{\&} -T)$
(97) Result of applying De Morgan's laws: $R \lor T$.
(98) Translation back into English: _HE IS RESPONSIBLE OR TRUSTWORTHY (OR BOTH)._

It is not true that the glyptodon is either not a reptile or else not extinct.

Let R: The glyptodon is a reptile; E: The glyptodon is extinct.

(99) Paraphrase: $-(-R \lor -E)$
(100) Result of De Morgan's laws: $R \mathrel{\&} E$.
(101) Translation back into English: _THE GLYPTODON IS A EXTINCT REPTILE_.

It is not the case that there is a first point in time or that time is not capable of running backwards.

Let P: There is a first point in time; R: Time is capable of running backwards.

(102) Paraphrase: $-(P \lor -R)$
(103) Result of De Morgan's laws: $-P \mathrel{\&} R$.
(104) Translation back into English: _THERE IS NOT A FIRST POINT IN TIME AND TIME IS CAPABLE OF RUNNING BACKWARDS_.

If two statements are logically equivalent, then at any row on the truth table they have (105) THE SAME / DIFFERENT truth values.   Hence if P and Q are logically equivalent, at any row where P takes the value T, Q takes the value (106) _T._ Now an argument is valid if, for every row at which the premises are all T, the conclusion is also (107) _T._   Hence, if P and Q are logically equivalent, the argument P so Q is (108) VALID / INVALID.

Now explain why, if P and Q are logically equivalent, the argument Q so P is valid.   (109) _IF P & Q ARE LOGICALLY EQUIVALENT THEN WHENEVER / ROW THEY HAVE THUS SAME TRUTH VALUES THUS IF P IS T SO IS Q THUS IF Q IS T SO IS P_.

14 / Building Truth Tables

This chapter shows how to build complex truth tables to test quite complicated argument forms for validity.

The abbreviation "$P \vdash Q$" means **(1)** P, so Q / <u>THE ARGUMENT FORM "P, SO Q" IS VALID</u>.

If two statements are logically equivalent, is it possible for one to take the value T at a row in the truth table where the other takes the value F? **(2)** YES / NO. If two statements are logically equivalent, is it possible that both should take the value F at some row in the truth table? **(3)** YES / NO.

Check the correct assertions that follow and cross out the incorrect ones. If you are unsure about any example, test by drawing a truth table.

(4) ___✓___ $P \vdash P \lor Q$.

~~(5)~~ _____ $-(P \lor Q) \vdash -(-P \& -Q)$.

(6) ___✓___ $---P \vdash -P$.

~~(7)~~ _____ $Q \vdash P \& Q$.

~~(8)~~ _____ $P \& Q \vdash -(-P \lor Q)$.

~~(9)~~ _____ $Q \lor P \vdash P$.

(10) ___✓___ $P \& Q \vdash Q \lor P$.

~~(11)~~ _____ $-P \& -Q \vdash -Q \lor -P$.

~~(12)~~ _____ $-(P \lor Q) \vdash -P \& Q$.

(13) ___✓___ $-(P \lor -Q) \vdash -P \& Q$.

~~(14)~~ _____ $----Q \vdash -Q$.

115

In some of the above assertions that you have checked as correct, the conclusion also implies the premise, so that the premise and the conclusion are
logically equivalent. **(15)** Which? 4 / 5 / 6 / 7 / 8 / 9 / 10 / 11 / 12 /
13 / 14.

Each of our examples so far involves only one base component and one
premise. Now we need to look at more complicated examples. First you
must get a sense of the meaning of quite intricate statements. For example:

> Either Chicago beat $\underline{M}$ontreal and lost to $\underline{S}$t. Louis, or it beat $\underline{P}$ittsburgh
> and lost to $\underline{P}$hiladelphia.

Before paraphrasing this into our notation, it is a good idea to put brackets
around the various components to make clear just what the connectives
connect. What are the connectives? **(16)** *Either, or, and, and*
Bracketing the parts of the statement, we get:

> Either [(Chicago beat $\underline{M}$ontreal) and (lost to $\underline{S}$t. Louis)] or [(it beat
> $\underline{P}$ittsburgh) and (lost to $\underline{P}$hiladelphia)].

We will use the underlined letters to stand for the various components in the
obvious way:

> M: Chicago beat Montreal.
> S: Chicago lost to St. Louis.
> P: Chicago beat Pittsburgh.
> H: **(17)** *Chicago lost to Philadelphia.*

Then we obtain (circle the correct answer): **(18)** $(M \& S \vee P \& H)$ /
$((M \& (S \vee P)) \& H)$ / $(\underline{(M \& S) \vee (P \& H)})$ / $(((M \& S) \vee P) \& H)$.
Since we do not bother with outside brackets, we can write simply:

$$(M \& S) \vee (P \& H)$$

Of the wrong answers above, the first is simply ambiguous. But the other
two correspond to perfectly good English statements. One of them paraphrases the following statement:

> [(Chicago beat Montreal) and either [(lost to St. Louis) or (beat Pittsburgh;)]
> and (it also lost to Philadelphia.)

(19) Bracket the parts of the statement. What is the paraphrase? **(20)**
$\underline{(M \& (S \vee P)) \& H}$ / $((M \& S) \vee P) \& H$.

(21)   Write out an English sentence corresponding to $((M \& S) \vee P) \& H$.

EITHER CHICAGO BEAT MONTREAL AND LOST TO ST. LOUIS, OR, IT BEAT PITTSBURG, AND IT ALSO LOST TO PHILADELPHIA.

Match the following statements against the appropriate paraphrases. Before trying to match, bracket the parts of the statements to avoid getting confused:

(22) __a__ $(R \vee E) \& (-C \vee P)$.

(a)   Either the road was blocked by snow or the engine broke down, and also, either he did not care much about coming or his passenger delayed him.

(23) __b__ $R \vee (E \& (-C \vee P))$.

(b)   Either the road was blocked by snow or, it is true both that the engine broke down and that either he did not care much about coming or his passenger delayed him.

(24) __c__ $((R \vee E) \& -C) \vee P$.

(c)   Either it is true both that either the road was blocked by snow or the engine broke down, and that he did not care much about coming, or else his passenger delayed him.

(25) __d__ $R \vee ((E \& -C) \vee P)$.

(d)   Either the road was blocked by snow, or else either the engine broke down and he did not care much about coming, or his passenger delayed him.

In a complicated statement scheme, we are following the convention of putting brackets around every conjunction and alternation. Moreover, if we wish to deny a compound statement, we put brackets around the compound and then write a bar in front of it. But to deny an atomic statement P, we don't bother to bracket the P, so we write (26) $-(P) \; / \; --P \; / \underline{-P}$ for the denial of P. But the denial of $P \vee Q$ is (27) $-P \vee Q \; / \; -P \vee -Q \; / \; \underline{-(P \vee Q)} \; / \; -(-P \vee -Q)$. Moreover, we don't bother with outer brackets, for these remove no ambiguity. Brackets are used only to avoid ambiguity.

The statement scheme $(P \vee Q) \& (R \vee S)$ is a conjunction; both conjuncts are themselves (28) CONJUNCTIONS / ALTERNATIONS.

The statement scheme $(P \& Q) \vee (R \& S)$ is an (29) CONJUNCTION / ALTERNATION. Both alternatives are (30) CONJUNCTIONS / ALTERNATIONS.

The truth value of a complex statement is built up in a systematic way from the truth value of the base components. Consider $(P \lor Q) \& (R \lor S)$. First recall that a conjunction is T if and only if both conjuncts are **(31)** _T_. An alternation is F if and only if both alternatives are **(32)** _F_. The conjuncts of $(P \lor Q) \& (R \lor S)$ are **(33)** _P ∨ Q_ and **(34)** _R ∨ S_. Suppose that P is T; Q is F; R is T; and S is F. What is the truth value of the conjunct $P \lor Q$? **(35)** _T_. What is the truth value of the conjunct $R \lor S$? **(36)** _T_. So under this assignment of truth values, both conjuncts are **(37)** _T_. Hence, the truth value of $(P \lor Q) \& (R \lor S)$ is **(38)** _T_.

Suppose that P is T; Q is F; R is F; and S is F. What is the truth value of $P \lor Q$? **(39)** _T_. What is the truth value of $R \lor S$? **(40)** _F_. What is the truth value of $(P \lor Q) \& (R \lor S)$? **(41)** _F_.

Under this assignment of truth values to P, Q, R, and S, what is the truth value of $P \lor Q$? **(42)** _T_. What is the truth value of $R \& S$? **(43)** _F_. What is the truth value of $(P \lor Q) \lor (R \& S)$? **(44)** _T_.

Every row in the truth table can be built up systematically in the same way. But first we must learn to draw tables for more than two components.

Suppose we have only one component. Then there are just two possibilities. The component may be T, and it may be F. We need a row in the truth table for each possibility. How many rows will there be in a truth table for P? **(45)** _Two_ How many base components are there in $-P$? **(46)** _ONE_ How many rows will we need for a truth table of $-P$? **(47)** _Two_ How many base components are there in a truth table for $(P \lor -P) \& (P \& P)$? **(48)** _ONE_ How many rows will we need? **(49)** _Two_

If there is just one base component, we need just **(50)** _Two_ rows in the truth table.

Now suppose we have two base components, P and Q, as in $P \lor Q$. The possibilities for P are just T and F. Now look at the first possibility, with P being T. If P is T, there remain two possibilities for Q, namely Q is T or Q is **(51)** _F_. Thus if P is T, there are two possibilities: the possibilities for Q divide P in half:

$$P \quad Q$$
$$T \lessgtr \begin{matrix} T \\ F \end{matrix}$$

If P is F, there remain **(52)** ONE / _TWO_ possibilities for Q, namely Q is **(53)** _T_ or Q is **(54)** _F_. Thus, if P is F there are **(55)** ONE / TWO possibilities. The possibilities for Q divide P in half:

$$P \quad Q$$
$$F \lessgtr \begin{matrix} T \\ F \end{matrix}$$

Combining these two part-tables, we have:

$$P \qquad Q$$

$$T <\begin{matrix} T \\ F \end{matrix}$$

$$F \qquad \begin{matrix} T \\ F \end{matrix}$$

or, as we have been doing all along:

P	Q
T	T
T	F
F	T
F	F

Thus with two components, we have four possibilities and four rows in the truth table. This is **(56)** JUST AS MANY / TWICE AS MANY possibilities as for one component. We get twice as many because every possibility for P is divided in two by the possibilities for Q.

We continue in this way when we have P, Q, and R. Every possibility for P and Q is divided in two by the possibilities for R. There were **(57)** _4_ possibilities for P and Q. There will be twice as many possibilities for P, Q, and R, or a total of **(58)** _8_ possibilities in all.

Here are the eight possibilities:

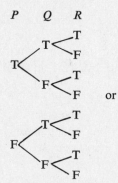

or

P	Q	R
T	T	T
T	T	F
T	F	T
T	F	F
F	T	T
F	T	F
F	F	T
F	F	F

In drawing a table for a statement with three base components, there will be **(59)** _8_ rows in the truth table. If there were four components, there would be twice as many rows as for three components, so there will be a total of **(60)** _16_ rows.

What happens here is formally similar to Venn diagrams. With just one term we drew just one circle, and there were two areas, inside and outside the

circle. With two terms, we had two circles and twice as many areas, namely
(61) _X_. With three terms we had twice as many areas again, namely
(62) _8_ . With four terms we will have to have **(63)** _16_ areas.

Now you should be able to draw truth tables for quite complicated forms.
Start with $P \& (Q \lor -R)$. This is a **(64)** CONJUNCTION / ALTERNATION.
One conjunct is P. The other is **(65)** _(Q ∨ -R)_ So the other conjunct is the **(66)** CONJUNCTION / <u>ALTERNATION</u> $Q \lor -R$. The first alternative is **(67)** _Q_. The second is $-R$, which is the denial of **(68)** _R_.
Thus $P \& (Q \lor -R)$ breaks down into P and $(Q \lor -R)$; the latter breaks
down into Q and $-R$; this last breaks down into R. We shall want a column
for each of these statement parts, as shown on the following table. Complete
the table:

(69)

P	Q	R	$-R$	$Q \lor -R$	$P \& (Q \lor -R)$
T	T	T	F	T	T
T	T	F	T	T	T
T	F	T	F	F	F
T	F	F	T	T	T
F	T	T	F	T	F
F	T	F	T	T	F
F	F	T	F	F	F
F	F	F	T	T	F

You can proceed systematically, filling in each blank. Thus in the first row,
P, Q, and R are all **(70)** T / F. So, $-R$ is **(71)** _F_. The alternatives of
$Q \lor -R$ are **(72)** _Q_ and **(73)** _-R_. Of these, Q is **(74)** _T_ in the
first row, and $-R$ is **(75)** _F_. So the truth value of $Q \lor -R$ is **(76)** _T_,
for an alternation takes the value F only when *both* alternatives are **(77)**
_F_. The conjuncts of $P \& (Q \lor -R)$ are **(78)** _P_ and **(79)** _(Q ∨ -R)_
In the first row, P is **(80)** _T_ and $Q \lor -R$ is **(81)** _T_. So the truth
value of $P \& (Q \lor -R)$ in the first row is **(82)** _T_.

You can complete every row in this same systematic way. Some people
find it shorter and quicker to use the fact that a conjunction is T if and only
if both conjuncts are **(83)** _T_ and an alternation is F if and only if both
conjuncts are **(84)** _F_.

$Q \lor -R$ is an **(85)** CONJUNCTION / <u>ALTERNATION.</u> So it is **(86)** _F_ if
and only if both components are **(87)** _F_. The components are **(88)** _Q_
and **(89)** _-R_. So run down the columns for Q and $-R$ and see if you can
find any row where both are F. There are two such rows. Enter F in the
same rows under $Q \lor -R$. Then in every other row enter T.

Similarly to fill in $P \& (Q \lor -R)$ run down the columns for P and
$Q \lor -R$, and whenever you find T in both rows, enter T under the conjunction. Enter **(90)** _F_ in every other row under the conjunction.

15 / Tests for Validity

This chapter contains some practical examples of tests for validity and provides further explanation of why truth tables provide tests of validity.

Cross out the false assertions:

(1) An invalid argument could have all premises T and the conclusion T.
(2) An invalid argument could have all premises T and the conclusion F.
(3) An invalid argument could have one or more premises F and the conclusion T.
(4) An invalid argument could have one or more premises F and the conclusion F.
(5) A valid argument could have all premises T and the conclusion T.
(6) A valid argument could have all premises T and the conclusion F.
(7) A valid argument could have all premises F and the conclusion T.
(8) A valid argument could have all premises F and the conclusion F.

You should by now be able to recognize some simple valid argument forms. Cross out the invalid argument forms in the following list. When you are in doubt, check your guess with a truth table.

(9) $P \lor Q$, $-P$, so Q.
(10) $-P \lor -Q$, Q, so P.
(11) Q, $-Q \lor -P$, so $-P$.
(12) P, so $P \lor Q$.
(13) $Q \lor P$, so Q.
(14) Q, so $P \& Q$.
(15) $P \& Q$, so Q.
(16) $P \lor Q$, so $Q \& P$.

What is the meaning of "$P \vdash Q$"?   (17) _THE ARGUMENT FORM P, so Q, IS VALID._

Cross out the incorrect assertions in this list; when in doubt check your answers with truth tables.   All involve De Morgan's laws.

(18) $P \vee Q \vdash -(-P \& -Q)$.
~~(19)~~ $-P \& Q \vdash -(-P \vee -Q)$.
(20) $-(P \vee -Q) \vdash -P \& Q$.
~~(21)~~ $P \& -Q \vdash -P \vee Q$.

Some of the following schemes of statements have incorrect bracketing. Some are ambiguous, others have more left brackets, "(", than right ones, ")", and so forth.   Cross out the incorrect bracketings.

(22) $(P \& Q) \vee -P$.
~~(23)~~ $(-P \vee -Q) \vee P \& Q$.
~~(24)~~ $P \& Q \vee R \& (-R \vee P)$.
~~(25)~~ $((P \& Q) \vee R) \& ((P \vee R) \& -P$.
~~(26)~~ $(Q \vee P) \vee (R \vee -P) \& (P \& Q)$.

Most of the examples so far considered are argument forms with only one premise.   The method of truth tables is readily extended to arguments with many premises.   For validity, we require that every row in which all the premises are (27) _T_ has a conclusion that is (28) _T_.   If we can find a single row in which all the premises are (29) _T_ and the conclusion is F, we know the argument form is invalid.

Test the two following arguments for validity by drawing a truth table.

(30) $P \vee -R, -R$, so P. — _INVALID_
(31) $P \vee -R, R$, so P. — _VALID_.

In the following examples:

1. Bracket the various parts of the English statements given.   Underline the conclusion of the argument.
2. Write out paraphrases of premises and conclusion.   Abbreviate using the indicated letters.
3. Test the resulting argument form for validity by using a truth table.
4. Say whether the argument is valid.

(32) Either (the faculty honored the dean's recommendation to nullify the penalties imposed on the five students) or (the dean resigned.)   In fact, (the students remained adamant,) but (the faculty did not honor the dean's recommendation.)   Hence, (the dean resigned) while (the students remained adamant.)

$H \vee D$
$S \& -H$
$So, D \& S$

$VALID$

Handwritten top margin: B∨F / 6 ≠ 8 / So, 6∨F   VALID

Handwritten left margin (33): VALID

(33) Either (the universe began at some moment in time,) or (it has been going on forever.) (God created the universe,) and (the universe has a definite beginning in time.) So either (God created the universe) or (the universe has been going on forever.)

Handwritten left margin (34): VF / =V B / B

(34) Either (God created the universe) or (the universe has been going on forever.) Either (the universe has been going on forever,) or (the universe has a definite beginning in time.) (The universe has a definite beginning in time.) Hence, (the universe has been created by God.)

Handwritten left margin (35): o, 6

(35) Abel: Either he did not enlist in the army, or he did not, after all, resolve to avoid combat.

Handwritten left margin: -E∨-R / =(ER)∨-T

Cain: In fact, either he enlisted in the army and at the same time resolved to avoid combat, or else he simply did not think what he was doing.

Handwritten left margin: So, -T

Abel: Therefore he simply did not think what he was doing.

Handwritten left margin: VALID

As well as providing practical tests of validity, truth tables can help explain why some arguments are valid and others are invalid. In this respect, they are like Venn diagrams, our tests for the validity of the syllogism. In the case of the syllogism, an argument is valid if the conclusion is diagramed as soon as the premises are all diagramed. If the information contained in the conclusion is true on the diagram as soon as the premises are diagramed, then all the information contained in the conclusion is **(36)** EXEMPLIFIED BY / CONTAINED IN the premises. We see from Venn diagrams that all the information contained in some conclusion can be contained in some premises. Naturally, if this is so, if all the information contained in the premises is correct, the information contained in the conclusion will be **(37)** CORRECT / INCORRECT. That is how it is possible to find some statements that follow from others.

Venn diagrams show how valid argument is possible. Truth tables have a similar merit. Take a familiar example, the argument form "$P \lor Q$, $-P$, so Q." This is **(38)** VALID / INVALID. Here is the truth table:

	P	Q	$P \lor Q$	$-P$	Q
1	T	T	T	F	T
2	T	F	T	F	F
3	F	T	T	T	T
4	F	F	F	T	F

There are two possibilities for P, namely, T and F. There are two possibilities for Q, namely, **(39)** ___T___ and **(40)** ___F___. There are thus **(41)** ONE / TWO / THREE / FOUR / FIVE / SIX / SEVEN / EIGHT possibilities for P and Q taken together. These possibilities are, as indicated on the truth table, TT, TF, FT, and, **(42)** _FF_. Are there any more possible combinations of truth values than these four? **(43)** YES / NO.

Notice that these four combinations exhaust the possibilities, no matter what P and Q may be. For example, take:

P: There is life on Mars.
Q: There is life on Venus.

The possibility corresponding to TT (row 1 on the truth table) is: There is life on Mars, and there is life on Venus. The possibility corresponding to TF is: There is life on Mars, but there is no life on Venus. What possibilities correspond to:

(44) FT: *THERE IS NO LIFE ON MARS BUT THERE IS LIFE ON VENUS -*
(45) FF: *THERE IS NO LIFE ON MARS AND THERE IS NO LIFE ON VENUS .*

We can subdivide these possibilities. For example, P can be divided into the possibility that there is only vegetable life on Mars, and the possibility that there is some other kind of life than vegetable life there. But looking just at P and Q, our four rows in the truth table (46) DO / DO NOT exhaust the possible combinations of truth values for P and Q.

Recall that an argument form is valid if there is no (47) INTERPRETATION / EXAMPLE of the argument form in which the premises are T and the conclusion is (48) *F*. For any interpretation of P and Q whatsoever, our truth table above contains all possible combinations of truth values. We see that there is (49) ONE / NO combination of truth values where both premises are T and the conclusion is F. So there cannot be an interpretation of P and Q in which both premises are T and the conclusion is (50) *F*. Hence, the argument form is (51) VALID / INVALID.

Truth tables show us that it is possible to combine simple statements using the connectives "$\lor$," "$-$," and "&" in such a way that there is no possibility of having the premises all T and the conclusion F. Thus in the case of arguments of the sort we have been examining, validity results from properties of the connectives.

Truth tables are also related to counterexamples in a direct way. The argument form "$-P \lor Q$, $-P$, so Q" is (52) VALID / INVALID. Here is the truth table:

	P	Q	$-P$	$-P \lor Q$	Q
1	T	T	F	T	T
2	T	F	F	F	F
3	F	T	T	T	T
4	F	F	T	T	F

The premises are both T in lines (53) *3* and (54) *4*. In line 3, the

conclusion is T.   But in line 4, the conclusion is **(55)** _F_.   This shows that
the argument form is **(56)** _INVALID_

A counterexample to an argument form is an interpretation of the form in
which all the premises are **(57)** _T_ and the conclusion is **(58)** _F_.   The
last line in the above truth table shows us how to find a counterexample.
All we need is an **(59)** INTERPRETATION / EXEMPLIFICATION of the letters P and
Q in which P and Q have the values assigned in row 4, namely P must be F
and Q must be **(60)** _F_.   This gives us plenty of scope.   We could have:

> P: Fifty human beings flew to Mars before 1950.
> Q: Thirty monkeys flew to Venus before 1940.

In this interpretation, we have, for the argument form " $-P \lor Q, -P,$ so Q";

> Either it is not true that 50 human beings flew to Mars before 1950, or
> else 30 monkeys flew to Venus before 1940.
> It is not true that 50 human beings flew to Mars before 1950.
> So, 30 monkeys flew to Venus before 1940.

In this interpretation, are the premises both true?   **(61)** YES / NO.   Is the
conclusion true or false?   **(62)** _F_.   Is this a counterexample?   **(63)**
YES / NO.

Using truth tables to find a row in which premises are T and conclusion is
F, construct your own counterexamples to the following argument forms:

(64) $-P \lor -Q,$ so $P \& Q.$
(65) $-(P \lor Q),$ so $-P \lor -Q.$ MISSPRINT
(66) $P,$ so $P \& Q.$

Drawing truth tables is often tedious.   You are already able to recognize
quite a few valid argument forms.   It is perhaps useful to give names to some
of the most common valid argument forms.   The names do not matter much
—what matters is the form itself.   If you have no trouble in recognizing
valid argument forms, then you don't have to bother to remember their
names.   But if you still have trouble, actually giving names to some simple
rules may help you remember them.

One useful rule is this:

---

*If two statements are logically equivalent, they can be inter-
changed without affecting the validity of an argument.*

For example, P and $--P$ **(67)** ARE / ARE NOT logically equivalent.   Is the following argument form "$P \lor Q$, $-P$, so Q" valid?   **(68)** YES / NO. Using our rule about logical equivalence, we conclude at once that:

and

$$--P \lor Q, -P \vdash Q$$

$$P \lor Q, ---P \vdash Q$$

We know the following logical equivalences:

1.   *De Morgan's laws.*
2.   *Double denial* ($--P$ and P *are logically equivalent.*)
3.   *Permutation of conjuncts or alternatives* ($P \lor Q$ *is logically equivalent to* $Q \lor P$, $P \mathbin{\&} Q$ *is logically equivalent to* $Q \mathbin{\&} P$.)

We know the following rule of inference:

From an alternation, plus a denial of one alternative, it is valid to infer the other alternative.

For example:

$$P \lor Q, -P \vdash Q$$

In this rule we are detaching one alternative from an alternation, so we call this the rule of *detaching an alternative.*

We also know that we can add additional alternatives, as "$P \vdash P \lor Q$," "$-Q \vdash -Q \lor --P$," and so forth.   We call this a rule for *weakening*, for the conclusion is **(69)** WEAKER / STRONGER than the premise.

We know "$P \mathbin{\&} Q \vdash P$" and "$P \mathbin{\&} Q \vdash Q$" because a conjunction implies its conjuncts.   Finally, we know that from two premises we can infer the conjunction of the two premises: P, $Q \vdash P \mathbin{\&} Q$.   Thus, we call these the rules of *conjunction.*

On the right are some examples of valid inference.   On the left are the names of some rules.   Match.

(70) _c_ Detaching an alternative.   (a) $-Q \vdash -Q \lor (P \lor R)$.
(71) _b_ Conjunction.   (b) $Q \mathbin{\&} R, P \lor S \vdash$
                                                    $(Q \mathbin{\&} R) \mathbin{\&} (P \lor S)$.
(72) _a_ Weakening.   (c) $--Q, P \lor -Q \vdash P$.

We can also combine several different rules of inference in a sequence, as follows:

1. $P \& Q \vdash P.$ Conjunction.
2.   „ $\vdash P \lor Q.$ Weakening.
3.   „ $\vdash Q \lor P.$ Permutation.

Here the ditto signs („) save us the trouble of writing out the premises again and again. Thus, line 3 is short for **(73)** $P \lor Q \vdash Q \lor P \mid P \& Q \vdash Q \lor P.$ The sequence 1–3 means:

Step 1 is correct, for it represents the rule of conjunction.
Step 2 is correct, for we pass from the conclusion of 1, namely P, to $P \lor Q$, by the rule of weakening.
Step 3 is correct, for we pass from the conclusion of 2, namely **(74)** _PVQ_,
to $Q \lor P$ by the rule of **(75)** _PERMUTATION_

Such a chain of inference is called a *deduction*.
Here are some simple deductions. At each stage we have given a reason, or left a blank for you to write the reason.

$-(P \& Q) \vdash -Q \lor -P$

Deduction:

1. $-(P \& Q) \vdash -P \lor -Q.$ De Morgan.
2.   „ $\vdash -Q \lor -P.$ **(76)** _PERMUTATION._

$-P \lor -Q \vdash -(Q \& P) \lor R$

Deduction:

1. $-P \lor -Q \vdash -(Q \& P).$ **(77)** _DE MORGAN_.
2.   „ $\vdash -(Q \& P) \lor R.$ Weakening.

$-(P \& Q) \lor -(R \& S) \vdash (-P \lor -Q) \lor (-R \lor -S)$

Deduction:

1. $-(P \& Q) \lor -(R \& S) \vdash (-P \lor -Q) \lor -(R \& S).$ De Morgan.

2.   „ $\vdash (-P \lor -Q) \lor (-R \lor -S).$
     (78) _DE MORGAN APPLIED TO LAST ALT._

We shall not use deductions much in the next few chapters, but they will become increasingly useful toward the end of this book. Hence, we shall keep introducing a few examples from time to time, in preparation for the concluding chapters.

16 / Truth Functional Connectives

This chapter explains a difficulty in paraphrasing the connective "if, then" which is of fundamental importance to deductive logic.

The statement:

He took her a present, and she did not thank him.

is a **(1)** CONJUNCTION / ALTERNATION. The conjuncts are **(2)** *HE TOOK HER A PRESENT* and **(3)** *SHE DID NOT THANK HIM*. The second conjunct is a **(4)** CONJUNCTION / DENIAL of the statement **(5)** *SHE DID THANK HIM*

The useful thing about "and" and "or," when it comes to drawing truth tables, is that once we know the truth value of the base components, we can work out the truth value of the compound. Thus, suppose we know that it is true that the person in question took her a present, and false that she thanked him. Then, "She did not thank him" is **(6)** T / F, and the whole statement, "He took her a present, and she did not thank him" is **(7)** T / F Does the truth value of the compound depend on the truth value of the components? **(8)** YES / NO.

If the truth value of a compound statement formed using a connective is uniquely determined by the truth values of the components connected by the connective, then the connective is called truth functional.

Is the ampersand truth functional? **(9)** _YES_ / NO. Is the wedge truth functional? **(10)** _YES_ / NO. Is the bar truth functional? **(11)** _YES_ / NO. Not all connectives are truth functional. Consider this pair of statements:

Joseph loves Lydia because she is kind.
Joseph loves Lydia and she is kind.

What are the connectives in these statements? **(12)** _Because_ and **(13)** _and_. Is "and" truth functional? **(14)** _YES_ / NO. We shall now show that "because" is not truth functional. A connective is truth functional if the truth value of the compound depends only on and is *uniquely* determined by the truth value of the **(15)** _components_ that are connected by the connective. To show that a connective is not truth functional, we must be able to show that the truth value of the compound is not uniquely determined by **(16)** _THE TRUTH VALUE OF THE COMPONENTS CONNECTED_

In the case of the statement:

Joseph loves Lydia because she is kind.

suppose both components are T. This means that it is T that Joseph loves Lydia, and T that **(17)** _SHE IS KIND_ Hearing that both components are T, do we know that Joseph loves Lydia because she is kind? Joseph loves Lydia, all right, and Lydia is kind, all right, but does Joseph love Lydia *because* she is kind? That is the question. Knowing that Joseph loves Lydia, and that she is kind, we still **(18)** DO / _DO NOT_ know for sure that he loves her *because* she is kind.

Perhaps the best way to demonstrate this is to tell two stories. In both stories, both components will be T, but in one story the whole compound will be F, whereas in the other story the compound will be T. Thus, even though both components are T, the compound might be T, or might be F. Thus the truth value of the compound **(19)** IS / _IS NOT_ uniquely determined by the truth value of the components.

> **Story One.** Joseph does love Lydia. Lydia is kind. However, Joseph is pretty indifferent to Lydia's kindness. He is infatuated with her because she is beautiful; the girl is in fact rather more attractive than anyone he has ever met, and that is why he is in love with her. He is in love with her because she is beautiful, not because she is kind.

In this story, is the compound statement:

Joseph loves Lydia because she is kind.

true? **(20)** _YES_ / NO. Are both components true? **(21)** _YES_ / NO.

Here, then, we have a story in which both components are **(22)** T̲ / F and the compound is **(23)** T / F̲.

> **Story Two.** Joseph does love Lydia. Lydia is kind. More-over, that is why Joseph loves Lydia—because she is kind. She is a rather ugly girl, but that doesn't bother Joseph. He has spent most of his life being bullied by people who take advantage of him, but finally he has met someone who is kind to him, and because of this he has fallen madly in love with her.

In this story, is the compound statement true? **(24)** Y̲E̲S̲ / NO. Are both components true? **(25)** Y̲E̲S̲ / NO. So this is a story in which both components are T and the compound is **(26)** T̲ / F.

In Story One, both components were **(27)** T̲ / F and the compound was **(28)** T / F̲. In Story Two, once again the components were **(29)** T̲ / F, but the compound this time was **(30)** T / F̲.

These two stories show that the connective "because" is not truth functional. A connective is truth functional if the truth value of the compound is **(31)** *UNIQUELY* determined by the truth value of the components. Given the truth value of the components, there must be a unique truth value for the **(32)** *Compound* formed by connecting the components. But in our stories, we see that although the components are both T, the truth value of the compound is not thereby determined. For the compound might have truth value T, as in Story **(33)** ONE / T̲W̲O̲, and it might have truth value F, as in Story **(34)** O̲N̲E̲ / TWO.

Now consider the statement:

> Joseph passed the course because the teacher liked him.

(35) Tell two stories, in both of which both components are T, but in one of which the compound is T, whereas in the other the compound is F. Write out the stories on your own paper. Then explain why your two stories show that "because" is not truth functional.

"Probably" is another connective that is not truth functional. Once again we take a concrete example. For the component take:

> Adam will win first prize in the lottery.

Using the connective, we get the compound:

> Probably Adam will win first prize in the lottery.

Suppose that as a matter of fact the component is T: Adam really will win first prize in the lottery. The mere truth of this component does not determine the truth value of the compound. Once again we tell two stories to demonstrate this.

> **Story One.** Adam has bought 99 percent of the tickets in the lottery. It is a fair lottery. Even before the draw, everyone agrees that it is very likely that Adam will win first prize. The draw is held, and he wins.

In this story, the component is **(36)** T / F. The statement:

> Probably Adam will win first prize in the lottery.

made before the draw, is also **(37)** T / F. Hence, in this story, both the component and the compound are **(38)** T / F.

> **Story Two.** Adam has bought only one ticket. There are 700,000 other tickets in the barrel about to be drawn. It is a fair lottery. It is extremely unlikely that Adam will win anything. By sheer chance, however, his ticket is the first to be drawn, and he wins first prize.

In this story, the component is **(39)** T / F. However, the statement:

> Probably Adam will win first prize in the lottery.

made before the draw, is not true; on the contrary, before the draw, it is not at all probable that Adam will win. Hence, in this story, the compound is F.

In both stories, the component was **(40)** T / F. In the first story the compound statement, uttered before the draw, was **(41)** T / F. In the second story, the compound statement, uttered before the draw, was **(42)** T / F. Thus, even though the component is **(43)** T / F, the truth value of the compound is not uniquely **(44)** DETERMINED by the truth value of the component. Hence, the connective "probably" is not **(45)** TRUTH FUNCTIONAL

Answer T or F:

(46) F If a connective is truth functional, the truth value of the components is uniquely determined by the truth value of the compound.

(47) T If the truth values of the components do not uniquely determine the truth value of the compound, then the connective is not truth functional.

One of the most important connectives is "if, then." Here is an extreme example.

(If)the present 7 percent investment tax credit is continued, then investment in new industrial plant will continue unabated. (If)such investment continues, then inflation will become even more rapid. (If)inflation becomes more rapid, then the differential between the poor and the middle classes will become even more marked. (If)the differential becomes even more marked, then racial harmony will be even more difficult to achieve than at present. Hence, unless the investment tax credit is discontinued, racial harmony will be even more difficult to achieve than at present.

Circle each "if" of an "if, then" statement in the above paragraph. You will find four of them.

In a statement of the form:

If P, then Q.

the component P is called the *antecedent*. This is because it comes "before" the rest of the statement. "Ante-" is a prefix meaning "before" or "in front of" as in the words "anteroom" and "antechamber." The Q is called the *consequent* because it indicates a consequence of the P. (48) Underline the antecedent of the *first* premise of the above argument and the consequent of the *last* premise of the above argument.

Do not confuse "premise" with "antecedent," nor "conclusion" with "consequent." "Premise" and "conclusion" apply to parts of (49) ARGUMENTS / IF, THEN STATEMENTS whereas "antecedent" and "consequent" apply to parts of (50) ARGUMENTS / IF, THEN STATEMENTS.

A. If he is at home, then he is ill.
B. She went to work. She works only when she is well. So, she is not sick now.

"He is at home" is the antecedent of A. "He is ill" is the (51) CONSEQUENT / CONCLUSION of A. "She went to work" is a(n) (52) ANTECEDENT / PREMISE of B. "She is not sick now" is the (53) CONSEQUENT / CONCLUSION of B.

Sometimes people confuse "if" and "only if." Here are some examples:

C. If you live in the tropics, you will get malaria.
D. Only if you live in the tropics will you get malaria.

Do these mean the same? (54) YES / NO.

E. If you complete every page in this work book, you will know the rudiments of elementary deductive logic.
F. Only if you complete every page in this work book will you know the rudiments of elementary deductive logic.

Do E and F mean the same? **(55)** YES / NO. It is easy to see they differ in meaning. For E is true: if you do complete this book, you will know the elements of logic. But F is false: completing this book is not the only way to master simple logic. There are lots of other good books. Since one statement is true and the other is false, the two must differ in meaning. Similarly for C and D. Perhaps D is true: only people who live in the tropics get malaria. But C is false: not everyone who lives in the tropics gets malaria.

Finally, note that the "direction" of an "if, then" statement matters. Contrast:

G. If Adam was ill, then he went home to bed.
H. If Adam went home to bed, then he was ill.

Now, here is a story in which H is false and G is true:

> Adam is an extremely lazy fellow.
> He will leave work and go home to bed on the slightest excuse.
> So, surely, if one day Adam was ill, then he went home to bed.

So G is true. But knowing that he went home to bed on another occasion, you cannot infer that he was ill—he may just have been pretending. Thus, H would be false. **(56)** Now write a story on your own paper in which H is T and G is F. Make sure that you get both parts right: H is to be T *and* G is to be F.

"If, then" is one of the most common connectives used in deductive argument. We have seen how to use truth tables to test for validity. It would be nice if we could draw a truth table for "if, then." But to draw a truth table for a connective, the connective must be truth functional. For suppose the connective were like "because," and not truth functional. Then, in the case of "because," when P is T, and Q is T, "P because Q" might be T and it might be F. So we would not know how to complete the column in the truth table under P because Q. In the row TT, we would not know whether to put in T or F. So we **(57)** COULD / COULD NOT draw up a truth table.

We now show that "if, then" is not strictly truth functional. Let us begin with another example:

If Joseph smokes marijuana this January, he will be a drug addict by Christmas.

(58) Underline the antecedent. Circle the consequent. We want to know if this statement is true. We find Joseph smoking marijuana in January. By Christmas, he is not taking any kind of drug at all. Then the antecedent is T and the consequent is **(59)** T / F. The whole statement is **(60)** T / F.

In this case the **(61)** A̲N̲T̲E̲C̲E̲D̲E̲N̲T̲ / PREMISE is **(62)** T̲ / F.   The **(63)** CON-
CLUSION / C̲O̲N̲S̲E̲Q̲U̲E̲N̲T̲ is **(64)** T / F̲.   The **(65)** ARGUMENT / COMPOUND
S̲T̲A̲T̲E̲M̲E̲N̲T̲ is **(66)** T / F.

> *An if, then statement cannot be true if the antecedent is true and
> the consequent is false.*

The easiest way to refute an if, then statement is to show that the antecedent
is T whereas the conclusion is F.   Someone says:

If you buy that motorcycle, you'll have an accident within a month.

Not believing him, you buy the cycle and don't have an accident within the
month.   Is what he said true?   **(67)** YES / N̲O̲.
  The compound statement is F, because as it turns out, the antecedent is T
and the consequent is **(68)** _F_ .
  Someone says:

If he types the manuscript himself, there will be no typing errors in it.

It turns out that he typed the manuscript himself, but it is full of typing
errors.   Is the compound statement true?   **(69)** YES / N̲O̲.   It is F because
the **(70)** _CONSEQUENT_ is F whereas the **(71)** _ANTECEDENT_ is T.
  This suggests that if we were to begin to build a truth table for "If P, then
Q" we would start this way:

P	Q	If P, then Q
T	T	
T	F	F
F	T	
F	F	

We have filled in the one row we have treated so far, namely the case in
which the antecedent is T, the consequent F, and the whole statement
(72) _F_ .
  Unfortunately we cannot fill in every row so easily.   This is because
despite the case of the true antecedent and the false consequent (where the
compound statement is **(73)** _F_) if, then statements are not strictly truth
functional.   Consider the last row in the truth table, where P and Q are both
(74) _F_ .   In this case the compound might be T, and it might be F, so the
truth value of the compound is not uniquely determined.   This is enough to

show that if, then statements are not (75) _Truth Functional_.
As before, we demonstrate this by telling two stories.

If an election is held, there will be civil disorder.

> **Story One.** In the nation of Bworo, there is an underground
> political party that plans to assassinate a large number of
> ministers of the government the day before an election is held.
> When this plot is discovered, everyone agrees that if an election
> is held, there will be civil disorder. Because of this fear, the
> election is postponed indefinitely until the underground move-
> ment is placated or defeated. There is no civil disorder.

The antecedent is (76) _An election is held_. The consequent
is (77) _There will be civil disorder_. In this story, the antecedent is
(78) T / _F_ and the consequent is (79) T / _F_. In this story, is it true that if
an election is held, there will be civil disorder? (80) _yes_ / NO. So in this
story, both components are (81) T / _F_, and the whole statement is (82)
_T_ / F.

> **Story Two.** In the nation of Tamba, there is a rather dictatorial
> regime that is interested in the permanent abolition of elections.
> In fact, because of current prosperity, the regime is fairly
> popular at present despite its authoritarian character. Fearing
> a decrease in popularity in the future, however, the government
> wishes to induce a fear of elections. So it circulates the rumor
> that if elections are held, there will be civil disorder. This is
> simply a lie put out by the propaganda machine. It is an
> effective lie, however, and elections are not held, and there is no
> civil disorder.

In this story, is the antecedent false? (83) _yes_ / NO. Is the consequent
false? (84) _yes_ / NO. What is the truth value of the compound statement?
(85) _False_ Presumably the compound statement, which we have called a
lie, is not true. Thus in this case, the components are both (86) T / _F_,
whereas the compound is (87) T / _F_.

In Story One, both components were (88) T / _F_, and the compound was
(89) _T_ / F. In Story Two, both components were (90) T / _F_ and the compound was (91) T / _F_. Hence, when both components are F, the truth
value of the compound is not uniquely determined by the truth value of the
components. Hence, "if, then" statements are not strictly (92) _____
Truth Functional -

Now use your own imagination to show that "if, then" is not a strictly
truth functional connective. Take as your example:

If he continues to date the boss's daughter, then he will be fired.

(93) On your own paper, compose two stories, in both of which the two components are F. However, arrange it so that in one story, the compound statement would be called T, whereas in the other, it would be called F. (94) Explain why your story shows that the connective "if, then" is not truth functional.

Although "if, then" is not strictly truth functional, we can often give it a rough paraphrase with an artificially constructed connective. We were able to complete one row in an attempted truth table for the connective "if, then." When the antecedent is T and the consequent is F, the compound is (95) T / F. This is the most important aspect of such statements: *they can never lead us from true antecedents to false consequents.*

We can see the point of this by looking at a very simple pattern of inference:

> If he went home, then he is ill.
> He went home.
> So, he is ill.

> If he is smart, he will not buy that car.
> He is smart.
> So, he will not buy that car.

Are these examples of the same form of argument? (96) YES / NO. In general, the form of this argument is:

> If *P*, then *Q*.
> *P*.
> So, *Q*.

We call a statement of the form "if *P*, then *Q*" a *conditional* statement. A conditional statement tells us that if we have the antecedent as a premise, we can infer the consequent. Given the antecedent, we can *detach* the consequent *Q* and assert it alone as the conclusion. So the above rule of inference is called *detachment of the consequent* or *detachment* for short.

An argument form is valid if there is no interpretation in which the premises are all (97) _T_ and the conclusion is (98) _F_.

Now suppose we wish to paraphrase "if, then" by a strictly truth functional connective that resembles "if, then." The most important point about this connective is that detachment should be valid. That is, if we represent this connective by an arrow ($\rightarrow$), then the following should be valid:

> $P \rightarrow Q$.
> *P*.
> So, *Q*.

Thus, we design the truth table for $P \rightarrow Q$ so that if P is T, and $P \rightarrow Q$ is T, then Q is T, too.

P	Q	$P \rightarrow Q$
T	T	T
T	F	F
F	T	
F	F	

If detachment is the chief thing we are interested in, then it does not much matter how we fill in the remaining rows under $P \rightarrow Q$. It turns out to be simplest to make them all T.

P	Q	$P \rightarrow Q$
T	T	T
T	F	F
F	T	T
F	F	T

$P \rightarrow Q$ is F if and only if P is T and Q is F.

Considerations of various sorts can be given in support of using this connective to paraphrase "if, then." For example, if you really don't think *Alphabet Soup* has a chance of winning the next race, you would not be surprised to hear someone say:

If *Alphabet Soup* wins the next race, then I'll eat my hat.

If *Alphabet Soup* does win, and the speaker doesn't eat his hat, then he has let us down. What he said was false. He broke his promise. But if the antecedent is F, and *Alphabet Soup* does not win, then, perhaps, what he said was T, exactly as we have drawn in the truth table for the arrow.

A stronger consideration results from comparing:

If reinforced concrete was not used, the building will collapse in the next earthquake.
Either reinforced concrete was used, or the building will collapse during the next earthquake.

These two statements convey very nearly the same fact: the building will fall down unless the proper materials were used in its construction. So we should like these two statements to be paraphrased in equivalent ways. Let R: reinforced concrete was used; C: the building will collapse in the next earthquake. Complete this table:

	R	C	$-R$	$-R \rightarrow C$	$R \vee C$
1	T	T	F	T	T
2	T	F	F	T	T
3	F	T	T	T	T
4	F	F	T	F	F

Since $-R \rightarrow C$ is F if and only if the antecedent is T and the consequent is **(99)** _F_, and since the antecedent is $-R$, $-R \rightarrow C$ is F if and only if $-R$ is **(100)** _T_ and C is **(101)** _F_. This is line **(102)** _4_ in the table. Do $-R \rightarrow C$ and $R \vee C$ have the same table? **(103)** YES / NO.

Here is another example:

If this newspaper is telling the truth, 1,500,000 people were massacred shortly after the defeat of the French in Indochina.

Either this newspaper is not telling the truth, or 1,500,000 people were massacred shortly after the defeat of the French in Indochina.

Do these two statements convey roughly the same fact? **(104)** YES / NO. Hence, they should have the same paraphrase. Letting N stand for the antecedent of the first statement, and M for the consequent, what is the paraphrase of the first statement? **(105)** _N → M_. Paraphrase the second statement. **(106)** _−N ∨ M_. On your own paper, draw a table to see if these two are logically equivalent. Are they? **(107)** YES / NO.

The fact that $-P \vee Q$ and $P \rightarrow Q$ are logically equivalent confirms our choice of the arrow to paraphrase "if, then." Notice that the arrow, as defined by the truth table **(108)** IS / IS NOT strictly truth functional whereas "if, then" **(109)** IS / IS NOT strictly truth functional. Thus our paraphrase is only approximate.

The truth value of:

The moon is made of green cheese $\rightarrow 2 + 2 = 4$.

is **(110)** T / F. This odd statement has a definite truth value. Since the antecedent is F and the consequent is T, the whole is **(111)** _T_.

An arrow statement is F if and only if the antecedent is **(112)** _T_ and the consequent is **(113)** _F_. So the truth value of:

The moon is made of green cheese → the moon is made of gorgonzola.
is **(114)** T / F. The truth value of:

There is water in the sea → 2 + 2 = 4.

is **(115)** T / F.

Compare the following odd statements:

If the moon is made of green cheese, then 2 + 2 = 4.
If the moon is made of green cheese, then the moon is made of gorgonzola.
If there is water in the sea, then 2 + 2 = 4.

These statements are so wild that it is hard to tell whether to call them true or false or just sheer nonsense. This points up a strong contrast between "if, then" and the arrow. $P \to Q$ is defined for any pair of statements P, Q. But for sufficiently fanciful choices of P and Q, "if P, then Q" does not have any very clearly defined truth value. Sometimes this is given as the reason for saying that "if, then" is not truth functional. But it is a bad reason, for we could ask whether "if P, then Q" is truth functional in every case where the truth value is defined. Our early examples, say in the case of the election and civil disorders, are examples where the truth value of a particular, individual statement, of the form "if P, then Q" is perfectly well defined on two different occasions of utterance, but on one occasion, it is T, and on another occasion it is F, even though the truth value of the components is F in both cases.

This has been a more philosophical chapter than preceding ones. As a summary of the chief logical points, write T or F in front of these statements:

(116) _T_ A connective is truth functional if and only if the truth value of the compound is uniquely determined by the truth value of the components.

(117) _T_ $P \to Q$ and $-P \lor Q$ are logically equivalent.

(118) _F_ The wedge is not truth functional.

(119) _F_ "Because" is truth functional.

(120) _F_ "If, then" is truth functional.

(121) _T_ The arrow is truth functional.

(122) _F_ A statement of the form $P \to Q$ is T if and only if P is T and Q is T.

(123) _T_ A statement of the form $P \to Q$ is F if and only if P is T and Q is F.

17 / The Conditional

This chapter completes the analysis of "if, then" statements begun in the last chapter.

Paraphrase:

D → M

(1) If Darwin was right, then men are descended from apes. *P → Q*

(2) If automobile insurance is operated by the state, then costs of insurance tend to decrease. *A → C*.

(3) Either the chairman will retire and peace will be restored, or he will not, and three of his committee members will resign. *(C·P)∨(C̄·R)*

(4) If Adam was the first man, then either Eve was the first woman, or Adam had a mother. *A → (E∨M)*

(5) If a cure is discovered, the boy will recover, but if a cure is not discovered, his case is hopeless. *(C → B)·(~C → H)*

If you let *P*: The plane crashed; *Q*: The quarry was unmarked; *R*: The rescue party found the pilot, what statements correspond to the following paraphrases?

(6) $P \to R$. *IF THE PLANE CRASHED, THEN THE RESCUE PARTY FOUND THE PILOT*

(7) $Q \to R$. *IF THE QUARRY WAS UNMARKED, THEN THE RESCUE PARTY FOUND THE PILOT.*

(8) $R \to Q$. *IF THE RESCUE PARTY FOUND THE PILOT, THEN THE QUARRY WAS UNMARKED*

(9) $-R \to (P \lor Q)$. *IF THE RESCUE PARTY DIDNT FIND THE PILOT THEN EITHER THE PLANE CRASHED OR THE QUARRY WAS UNMAR*

(10) $-R \to (-P \to Q)$. *IF THE RESCUE PARTY DID NOT FIND THE PILOT THEN, IF THE PLANE DID NOT CRASH, THE QUARRY WAS UNMARKED.*

What is the only row in the truth table in which $P \to Q$ is F?

140

(11) ___*P is T + Q is F*___. What is the only row in the truth
table at which $-P \to -Q$ is F? **(12)** When P is _F_ and Q is _T_.
What is the only row in the truth table at which $P \to -Q$ is F? **(13)** When
P is _T_ and Q is _T_.

On your own paper, draw truth tables to test the following argument
forms for validity and check the valid forms.

(14) ___✓___ $P, P \to Q$, so Q.

(15) _____ $P \to Q$ so $Q \to P$.

(16) ___✓___ $P \to Q, Q \to R$, so $P \to R$.

(17) _____ $P \to Q, -Q$, so P.

On your own paper, test the following arguments for validity. First
bracket the parts of the statements in question and distinguish the premises
from the conclusion. Then paraphrase the argument. Then test for
validity. Finally, state whether the argument is valid.

H v A
-H -> A
(18) Either (he is not at <u>home</u>) or (he is <u>asleep</u>) So, if (he is at <u>home</u>) (he is
<u>asleep</u>)

ALID
(19) If (he is at <u>home</u>) (he is <u>asleep</u>) So, either (he is not at <u>home</u>) or (he is
<u>asleep</u>)

$H \to A$
$So - H v A$
VALID

-> S
J -> S
J v J
VALID
(20) If (Adam gets a <u>job</u>) (he will be able to <u>support his family</u>) If (he
receives <u>welfare assistance</u>) then (he will be able to <u>support his family</u>)
So, either (he will get <u>welfare assistance</u>) or (he will get a <u>job</u>)

(21) If (Joseph does not <u>propose now</u>) (he will not <u>marry Lydia</u>) If (Joseph
does not <u>propose now</u>) (he will remain a <u>bachelor all his life</u>) So, if
(he does not <u>propose now</u>) (he will both not <u>marry Lydia</u>) and (remain a
<u>bachelor all his life</u>)

$-P \to M$
$-P \to B$
$So,$
$-P \to (M \cdot B)$
VALID

-> A
-(B·-A)
VALID
(22) If (Adam has the same <u>blood group</u>) then (he will <u>allow a transfusion</u>)
So at least we can be sure of this: it is not the case both that (he has
the right <u>blood group</u>) and (that he will not <u>allow a transfusion</u>)

It is important to notice the "direction" of the conditional: crudely, the
direction is the direction of the arrow in a correct paraphrase. Here are
two statements and two statement schemes for conditionals:

> H: The plane was hijacked.
> M: The plane was flying to Miami.

A. $H \to M$.
B. $M \to H$.

Match the schemes with the following statements:

(23) ___A___ If the plane was hijacked, it was flying to Miami.

(24) __*B*__ The plane was hijacked if it was flying to Miami.

(25) __*A*__ The plane was flying to Miami if it was hijacked.

(26) __*B*__ If the plane was flying to Miami, it was hijacked.

These examples show that:

> If *P*, *Q*.
> If *P*, then *Q*.

and

> *Q* if *P*.

are to be paraphrased in **(27)** THE SAME / A DIFFERENT way, namely as **(28)** *P* → *Q* / *Q* → *P*. The rule of thumb is: the connective "if" (of "if, then") always comes before the **(29)** ANTECEDENT / PREMISE / CONSEQUENT.

Do not confuse "if" with "only if"; they differ. "If" also differs from "if and only if." Suppose we want to indicate, in English, that the arrow holds both ways, that is, that:

> *P* → *Q* and *Q* → *P*.

Then we can say something of the form:

> *P* if and only if *Q*.

For example, let *P*: The number of states in the Union is even; *Q*: The number of states in the Union is a number divisible by 2. Since "even" means "divisible by 2," clearly *P* and *Q* imply each other. We can say,

> The number of states in the Union is even, if and only if, the number of states in the Union is a number divisible by 2.

Since "if and only if" is the arrow pointing both ways, we represent it by a double arrow (↔). So the previous statement is paraphrased *P* ↔ *Q*. We can let *P* ↔ *Q* be an abbreviation for (*P* → *Q*) & (*Q* → *P*).

(30) On your own paper draw a truth table for *P* ↔ *Q* —that is, draw a truth table for (*P* → *Q*) & (*Q* → *P*). If *P* is T and *Q* is F, is *P* ↔ *Q* T? **(31)** YES / NO. *P* ↔ *Q* is T if and only if *P* and *Q* have **(32)** THE SAME / DIFFERENT truth values. Can *P* ↔ *Q* be T if *P* is F? **(33)** YES / NO. If *P* ↔ *Q* is T and *P* is F, what is the truth value of *Q*? **(34)** __*F*__.

Here are two statements:

A. Adam will retire if and only if his son Abel is made president of the company.

B.   Adam will retire if his son Abel is made president of the company.

Paraphrase statement A: **(35)** _$R \leftrightarrow P$_ .   Does statement A mean the same as statement B?   **(36)** YES / NO.

Paraphrase statement B: **(37)** _$P \rightarrow R$_.

The difference between these two statements is as follows.   According to B, news that Abel is going to be made president will be *sufficient* to get Adam to retire.   But it may not be *necessary* to promote Abel.   Perhaps a golden handshake of 80,000 shares of stock in the company will also induce Adam to retire.   But according to A, Adam is just not going to quit until his son is made president.   According to A, Adam can't be bought off whereas B is neutral.   It tells us what is *sufficient* to get Adam to retire, but is *neutral* as to whether that is also *necessary*.

A is paraphrased:

$$R \leftrightarrow P$$

or

$$(R \rightarrow P) \& (P \rightarrow R)$$

B, which is *R* if *P* (or, if *P*, *R*) is paraphrased:

$$P \rightarrow R$$

What about $R \rightarrow P$?   In A we had the connective **(38)** <u>IF AND ONLY IF</u> / IF / ONLY IF.   In B we had the connective **(39)** IF AND ONLY IF / IF / ONLY IF. Hence, in order to express the direction opposite to B, namely $R \rightarrow P$, we will use "only if":

C.   Adam will retire *only if* his son Abel is made president of the company.

The paraphrase of B is **(40)** _$P \rightarrow R$_ Since C is the opposite direction to B, the paraphrase of C must be: **(41)** _$R \rightarrow P$_.

The rule for "only if" is:

"Only if" comes before the consequent.

The rule for "if" (not "only if") is:

"If" comes before the antecedent.

If you are in doubt about these two connectives, memorize these two rules. If you need a quick memory guide, notice that the "i" of "if" comes earlier in the alphabet than the "o" of "only if" and the "a" of "antecedent" comes before the "c" of consequent.   Remember:

If—antecedent	*Only if—consequent.*

Match:

(42) _e_ _f_ $P \to Q$.

(43) _d_ _g_ $Q \to P$.

(d) *P* if *Q*.
(e) If *P*, *Q*.
(f) *P* only if *Q*.
(g) Only if *P*, *Q*.

Notice that "*P* only if *Q*" is paraphrased in the same way as **(44)** "*P* if *Q*." / "If *P*, then *Q*." / "If *Q*, then *P*."   Notice that "If *P*, then *Q*" is paraphrased in the same way as **(45)** "Only if *P*, *Q*." / "Only if *Q*, *P*."   This is exactly parallel to the use of "only" in syllogisms.   Look back at page 44, and in the reminder-square there you will see that "All *F* are *G*" is logically equivalent to **(46)** "Only *F* are *G*." / "Only *G* are *F*."

Paraphrase:

(47) Joseph will be rewarded only if the courage he displayed is drawn to the council's attention. $R \to C$

(48) The cars will be withdrawn for repairs if the brakes are faulty. $B \to C$

(49) Only if these people are telling the truth do we have any evidence for the existence of flying saucers. $E \to P$

Another conditional connective is "unless."   Suppose you believe that:

Joseph did not pass unless he worked harder than he did last year.

You learn later that:

Joseph did pass.

You would conclude that **(50)** JOSEPH DID NOT WORK HARDER THAN HE DID LAST YEAR / JOSEPH DID WORK HARDER THAN HE DID LAST YEAR.

To take another example, suppose you believe that:

Adam will not marry Eve unless she is rich.

You later hear that:

Adam married Eve.

You would conclude that **(51)** EVE IS NOT RICH / <u>EVE IS RICH</u>.

In each of these two examples the "unless" statement is of the form **(52)** "<u>−P unless Q</u>" / "Unless P, Q." Here, −P is, for example, "Joseph did not pass" or "Adam will not marry Eve." When we are told P: "Joseph passed" or "Adam married Eve," we infer Q: "Joseph worked harder" or "Eve is rich." Schematizing this, we get:

> −P unless Q.
> P.
> So, Q.

This looks like a kind of *detachment*. The rule we called detachment (of the consequent) is,

> $P \rightarrow Q$.
> P.
> So, Q.

This suggests that

> −P unless Q.

is to be paraphrased,

$$P \rightarrow Q.$$

The rule for paraphrasing unless is:

"Unless" comes before the consequent. The other component is a denial of the antecedent.

Use this rule to match the following:

(53) _a_ _e_ $-P \rightarrow Q$.

(54) _b_ _d_ $-Q \rightarrow P$.

(55) _c_ _f_ $P \rightarrow Q$.

(a) P unless Q.
(b) Q unless P.
(c) −P unless Q.
(d) Unless P, Q.
(e) Unless Q, P.
(f) Unless Q, −P.

Paraphrase:

(56) Unless he retires, he will be fired. $-F \rightarrow R$.

(57) Unless the missionaries are expelled, the nationalist party will need
to be placated. $-N \rightarrow M$.

(58) He will not run unless there is a draft. $R \rightarrow D$.

(59) He will be angry unless he gets the job $-A \rightarrow J$.

Match:

(60) _e_ If P, then $-Q$.

(61) _j_ $-P$ if and only if Q.

(62) _c_ P unless Q.

(63) _a_ P only if Q.

(64) _m_ $-P$ if and only if $-Q$.

(65) _f_ Only if $-P$, Q.

(66) _d_ Unless P, Q.

(67) _k_ P if and only if Q.

(68) _g_ $-Q$ if $-P$.

(69) _i_ Q if and only if $-P$.

(70) _h_ Q unless $-P$.

(a) $P \rightarrow Q$.
(b) $Q \rightarrow P$.
(c) $-P \rightarrow Q$.
(d) $-Q \rightarrow P$.
(e) $P \rightarrow -Q$.
(f) $Q \rightarrow -P$.
(g) $-P \rightarrow -Q$.
(h) $-Q \rightarrow -P$.
(i) $Q \leftrightarrow -P$.
(j) $-P \leftrightarrow Q$.
(k) $P \leftrightarrow Q$.
(m) $-P \leftrightarrow -Q$.

18 / Deduction

This chapter shows how to make deductions involving truth functional connectives.

Examples of arguments with four or more base components require enormous truth tables.   Sometimes there are short cuts in testing by truth tables, but a big truth table can very quickly become unmanageable.   So it helps to know some simple steps in arguments that you can recognize immediately and instinctively.   You should already know the following.

1. Two statements that are logically equivalent are always **(1)** INTER-CHANGEABLE / REPLACEABLE in any argument.
2. $--P$ is logically equivalent to **(2)** $-P$ / <u>P</u>.
3. De Morgan's laws of logical **(3)** <u>$EQUIVALENCE$</u> According to these laws, for example, $P \lor Q$ is logically equivalent to **(4)** $\overline{-(-P \& Q)}$, and $-(-P \& Q)$ is logically equivalent to **(5)** $\underline{P \lor -Q}$ If you hesitate about these questions, review Chapter 13 before going on.
4. The rule of permutation, according to which $P \& Q$ is logically equivalent to **(6)** $P \lor Q$ / <u>$Q \& P$</u>, and $P \lor Q$ is logically equivalent to **(7)** <u>$Q \lor P$</u>.
5. The rule of weakening, according to which: (circle the correct assertions) **(8)** $P \lor Q \vdash P$ / <u>$P \vdash P \lor Q$</u> / $Q \vdash P \lor Q$.
6. The rules of conjunction, according to which **(9)** $P \vdash P \& Q$ / <u>$P, Q \vdash P \& Q$</u> / <u>$P \& Q \vdash P$</u> / <u>$P \& Q \vdash Q$</u>.   (Circle three of these assertions).
7. Two rules of detachment, one for detaching an alternative, and one for detaching a consequent.

Cross out the incorrect detachments:

(10) $P, P \rightarrow Q \vdash Q.$
(11) $-P, -P \vee Q \vdash Q.$
(12) $P, -P \rightarrow Q \vdash -Q.$
(13) $-Q \vee P, -P \vdash -Q.$
(14) $P \vee -Q, Q \vdash -P.$
(15) $-P, -P \rightarrow Q \vdash Q.$

Cross out the incorrect applications of the above rules.

(16) $-(P \vee Q) \& R \vdash -(-(P \vee Q) \vee -R).$
(17) $-(P \vee Q) \& R \vdash (-P \& -Q) \vee R.$
(18) $-(P \vee Q) \& R \vdash -((P \vee Q) \vee -R).$
(19) $(P \& Q) \& R \vdash R.$
(20) $P \vee Q \vdash (P \vee Q) \vee -R.$
(21) $-R \vdash -R \& Q.$
(22) $P \& Q \vdash -Q \& -P.$
(23) $(P \& Q) \vee R \vdash R \vee (P \& Q).$

Match.

(24) _b_ Conjunction.

(25) _a_ Permutation.

(26) _d_ Detachment of alternative.

(27) _f_ De Morgan.

(28) _g_ Double denial.

(29) _e_ Detachment of consequent.

(30) _c_ Weakening.

(a) $P \vee Q \vdash Q \vee P.$
(b) $P \& Q \vdash P.$
(c) $P \vee Q \vdash (P \vee Q) \vee (R \& S).$
(d) $-(P \& Q),$ $R \vee (P \& Q) \vdash R.$
(e) $P \vee -Q, (P \vee -Q) \rightarrow (R \vee S) \vdash R \vee S.$
(f) $-(P \vee Q) \rightarrow R \vdash (-P \& -Q) \rightarrow R.$
(g) $--P \vdash ----P.$

The two kinds of detachment are not very different. $P \rightarrow Q$ takes the value F if and only if P is (31) _T_ and Q is (32) _F_. Under what circumstances does $-P \vee Q$ take the value F? (33) _PT QF_. It follows that $P \rightarrow Q$ and $-P \vee Q$ are logically (34) _EQUIVALENT_ We call this the rule of *wedge-arrow equivalence*.

$P \rightarrow Q$ is logically equivalent to $-P \vee Q.$

---

18 / Deduction

This chapter shows how to make deductions involving truth functional connectives.

Examples of arguments with four or more base components require enormous truth tables.   Sometimes there are short cuts in testing by truth tables, but a big truth table can very quickly become unmanageable.   So it helps to know some simple steps in arguments that you can recognize immediately and instinctively.   You should already know the following.

1. Two statements that are logically equivalent are always **(1)** INTER-CHANGEABLE / REPLACEABLE in any argument.
2. $--P$ is logically equivalent to **(2)** $-P$ / $\underline{P}$.
3. De Morgan's laws of logical **(3)** _EQUIVALENCE_ According to these laws, for example, $P \lor Q$ is logically equivalent to **(4)** $-(-P \& Q)$, and $-(-P \& Q)$ is logically equivalent to **(5)** $P \lor -Q$ If you hesitate about these questions, review Chapter 13 before going on.
4. The rule of permutation, according to which $P \& Q$ is logically equivalent to **(6)** $P \lor Q$ / $\underline{Q \& P}$, and $P \lor Q$ is logically equivalent to **(7)** $\underline{Q \lor P}$.
5. The rule of weakening, according to which: (circle the correct assertions) **(8)** $P \lor Q \vdash P$ / $\underline{P \vdash P \lor Q}$ / $\underline{Q \vdash P \lor Q}$.
6. The rules of conjunction, according to which **(9)** $P \vdash P \& Q$ / $\underline{P, Q \vdash}$ $\underline{P \& Q}$ / $\underline{P \& Q \vdash P}$ / $\underline{P \& Q \vdash Q}$.   (Circle three of these assertions).
7. Two rules of detachment, one for detaching an alternative, and one for detaching a consequent.

Cross out the incorrect detachments:

(10) $P, P \to Q \vdash Q.$
~~(11)~~ $-P, -P \lor Q \vdash Q.$
~~(12)~~ $P, -P \to Q \vdash -Q.$
(13) $-Q \lor P, -P \vdash -Q.$
~~(14)~~ $P \lor -Q, Q \vdash -P.$
(15) $-P, -P \to Q \vdash Q.$

Cross out the incorrect applications of the above rules.

~~(16)~~ $-(P \lor Q) \& R \vdash -(-(P \lor Q) \lor -R).$
~~(17)~~ $-(P \lor Q) \& R \vdash (-P \& -Q) \lor R.$
(18) $-(P \lor Q) \& R \vdash -((P \lor Q) \lor -R).$
(19) $(P \& Q) \& R \vdash R.$
(20) $P \lor Q \vdash (P \lor Q) \lor -R.$
~~(21)~~ $-R \vdash -R \& Q.$
~~(22)~~ $P \& Q \vdash -Q \& -P.$
(23) $(P \& Q) \lor R \vdash R \lor (P \& Q).$

Match.

(24) _b_ Conjunction.

(25) _a_ Permutation.

(26) _d_ Detachment of alternative.

(27) _f_ De Morgan.

(28) _g_ Double denial.

(29) _e_ Detachment of consequent.

(30) _c_ Weakening.

(a) $P \lor Q \vdash Q \lor P.$
(b) $P \& Q \vdash P.$
(c) $P \lor Q \vdash (P \lor Q) \lor$
      $(R \& S).$
(d) $-(P \& Q),$
      $R \lor (P \& Q) \vdash R.$
(e) $P \lor -Q, (P \lor -Q) \to$
      $(R \lor S) \vdash R \lor S.$
(f) $-(P \lor Q) \to R \vdash$
      $(-P \& -Q) \to R.$
(g) $--P \vdash ----P.$

The two kinds of detachment are not very different. $P \to Q$ takes the value F if and only if P is (31) _T_ and Q is (32) _F_. Under what circumstances does $-P \lor Q$ take the value F? (33) _PT QF_. It follows that $P \to Q$ and $-P \lor Q$ are logically (34) _EQUIVALENT_ We call this the rule of *wedge-arrow equivalence*.

$P \to Q$ is logically equivalent to $-P \lor Q.$

According to the rule for detaching a consequent; $P, P \rightarrow Q \vdash$ **(35)** _Q_.
According to the rule for detaching an alternative; $P, -P \vee Q \vdash$ **(36)** _Q_.
But since $-P \vee Q$ and **(37)** _P → Q_ are logically equivalent
according to the rule of wedge-arrow equivalence, these two rules hardly
differ. Hence, we refer to either rule simply as *detachment*.

Thanks to wedge-arrow equivalence we know how to express statements
using an arrow in terms of the wedge. Thanks to De Morgan's laws, we
know to express statements using a wedge in terms of the ampersand. So
we can express the arrow in terms of the ampersand too. For example,
$P \rightarrow Q$ is logically equivalent to **(38)** $P \vee Q$ / $-\underline{P \vee Q}$ / $-Q \vee P$. Then
in turn $-P \vee Q$ is logically equivalent to **(39)** $-P \& Q$ / $\underline{-(P \& -Q)}$ /
$P \& -Q$. So $P \rightarrow Q$ is logically equivalent to **(40)** $\underline{-(P \& -Q)}$ /
$(P \& -Q)$.

Notice that this logical equivalence states a familiar fact about the arrow.
$P \rightarrow Q$ is false only if P is **(41)** _T_ and Q is **(42)** _F_. That is to say,
according to $P \rightarrow Q$, it is not true that P is true and Q is false. That is,
$-(P \& -Q)$.

Express the following using only the ampersand and the bar.

(43) $-P \rightarrow Q$. _— (−p & −q)_.
(44) $-(Q \rightarrow P)$. _q & −p_.
(45) $-(-P \rightarrow Q)$. _−p & −q_.

Another useful rule is called *contraposition*. Is $P \rightarrow Q$ logically equivalent
to $Q \rightarrow P$? **(46)** YES / NO. **(47)** Draw a truth table to check that $P \rightarrow Q$
is logically equivalent to $-Q \rightarrow -P$.

$P \rightarrow Q$ and $-Q \rightarrow -P$ are logically equivalent.

We call this rule *contraposition* and include as contraposition anything that
merely involves deleting double bars. For example:

$-P \rightarrow Q$ is logically equivalent to $-Q \rightarrow --P$ or $-Q \rightarrow P$.

Apply contraposition and delete double bars from the following:

(48) $Q \rightarrow -P$. _P → −Q_.
(49) $-P \rightarrow -Q$. _Q → P_.
(50) $-Q \rightarrow (R \vee P)$. _−(R∨P) → Q_.

Notice that we can deduce that contraposition is valid, as follows.

1. $P \to Q \vdash -P \vee Q.$ Wedge-arrow.
2.   ,, $\vdash Q \vee -P.$ Permutation.
3.   ,, $\vdash -Q \to -P.$ Wedge-arrow.

Thus $P \to Q \vdash -Q \to -P.$ Make a similar deduction to show that $-P \to -Q \vdash Q \to P.$

(51)

$-P \to -Q \vdash --P \vee -Q$ W.A.

$\vdash P \vee -Q$ DOUBLE DENIAL

$\vdash -Q \vee P$ PERMUTATION

$\vdash Q \to P$ W.A.

A final useful rule is *association*:

> $(P \vee Q) \vee R$ and $P \vee (Q \vee R)$ are logically equivalent.
> $(P \,\&\, Q) \,\&\, R$ and $P \,\&\, (Q \,\&\, R)$ are logically equivalent.

Here are some examples of deductions. In more complicated deductions, we number the steps for ease of referring back.

$-P \vee -Q, -R \to (P \,\&\, Q) \vdash R$

Deduction:

1. $-P \vee -Q, -R \to (P \,\&\, Q) \vdash -(P \,\&\, Q)$
                First premise, De Morgan.

2.   ,, $\vdash -(P \,\&\, Q) \to R.$
                Second premise, contraposition,

3.   ,, $\vdash R.$
                1, 2, detachment.

Line 1 applies De Morgan's laws to the first premise. Line 2 applies contraposition to the **(52)** FIRST / SECOND premise. Line 3 derives R by detachment on the results of lines 1 and 2.

All of the following deductions are valid throughout. None involves any steps other than those we have just studied. In each case, justify every step as in the previous example, by writing the name of the rule alongside the lines that use it.

$-P \,\&\, -Q, R \to (P \vee Q) \vdash -R$

Deduction:

1. $-P \,\&\, -Q, R \to (P \vee Q) \vdash -(P \vee Q).$ **(53)** DE MORGAN
2.   ,, $\vdash -(P \vee Q) \to -R.$ **(54)** CONTRAPOSITION
3.   ,, $\vdash -R.$ **(55)** 1, 2, DETACHMEN

70. $-(p \lor q) \to -R, \; R \vdash p \lor q$

$\vdash R \to -(P \lor Q)$ CONTRA

$\vdash p \lor q$ DETACH.

71. $-(p \lor q) \to -R, \; R \vdash -(-p \& -q)$

$\vdash R \to (P \lor Q)$ CONTRA

$\vdash P \lor Q$ DETACH.

$\vdash -(-P \& -q)$ DE.M.

72. $-p \to -q, \; p \to R, \; Q \vdash R$

$\vdash Q \to P$ CONTRA

$\vdash p$ DETACH

$\vdash R$ DETACH.

73. $(p \lor q) \to -R \vdash R \to (-P \& -q)$

$\vdash R \to -(p \lor q)$ CONTRA

$\vdash R \to (-p \& -q)$ DeM

74. $p \to q \vdash -(-q \& p)$

$\vdash -p \lor q$ WEDGE ARROW

$\vdash q \lor -p$ ~~CONTR~~ PERMUTATION

$\vdash -(-q \& p)$ De M.

75. $(-p \lor -q) \lor R, \; P \& q \vdash R$

$\vdash -(-p \lor -q)$ DeM

$\vdash R$ DETACHMENT.

$$-(-R \lor -S) \vdash S$$

Deduction:

1. $-(-R \lor -S) \vdash R \& S.$ (56) _DE MORGAN_ .
2.   ,, $\vdash S.$ (57) _CONJUNCTION_ .

$$Q \vdash P \to Q$$

Deduction:

1. $Q \vdash -P \lor Q.$ (58) ~~DE MORGAN~~ _WEAKENING_
2. ,, $\vdash P \to Q.$ (59) _WEDGE ARROW_ .

$$P, Q \vdash -(-P \lor -Q)$$

Deduction:

1. $P, Q \vdash P \& Q.$ (60) _CONJUNCTION_ .
2.   ,, $\vdash -(-P \lor -Q).$ (61) _DE MORGAN_ .

$$P, P \to Q, Q \to R \vdash R$$

Deduction:

1. $P, P \to Q, Q \to R \vdash Q.$ (62) _DETACHMENT_ .
2.   ,, $\vdash R.$ 1, Premise $Q \to R$, and detachment.

At line 1 in the last example, we got Q from the two premises (63) _P_ and (64) _P→Q_ by detachment. At line 2, we got the conclusion of 2, namely, (65) _R_, from the conclusion of 1, namely, Q, and one of the premises, namely (66) _Q→R_, by another detachment.

$$P, -Q \to -P, -R \to -Q \vdash -R$$

←MISSPRINT SHOULD BE JUST R

Deduction:

1. $P, -Q \to -P, -R \to -Q \vdash P \to Q.$ (67) _CONTRAPOSITION_ .
2.   ,, $\vdash Q \to R.$ Premise, contraposition.
3.   ,, $\vdash Q.$ (68) 1, Premise, _DETACHMENT_
4.   ,, $\vdash R.$ (69) 2, 3, _DETACHMENT_ .

Now construct deductions for the following assertions on your own paper:

(70) $-(P \lor Q) \to -R, R \vdash P \lor Q.$
(71) $-(P \lor Q) \to -R, R \vdash -(-P \& -Q).$
(72) $-P \to -Q, P \to R, Q \vdash R.$
(73) $(P \lor Q) \to -R \vdash R \to (-P \& -Q).$

(74) $P \rightarrow Q \vdash -(-Q \& P)$.
(75) $(-P \vee -Q) \vee R, P \& Q \vdash R$.

In each of these examples, the trick is to apply one of our equivalences and try to get a stage where you can use detachment. For example, in (70), the conclusion is $P \vee Q$. You could get this by detachment if you got something arrow $P \vee Q$. But in the premise we see $-(P \vee Q)$ arrow something. This suggests that you apply contraposition to the premise and then see if detachment will work. Assertion (71) is obtained by continuing the deduction of (70), for the conclusion of (71) is equivalent to the conclusion of (70) by De Morgan.

Cross out the incorrect assertions below. Use any method you like. It will probably be quickest if you are fairly quick at deductions and can see when an inference is valid. But if you are not quick, it might be best to do truth tables for all of these and then to construct deductions for all the correct assertions below. After you have done that, you should have little trouble knowing what follows from what in cases like these.

(76) $P \rightarrow Q, Q \vdash P$.
(77) $P \vee Q, -Q \vdash -P$.
(78) $-(P \vee Q) \vdash -P \& -Q$.
(79) $P \rightarrow Q \vdash Q \rightarrow P$.
(80) $P \rightarrow Q, Q \rightarrow R, P \vdash R$.
(81) $P \rightarrow Q, -R \rightarrow -Q, P \vdash R$.
(82) $-P \vee Q, -R \rightarrow -Q, P \vdash R$.
(83) $P \rightarrow Q, P \rightarrow R, P \vdash Q \& R$.
(84) $---P \vdash --P$.
(85) $-P \vee Q, -R \vee Q \vdash (P \vee R) \vee Q$.
(86) $(P \vee R) \vee Q \vdash P \vee (R \vee Q)$.
(87) $P \& Q \vdash P \vee Q$.
(88) $P \vee Q \vdash P \& Q$.
(89) $-P, R \rightarrow P \vdash -R$.

19 / Conditional Proof

This chapter provides a final useful rule for making deductions.

What does "$P, Q \vdash R$" mean? **(1)** _____ *THE ARGUMENT FORM P, Q SO R IS VALID*
Notice that if $P \vdash Q$, then $P, R \vdash Q$ for any arbitrary premise R whatsoever.
For if the argument, P so Q, is valid, it is not possible for P to be true and
for Q to be **(2)** _*F*_. Hence it is not possible for P and R to be true and
Q to be false.

If $P \vdash Q$ and $Q \vdash R$, is it true that $P \vdash R$? **(3)** <u>YES</u> / NO. The answer is
yes, because if whenever P is true, Q is true (as required by $P \vdash Q$) and if
whenever Q is true, R is true, then whenever P is true, R is true.

(4) Is it true that if $P \vdash Q$, $Q \vdash R$, and $R \vdash S$, then $P \vdash S$? <u>YES</u> / NO.
(5) Is it true that if $P \vdash Q$, then also $Q \vdash P$ in every case? YES / <u>NO</u>.
(6) Is it true that if $P \vdash Q$ and $Q \vdash R$, then $P, S \vdash R$? <u>YES</u> / NO.

There is obviously a close connection between the arrow and valid argument. For example, we know the rule of detachment, according to which
the following is valid: **(7)** $P, P \rightarrow Q \vdash$ _*Q*_. Remember that $P \rightarrow Q$ is the
paraphrase of **(8)** P unless Q / <u>If P then Q</u> / Only if P, Q. It is natural
that we can go from P and, if P then Q, to Q. The conditional, "if P then
Q," is like a ticket on an airplane letting you go from P to Q. For this
reason the philosopher Gilbert Ryle has called conditional statements
"inference tickets." If somebody tells you that:

If there is no tax increase, then there will be more inflation.

you are told that you can infer more inflation from no tax increase. This
fact is summed up in the rule we call detachment.

Now the reverse of detachment should also hold. Suppose you can validly infer more inflation from no tax increase. Then, surely, if there is no tax increase there will be more inflation. This is the reverse of detachment. Having got a valid inference, we know a certain conditional holds.

The reverse of detachment is called *conditional proof*. This rule says that if you can deduce Q from P, you are entitled to assert $P \rightarrow Q$. Thus if you can assert $P \vdash Q$, you can also assert $\vdash P \rightarrow Q$. More generally, suppose that we can assert $R, P \vdash Q$. The rule of conditional proof tells us we can then assert $R \vdash P \rightarrow Q$.

Think of the conditional as an airplane ticket that enables you to go from P to Q. If you have a ticket $P \rightarrow Q$, and you are in P, then you can go to (9) _Q_. Now suppose you have gone to the ticket office and paid your money to get from P to Q. Then you are entitled to that journey and are issued a ticket to show this. The ticket is (10) _$P \rightarrow Q$_ / $Q \rightarrow P$. Doing the deduction is like paying your money.

Let us see how to use this rule in proofs, starting with a proof that, $P \rightarrow Q$, $Q \rightarrow R \vdash P \rightarrow R$. Such an inference form is certainly valid. Here is an example of an argument in this form:

> If he is guilty, then he will be fined.
> If he is fined, then he will be bankrupt.
> So, if he is guilty, then he will be bankrupt.

This inference is obviously (11) _VALID_ / INVALID. Now we use conditional proof to show that all inferences of this form are valid.

1. $P, P \rightarrow Q, Q \rightarrow R \vdash Q$.   Detachment from P and $P \rightarrow Q$.
2. $P, P \rightarrow Q, Q \rightarrow R \vdash R$.   1, premise, detachment.
3. $P \rightarrow Q, Q \rightarrow R \vdash P \rightarrow R$.   Conditional proof.

Notice that at lines 1 and 2 we have the same premises, namely (12) _P_, (13) _$P \rightarrow Q$_, and (14) _$Q \rightarrow R$_. Line 2 tells us that we can deduce R from these premises. That is, we can deduce R from P taken together with $P \rightarrow Q$ and (15) _$Q \rightarrow R$_. At line 2, we have "paid our money." At line 3 we get a ticket telling us that, given the remaining premises $P \rightarrow Q$ and (16) _$Q \rightarrow R$_, we are entitled to go from P to R. This is expressed by the conditional (17) $R \rightarrow P$ / _$P \rightarrow R$_. Notice that from line 2 we can proceed as above to line 3, but we can also go to:

2. $P, P \rightarrow Q, Q \rightarrow R \vdash R$.
4. $P, Q \rightarrow R \vdash (P \rightarrow Q) \rightarrow R$.   Conditional proof.

Also we can bring over the third premise and leave the other two:

2. $P, P \rightarrow Q, Q \rightarrow R \vdash R$.
5. $P, P \rightarrow Q \vdash (Q \rightarrow R) \rightarrow R$. Conditional proof.

Each of lines 3, 4, or 5 is got from 2 by following the rule of **(18)** *Conditional Proof*

Here are five attempted applications of conditional proof. Two are mistakes. Cross them out.

(19) Suppose $P, Q, R \vdash S$ is the result of some deduction. Then we get $Q, R \vdash P \rightarrow S$ by conditional proof.

(20) Suppose $P, Q, R \vdash S$ is the result of some deduction. Then we get $P, R \vdash S \rightarrow Q$ by conditional proof.

(21) Suppose $P, Q, R \vdash S$ is the result of some deduction. Then we get $P, R \vdash Q \rightarrow S$ by conditional proof.

(22) Suppose $P, Q, R \vdash S$ is the result of some deduction. Then we get $R, S \vdash P \rightarrow Q$ by conditional proof.

(23) Suppose $P, Q, R \vdash S$ is the result of some deduction. Then we get $P, Q \vdash R \rightarrow S$ by conditional proof.

The rule of detachment says, from P and $P \rightarrow Q$, you can infer **(24)** _Q_. Conditional proof says that if you have a proof of Q from P and some other premises, then you can assert that **(25)** _$P \rightarrow Q$_ follows from those other premises alone.

Here are some examples. If the premises in one line are exactly the same as in the previous line, we don't bother to copy them out. But as soon as we apply conditional proof, we "absorb" one of the premises into the conclusion. Thus the premises **(26)** ARE / ARE NOT all the same after applying conditional proof and we must rewrite the remaining premises to avoid any confusion.

$P \rightarrow (P \rightarrow Q) \vdash P \rightarrow Q$

Deduction:

1. $P, P \rightarrow (P \rightarrow Q) \vdash P \rightarrow Q$. **(27)** _Premise Detachment_.
2. $P, P \rightarrow (P \rightarrow Q) \vdash Q$. By detachment, using the premise P and the conclusion of line 1.
3. $P \rightarrow (P \rightarrow Q) \vdash P \rightarrow Q$. **(28)** _Conditional Proof_

Is the conclusion in line 1 the same as the conclusion in line 3? **(29)** YES / NO.
Are all the premises in line 1 in line 3? **(30)** YES / NO. Line 1 says **(31)** _$P, P \rightarrow (P \rightarrow Q) \vdash P \rightarrow Q$_.
Line 3 says **(32)** _$P \rightarrow (P \rightarrow Q) \vdash P \rightarrow Q$_.

Thus, although lines 1 and 3 have the same conclusion, line 3 asserts that the argument form "$P \to (P \to Q)$, so $P \to Q$" is valid.   Does line 1 assert this? **(33)** YES / NO.

$P \to Q \vdash (Q \to R) \to (P \to R)$

Deduction:

1. $P, P \to Q, Q \to R \vdash R$ ⟶ By detachment applied twice.

2. $P \to Q, Q \to R \vdash P \to R$ ⟶ **(34)** *CONDITIONAL PROOF*
3. $P \to Q \vdash (Q \to R) \to (P \to R)$ ⟶ **(35)** *CONDITIONAL PROOF*

Notice here we have applied conditional proof twice in a row, absorbing successively two premises into the conclusion.   At line 3, we brought the premise **(36)** *Q → R* over and made it the antecedent of the conditional.   Suppose we had brought over the other premise instead.   Then we would have got not 3 but 4.

4. $Q \to R \vdash$ **(37)** *(P → Q) → (P → R)*

At line 2, we brought the premise **(38)** *P* over and absorbed it as the antecedent of the conditional.   Suppose we had brought over $P \to Q$ instead.   Then we would have got not 2 but 5.

5. $P, Q \to R \vdash$ **(39)** *(P → Q) → R*

$P \to Q, P \to R \vdash P \to (Q \& R)$

Deduction:

1. $P, P \to Q, P \to R \vdash R$.   **(40)** *DETACHMENT*.
2.   „ $\vdash Q$.   **(41)** *DETACHMENT*.
3.   „ $\vdash Q \& R$.   1, 2, conjunction.
4. $P \to Q, P \to R \vdash P \to (Q \& R)$.   **(42)** *CONDITIONAL PROOF*.

The above example, like most others we have looked at, is just common sense.   The premises tell us that if P is true, Q is true, and also that if P is true, R is true.   So, if P is true, both Q and R must be true.   In concrete terms, suppose we are given the premises,

If he is ill, he will go to the hospital.
If he is ill, he needs a doctor.
So, **(43)** *IF HE IS ILL, HE WILL GO TO THE HOSPITAL AND HE NEEDS A DOCTOR.*

De Morgan's laws reminded us that there is a great symmetry between the wedge and the ampersand.   This symmetry also appears in rules of inference. For example, our permutation rule applies to both the wedge and the ampersand.

(44) $P \vee Q \vdash$ ___*Q ∨ P*___ by permutation.
(45) $P \& Q \vdash$ ___*Q & P*___ by permutation.

Paralleling the rule of conjunction:

   $P \& Q \vdash P$, and $P \& Q \vdash Q$.

we have the rule of weakening:

   $P \vdash P \vee Q$, and $Q \vdash P \vee Q$.

There is also a parallel to the rule derived above at (42):

   $P \to Q, P \to R \vdash P \to (Q \& R)$.

We shall call it simply the *alternative rule*.

The alternative rule:

$$P \to R, Q \to R \vdash (P \vee Q) \to R$$

The alternative rule is new.   Unlike the corresponding rule for the ampersand, it cannot be derived from the other rules we have given.   Notice that it too is just common sense.   A girl is anxious to see Joseph.   She knows that if he comes to school she will see him tomorrow.   She knows that if he goes to hear the *Jefferson Airplane* in the evening she will see him tomorrow. So she knows that if he either goes to school tomorrow or goes to hear the *Jefferson Airplane* in the evening, she will (46) *SEE JOSEPH*.   This is a special instance of the rule we have called the (47) *ALTERNATIVE* rule.

Cross out the incorrect assertions:

(48) $P \to (Q \vee R), S \to (Q \vee R) \vdash (P \vee S) \to (Q \vee R)$.
(49) $P \to Q, P \to R \vdash P \to (Q \vee R)$.
(50) $P \to Q, R \to Q \vdash (R \& P) \to Q$.
(51) $P \vee Q \vdash P \& Q$.
(52) $(P \vee Q) \to R \vdash (P \& Q) \to R$.

The last example is correct, as the following deduction shows:

1. $P \& Q, (P \lor Q) \to R \vdash P$.   (53) *CONJUNCTION*.
2. $P \& Q, (P \lor Q) \to R \vdash P \lor Q$.   (54) *WEAKENING*.
3. $P \& Q, (P \lor Q) \to R \vdash R$.   (55) *DETACHMENT*.
4. $P \lor Q \to R \vdash (P \& Q) \to R$.   (56) *CONDITIONAL PROOF*

Is $(P \& Q) \to R \vdash (P \lor Q) \to R$ correct? (57) YES / NO. If in doubt, draw a truth table.

   It is probably not very obvious how one can discover rules using conditional proof. Here is a fairly difficult example that may help.

$$P \to (Q \to R) \vdash (P \to Q) \to (P \to R).$$

The conclusion here is (58) *$(P \to Q) \to (P \to R)$*. The central connective in the conclusion is the (59) AMPERSAND / WEDGE / ARROW. One rule naturally leading to a conditional is (60) _*CONDITIONAL*_ proof. Let us start from the bottom of the deduction we are seeking for. At the bottom we see:

5. $P \to (Q \to R) \vdash (P \to Q) \to (P \to R)$.

Now if we got this by conditional proof, on the next line (61) ABOVE / BELOW we would see:

4. $P \to (Q \to R), P \to Q \vdash P \to R$.

The conclusion at this line is (62) *$P \to R$*. The central connective in the conclusion is (63) *THE ARROW*. One rule naturally leading to a conditional is (64) *CONDITIONAL PROOF*.
   If 4 was got by conditional proof, then the line above 4 must have been:

3. $P \to (Q \to R), P \to Q, P \vdash R$.

   Now if you look carefully at this, you will see that from the premises $P \to (Q \to R)$ and P you can detach (65) *$Q \to R$*. Moreover, from the premises $P \to Q$ and P you can detach (66) *Q*. Thus, from these premises we can get Q and $Q \to R$ from which we detach R and get to 3. Thus we can now set about our deduction:

1. $P \to (Q \to R), P \to Q, P \vdash Q \to R$.   (67) *DETACHMENT*.
2.   „ $\vdash Q$.   (68) *DETACHMENT*.

Now give the remaining steps in the proof.   The next step is to get 3 by detachment and then work down to 4 and 5.   Proceed:

(69) 3. $P \to (Q \to R)$, $P \to Q$, $P \vdash R$

(70) 4. $P \to (Q \to R)$, $P \to Q \vdash P \to R$

(71) 5. $P \to (Q \to R) \vdash (P \to Q) \to (P \to R)$

Which of the following assertions are correct? *69 — DETACHMENT*
CROSS OUT THE INCORRECT *70 — CONDITIONAL PROOF*
71 CONDITIONAL PROOF

(72)   If $P, Q \vdash R$, then $P \vdash Q \to R$.

(73)   If $P, Q \vdash R$, then $P \vdash -R \to -Q$.

~~(74)~~   If $P, Q \vdash R$, then $R \vdash P \to Q$.

(75)   If $P, Q \vdash R$, then $P \vdash -Q \lor R$.

(76)   If $P \vdash Q$ and $Q \vdash R$, then $P \vdash R$.

(77)   If $P \vdash Q$, then $P, R \vdash Q$.

(78)   If $P \vdash Q$ and $P \vdash R$, then $P \vdash Q \& R$.

(79)   If $P \vdash Q$ and $R \vdash S$, then $P, R \vdash Q \& S$.

Assertion 79 is correct, for if $P \vdash Q$, then $P, R \vdash Q$, since an additional premise can't hurt a valid argument.   Also, if $R \vdash S$, then $P, R \vdash S$.   Then we get $P, R \vdash Q \& S$ by using the rule of (80) *CONJUNCTION*

20 / Tautologies

This chapter gives some theoretical aspects of truth tables and deduction.

Which of the following is a correct application of conditional proof? **(1)** IF WE HAVE DEDUCED THAT $P, Q \vdash R$, THEN $P \vdash R \to Q$. / IF WE HAVE DEDUCED THAT $P, Q \vdash R$, THEN $P \vdash Q \to R$.

One trivial pattern of inference we have ignored is $P \vdash P$. We call this "identity." If an argument form is valid, then its conclusion cannot be **(2)** _F_ when all the premises are **(3)** _T_. Now P cannot be F when P is T, hence the argument form "P, so P" is certainly valid. Now suppose we apply conditional proof to $P \vdash P$. That is, we absorb the premise P into the antecedent of a conditional:

1. $P \vdash P$.   Identity.
2. $\vdash P \to P$.   Conditional proof.

Here we have a surprising result: $P \to P$ appears to be derived from no premises whatsoever. However, draw a truth table for $P \to P$:

(4)

P	$P \to P$
T	_T_
F	_T_

Is there any row in the truth table where $P \to P$ takes the value F? **(5)** YES / NO. Now an argument form is valid if there is no way of assigning T to all the premises and F to the conclusion. $P \to P$ can never be assigned the value **(6)** _F_. Hence, *no matter what Q is*, the argument form $Q \vdash P \to P$

160

is going to be **(7)** V~~ALID~~ / INVALID because no matter what values are assigned to Q, there is no way of assigning **(8)** _F_ to $P \rightarrow P$ and hence no way of assigning truth values to components so as to make the premise Q true and the conclusion $P \rightarrow P$ **(9)** _F_.

Since no matter what premise Q we choose, the argument form "Q, so $P \rightarrow P$" is valid, it is natural to think of the statement "$P \rightarrow P$" itself as being valid. There are plenty of other valid statements. For example, we know that $\vdash P \rightarrow P$, and we can infer from this that $\vdash -P \vee P$ by the rule of **(10)** ~~DE MORGANS LAWS~~ WEDGE ARROW

(11) On a separate sheet of paper draw a truth table for $-P \vee P$. Does it take the value F at any row in the table? **(12)** YES / NO.

A statement or statement scheme that takes the value T at *every* row in the truth table is called a *tautology*. On your own paper, draw tables to determine which of the following are tautologies:

(13) $(P \,\&\, (-Q \rightarrow -P)) \rightarrow Q.$ — TAUTOLOGY

(14) $(-P \rightarrow Q) \rightarrow -(P \,\&\, -Q).$ — NO —

(15) $((P \rightarrow P) \rightarrow Q) \rightarrow P.$ — NO —

(16) $((P \rightarrow Q) \rightarrow P) \rightarrow P.$ — TAUTOLOGY

For any tautology P, we can also deduce that $\vdash P$, i.e., P is valid. For example, here is the deduction for 16, which is a tautology. State the rules of inference used:

$((P \rightarrow Q) \rightarrow P) \rightarrow P.$

Deduction:

1.	$P \vdash P.$	**(17)** IDENTITY
2.	$\vdash P \rightarrow P.$	**(18)** CONDITIONAL PROOF
3.	$P \,\&\, -Q \vdash P.$	**(19)** CONJUNCTION
4.	$\vdash (P \,\&\, -Q) \rightarrow P.$	**(20)** CONDITIONAL PROOF
5.	$\vdash -(-P \vee Q) \rightarrow P.$	**(21)** DE MORGANS LAW
6.	$\vdash -(P \rightarrow Q) \rightarrow P.$	**(22)** WEDGE ARROW
7.	$\vdash (-(P \rightarrow Q) \vee P) \rightarrow P.$	2, 6, rule of alternatives.
8.	$\vdash ((P \rightarrow Q) \rightarrow P) \rightarrow P.$	**(23)** WEDGE ARROW.

Now construct a deduction for 13.

$(P \,\&\, (-Q \rightarrow -P)) \rightarrow Q.$

Deduction:

(24)

1.	$P \,\&\, (-Q \rightarrow -P) \vdash P$	CONJUNCTION
2.	"	$\vdash -Q \rightarrow -P$	"
3.	"	$\vdash P \rightarrow Q$	CONTRAPOSITION
4.	"	$\vdash Q$	DETACHMENT OF 1, 3
5.	"	$\vdash (P \,\&\, (-Q \rightarrow -P)) \rightarrow Q$	CONDITIONAL PROOF

If P is a tautology, then the argument form "Q, so P" is valid for any Q whatsoever. Can you explain why?

(25) *IF THERE IS NO ROW WHERE P IS F THEN Q CAN'T BE T AND P F*.

The argument form "P, so Q" is valid if and only if $P \rightarrow Q$ is a tautology. To show this, we have to show that if P, so Q is valid, then $P \rightarrow Q$ is a tautology, and if $P \rightarrow Q$ is a tautology, then P, so Q is valid. We must show **(26)** ONE / TWO things, corresponding to the two different directions of "if and only if."

If P, so Q is valid, then there is no assignment of truth values so that P takes the value **(27)** *T* and Q takes the value **(28)** *F*. But $P \rightarrow Q$ takes the value F if and only if P takes T and Q takes **(29)** *F*. We have just said there is no such possibility. So $P \rightarrow Q$ always takes the value **(30)** *T*. Hence, $P \rightarrow Q$ is a **(31)** *TAUTOLOGY*

On the other hand, if $P \rightarrow Q$ is a tautology, then there is no row where P takes the value T and Q takes the value F. But the argument form "P, so Q" is invalid only if at some row, P takes the value **(32)** *T* and Q takes the value **(33)** *F*. We have just shown there is no such row, so the argument form is **(34)** *VALID*.

(35) On your own paper prove that the argument form "P, Q, R, so S" is valid, if and only if $((P \& Q) \& R) \rightarrow S$ is a tautology.

Recall that two statements are logically equivalent if they never differ in truth value. Whenever one takes T at some row in the table, the other takes the value **(36)** *T*; whenever one takes F, so does the other. A biconditional $P \leftrightarrow Q$ takes the value T at some row in the table if and only if at that row P and Q have **(37)** THE SAME / DIFFERENT truth values.

(38) On your own paper explain why two statements P and Q are logically equivalent if and only if $P \leftrightarrow Q$ is a tautology. **(39)** Draw up a truth table for $P \& -P$. Is there any row at which it takes the value F? **(40)** YES / NO. Is there any row at which it takes the value T? **(41)** YES / NO.

A statement or statement scheme that takes the value F at every row in the truth table is called a *contradiction*. Draw truth tables to find out which of the following are contradictions:

CROSS THOSE THAT ARN'T CONTRADICTIONS

(42) $-(P \vee -P)$.

(43) $(P \vee Q) \leftrightarrow -(Q \vee P)$.

(44) $-P \vee (Q \& P)$.

The denial of a tautology is a contradiction, and the denial of a contradiction is a tautology. Explain why.

(45) *A TAUTOLOGY IS T IN EVERY ROW AND SINCE THE DENIAL WOULD MAKE IT F IN EVERY ROW IT WOULD BE A CONTRADICTION AND VICE VERSA ...*

Suppose you had an oracle called "Oscar," which could tell you when a statement was a contradiction. You want to know whether some statement is a tautology or not. You cannot ask Oscar directly, because he will answer only one kind of question, namely, "Is 'so and so' a contradiction?" All the same, you can use Oscar to recognize tautologies. For the denial of a tautology is a **(46)** _CONTRADICTION_ So if you want to know whether statement P is a tautology, you ask Oscar whether $-P$ is a contradiction. What will Oscar answer if P is a tautology? He will answer "$-P$ **(47)** IS / IS NOT a contradiction." What will he answer if P is not a tautology? **(48)** "_-P IS NOT CONTRADICTION_

The argument form "P, so Q" is valid if and only if **(49)** $P \to Q$ / $Q \to P$ / $P \leftrightarrow Q$ is a tautology. How would you use Oscar to discover whether an argument form is valid in virtue of the truth functional connectives? **(50)** _IS P <-> Q A TAUTOLOGY?_

A different oracle is called "Pard." It can answer only one kind of question. Given a biconditional of the form $P \leftrightarrow Q$, it can tell you whether the biconditional is a tautology.

P and Q are logically equivalent if and only if **(51)** $P \to Q$ / $Q \to P$ / $P \leftrightarrow Q$ is a **(52)** TAUTOLOGY / CONTRADICTION. How would you use Pard to find out if two statements are logically equivalent? _(P – PREMISE / Q – CONCLUSION)_ **(53)** _P – (P → Q) A CONTRADICTION?_

The statement scheme "$P \lor -P$" is a **(54)** TAUTOLOGY / CONTRADICTION. Thus it takes **(55)** T / F at every row in the truth table. Now suppose that $Q \leftrightarrow (P \lor -P)$ is a tautology. Then at each row, Q and $P \lor -P$ must take **(56)** THE SAME / DIFFERENT truth values. Hence, at every row in the truth table, Q must take the value **(57)** _T_. Hence, Q must be a **(58)** _TAUTOLOGY_

How would you use Pard to find out if any arbitrarily chosen statement is a tautology? **(59)** _EX IF YOU WANT TO KNOW IF Q IS A TAUTOLOGY ASK IF: IS Q <-> (PV-P) IS A TAUTOLOGY._

Oscar can answer only one kind of question directly: he can tell you whether a statement is a contradiction. But he is also able to help you find out if a statement is a tautology; to find out whether P is a tautology, you ask Oscar whether $-P$ is a contradiction. Hence, Oscar **(60)** CAN / CANNOT help you find out if a biconditional is a tautology. Can you find out anything using Pard that you cannot find out using Oscar? **(61)** YES / NO.

We saw that Pard is able to tell us indirectly whether an arbitrary statement Q is a tautology. We ask Pard, "Is $(P \lor -P) \leftrightarrow Q$ a tautology?" If he answers **(62)** YES / NO, we know that Q is a tautology. How would you use Pard to find out whether Q is a contradiction? **(63)** _ASK IF -Q <-> (PV-P) IS A TAUTOLOGY_ .

Is there any question we could answer using Oscar that we could not answer using Pard? **(64)** YES / NO.

A consultation with Oscar costs $3 a question; a consultation with Pard costs $7.50. If you simply wanted answers to questions, and you wanted to economize, would you ever have good reason for going to consult Pard? **(65)** YES / NO.

A third oracle, called "Roger," answers yet another kind of question. Given any two statements (not statement schemes, but actual statements), call them P and Q, he is able to tell you whether the biconditional $P \leftrightarrow Q$ is true. Pard tells you whether $P \leftrightarrow Q$ is a tautology, but that is different. For example, both of the following biconditionals are true:

A. Sea water is salty. $\leftrightarrow$ It is not the case that sea water is not salty.
B. Sea water is salty. $\leftrightarrow$ The sun is larger than the earth.

Only one is a tautology. Which is it? **(66)** A / B. Notice that B is certainly true, for the truth value of "Sea water is salty" is **(67)** _T_ and the truth value of "The sun is larger than the earth" is **(68)** _T_. Hence, both components of B have **(69)** THE SAME / DIFFERENT truth values. The biconditional is true if and only if both components have **(70)** THE SAME / DIFFERENT truth values. So biconditional B is true. However, A is not only true but also a tautology, for no matter what the truth value of the components, they both have the same truth value. Thus, the components of A are logically **(71)** _EQUIVALENT._ But the components of B are not logically equivalent, for although both components are in fact true, it would be perfectly possible for them to differ in truth value, for example, if enough of a salt-precipitating chemical is added to sea water, we might free the seas of salt, so the first component of B would be **(72)** _F_ whereas the second component would still be **(73)** _T_.

One of the following is a tautology, one is a contradiction, and one is true but not a tautology:

A. China has a larger population than India. $\leftrightarrow$ It is false that China has a larger population than India.
B. India has a larger population than China. $\leftrightarrow$ America has a larger population than India.
C. America has a larger population than India. $\leftrightarrow$ It is false that America does not have a larger population than India.

Which is which? A is a **(74)** _CONTRADICTION._ B is **(75)** _TRUE_. C is a **(76)** _Tautology_.

Notice A is a contradiction, even though the first component of A is T. Both B and C are T even though all components are F. This is because a biconditional requires that both components have the same truth value, but both can be F.

Now Pard can tell you whether a biconditional is a tautology, but Roger can tell you whether a biconditional is true. Can you use Pard to discover whether there is life on Mars? **(77)** YES / ＮO.

Yet Roger could tell you whether there is life on Mars. For, take any statement that you know is true, say, "Sea water is salty." Ask Roger whether the following biconditional is true:

There is life on Mars. ↔ Sea water is salty.

What will Roger answer if there is life on Mars? **(78)** _＿＿Ｔｒｕｅ＿＿＿＿_.
What will he answer if there is no life on Mars? **(79)** _＿＿Ｆａｌｓｅ＿＿＿_.

Roger can also tell you whether some statement is a tautology. You ask him if the following biconditional is true:

The statement is a tautology. ↔ Sea water is salty.

What will Roger answer if the statement in question is not a tautology? He will answer: "This biconditional is **(80)** T / ＿F."

Pard's services are available for your lifetime for a payment of $30; Oscar's for $18, and Roger's for $350. Which is the best purchase? **(81)** OSCAR / PARD / ＲOGER.

Answer "T" or "F":

(82) _＿Ｔ＿_ The argument form "*P*, so *Q*" is invalid if at every row in the truth table where *P* is T, *Q* is F.

(83) _＿Ｆ＿_ The argument form "*P*, so *Q*" is invalid only if at every row in the truth table where *P* is T, *Q* is F.

(84) _＿Ｔ＿_ If the argument form "*P*, so *Q*" is valid, then $P \to Q$ is a tautology.

(85) _＿Ｔ＿_ Only if the argument form "*P*, so *Q*" is valid, is $P \to Q$ a tautology.

(86) _＿Ｆ＿_ The argument form "*P*, so *Q*" is valid if, and only if, $P \leftrightarrow Q$ is a tautology.

(87) _＿Ｔ＿_ $P \leftrightarrow Q$ is a tautology if, and only if, $P \vdash Q$ and $Q \vdash P$.

(88) _＿Ｔ＿_ *P* is a tautology if, and only if, $-P$ is a contradiction.

(89) _＿Ｆ＿_ A biconditional is a tautology if, and only if, it is true.

(90) _＿Ｔ＿_ If an oracle could tell you whether any given biconditional is true, you could find out the truth value of any statement whatsoever.

(91) _＿Ｔ＿_ If an oracle could tell you whether any given biconditional is a tautology, you could use it to find out whether any given statement is a contradiction.

(92) _T_ If an oracle could tell you whether any given statement is true, you could find out whether any given biconditional is true.

(93) _F_ If an oracle could tell you whether any given biconditional is a tautology, you could use it to find out whether any given statement is true.

(94) _F_ If the statement P is a tautology, then $P \to Q$ is a tautology for any Q whatsoever.

(95) _T_ If P is a tautology, then no matter what statement Q you choose, the argument form "Q, so P" is valid.

(96) _T_ If P is a contradiction, then the argument form "P, so Q" is valid.

(97) _F_ If P is a contradiction, then $P \to Q$ is never a tautology.

(98) _F_ If $P \to Q$ is a tautology, then Q is too.

Another important idea is *consistency*. In the case of statements that can be put on Venn diagrams, we said any set of statements is consistent if they can all be diagramed on the same diagram. For this shows they can all be true together. The same idea applies in the case of truth functions. Two statement schemes are consistent if they can both take the value T together, that is, if there is some row on the truth table where they are all true. In general, a set of statements is consistent if there is some row on the truth table where they are all (99) _T_.

Notice we say *some* row, not every row. Consistency demands only that it is possible for all statements to be true at once. On the other hand, a set of statements is not consistent, or is *inconsistent*, if there is (100) SOME / NO row on the truth table where all the statements take the value T at once. Merely having some row where not all are T shows nothing. For there might be another row where all are T, and if so, the set of statements is (101) CONSISTENT / INCONSISTENT.

Draw truth tables and then determine whether the following sets of statement schemes are consistent. You must draw a table to compare truth values for each scheme. If you can find a single row where every statement scheme in the list is T, then you know that these schemes are consistent. But if there is no single row where all are (102) _T_, then they are inconsistent.

(103) $P \lor Q.$ $-P \,\&\, -Q.$ INCONSISTENT

(104) $P \to Q.$ $Q \to R.$ $R.$ CONSISTENT

(105) $Q \to R.$ $P \to R.$ $P \,\&\, -R.$ INCONSISTENT

(106) $-P \lor Q.$ $-Q \lor R.$ $-R \lor P.$ CONSISTENT,

Now paraphrase the following sets of statements and draw truth tables to discover whether they are jointly consistent.

107. $w \to m$
$m \to n$
$w \to -n$
CONSISTENT -

(**107**) If the war is drawn to an end, there will be ample money for domestic policies. If there is ample money for domestic policies, then the nation's urban problems will be mostly solved. Even if the war is ended, however, most of the nation's urban problems will remain unsolved.

$p \to a$
$a \to S$
$-S$
CONSISTENT

(**108**) If she is pregnant, she will try to get an illegal abortion. If she tries to get an illegal abortion, she will succeed. But she will not succeed in getting an illegal abortion.

$3 v - C$
$C \to 6$
$6 \to -B$

(**109**) Either the earth began at a definite time, or the earth was not created at all. If the earth was created, then there is a God. If there is no God, the earth did not begin at a definite time. Even if there is a God, there is no definite time at which the earth began.

$b \to -B$
CONSISTENT

(**110**) Slutski and Pritchard's sales of ball bearings did not increase last year. If Slutski and Pritchard did not increase their sales of ball bearings, the creditors will demand further guarantees. Luckily, Slutski and Pritchard did sell more ball bearings last year. However, their creditors still demand further guarantees.

S
$-S \to g$
INCONSISTENT.

S
g

In these examples, we are concerned with the consistency of some set of statements. We want to know whether it is possible for them all to be true together. If it is impossible that all should be true together, then the set of statements is (**111**) CONSISTENT / INCONSISTENT. But if there is some row in the truth table where all take the value true, then the set is (**112**) CONSISTENT / INCONSISTENT.

Notice that in the last paragraph we have said (**113**) SOMETHING / NOTHING about arguments. Are any of the sets of statements 107–110 arguments? (**114**) YES / NO. Each of 107–110 is a set of statements, but there is no argument. Of course, we could use the very same statements to form arguments. For example, the statements in 108 could be used as the premises to prove the conclusion that the girl in question is not pregnant. Would the argument resulting be valid? (**115**) YES / NO.

In this book we concentrate so much on valid *arguments*, that some students start thinking that anything discussed here is an argument. But 107–110 (**116**) ARE / ARE NOT arguments. Does it make any sense to speak of the premises of 107–110? (**117**) YES / NO.

Something is wrong with the following assertion. (**118**) Correct it:

CHANGE PREMISES TO STATEMENTS.

To discover whether a set of statements is jointly consistent, draw a truth table. If there is any row where all the premises are T, then the statements are consistent, but if there is no row where all the statements are T, then they are inconsistent.

Are there any premises in the following statement? (**119**) YES / NO.

If it rains on Thursday, Joseph won't take Lydia to the picnic.

The component "Joseph won't take Lydia to the picnic" is called the **(120)**
ANTECEDENT / CONSEQUENT of this conditional.   What is the name given to
the component "It rains on Thursday"?   **(121)** *ANTECEDENT* Arguments have premises and conclusions.   Conditional statements have antecedents and consequents.   Validity and invalidity are properties of arguments.   Consistency and inconsistency are properties of sets of statements.

21 / Reduction to Absurdity

So far we have examined arguments that are intended to prove a conclusion by deducing it from acceptable premises. Another use of argument is to show that some statements are false by showing that they imply known falsehoods. We conclude our examination of truth functional logic by studying this kind of argument. There are also review questions at the end of this chapter.

(1) What does $P \vdash Q$ mean? *THE ARGUMENT FORM $P \subset Q$ IS VALID*

(2) If $P \vdash Q$, and P is T, what is the truth value of Q? __T__ / F.

(3) If $P \vdash Q$, and P is F, does the truth value of Q have to be F? YES / __NO__.

(4) If $P \vdash Q$, and Q is T, does the truth value of P have to be T? YES / __NO__.

(5) If $P \vdash Q$, and Q is F, what is the truth value of P? T / __F__.

This last fact provides a useful way of refuting some statements. For example, suppose that someone says, "Convicted murderers must be executed in order to deter other would-be murderers." If you disagree, you might argue, "If that is true, then states that have abolished capital punishment should have experienced an increased murder rate. Experience shows that in such states, the murder rate has, if anything, decreased after the abolition of capital punishment. So what you are claiming is not true." (6) Underline the assertion that this argument is rebutting. This assertion has certain consequences, which, it is here claimed, are (7) __T__ / F. Hence, the statement itself must be (8) T / __F__. For in general, if $P \vdash Q$ and Q is F, then P must be (9) T / __F__.

So far in this book, we have mostly been considering arguments that are used to prove that some statement is true.   But we can have the opposite interest: we may want to show that something is false.   Often the way we argue is in the following pattern:

$$P \to Q, \ - Q, \text{ so } -P.$$

It is easy to see that this is valid.   The argument form is valid so long as the **(10)** PREMISES / CONCLUSION is T whenever the **(11)** PREMISES / CONCLUSION are T.   If the premises are T, then $- Q$ is **(12)** T / F.   Hence, Q is **(13)** T / F.   If the premises are both T, then $P \to Q$ is **(14)** T / F.   Hence, P is **(15)** T / F.   Hence, $-P$ is **(16)** T / F.   So when both premises are T, the conclusion, $-P$, is **(17)** T / F.   Hence, the argument form is **(18)** VALID / INVALID.   We can also see this by deduction.   State the rules of inference used:

$P \to Q, \ -Q \vdash -Q \to -P.$ **(19)** _Contraposition_.

  „ $\vdash -P.$ **(20)** _Detachment -_.

A person who believes that the earth is flat might produce the following argument:

> You say the earth is round.   But if the earth is round there would be places on the other side of the earth where people would simply fall off. There are no such places.   Therefore, the earth is not round.

What is his conclusion?   **(21)** _The Earth is not Round_.   Is his argument in the above form?   **(22)** YES / NO.   Is it valid?   **(23)** YES / NO. How would you criticize this argument?   **(24)** _There is a false premise (that people would fall off_)

The question of whether people could fall off the earth, is, of course, a question of **(25)** PHYSICS / LOGIC.   The truth or falsity of the premises in the above argument **(26)** IS / IS NOT a matter of logic.   In general, whether a premise is true is not a matter of logic.   But there is a special case.   What is the name of a statement that takes the value T at every row in a truth table? **(27)** _Tautology_.   What is the name of a statement that takes the value F at every row?   **(28)** _Contradiction_. If we can show that a statement P implies a contradiction, then we know that P itself must be **(29)** T / F.   A contradiction cannot possibly be **(30)** T / F.   It would be *absurd* to think a contradiction is true.   Hence, an argument showing P is false, by deriving a contradiction from it, used to be called *reductio ad absurdum*, or, reduction to **(31)** FALSEHOOD / ABSURDITY.

Probably the two most common uses of this kind of argument are in law and in mathematics.   For example, a witness claims he was in Harry's bar at 11:20 P.M. last Tuesday night.   He also says he caught the 10:50 clipperjet to San Francisco. These assertions, taken together with what we know about airports, imply an inconsistency. Hence, the lawyer urges that the witness is **(32)** TELLING THE TRUTH / LYING.

In mathematics, reduction to absurdity is one of the most useful tools. Here is a famous example. At one time Greek mathematicians probably believed that all lengths could be measured as multiples of some convenient unit. This is equivalent to saying, as we should express it today, that all numbers are rational fractions, i.e., they can be expressed as n/m, where n and m are whole numbers. But consider the diagonal of a square that is one foot long on each side. By Pythagoras' theorem, this diagonal must be $\sqrt{2}$ feet long. This is not a rational fraction. For suppose $\sqrt{2} = m/n$, where m and n are whole numbers with no common divisor. Then

$$2 = \frac{m^2}{n^2}$$

or

$$2n^2 = m^2$$

So m^2 is even. So there must be some number k so that $m^2 = (2k)^2 = 4k^2$. So,

$$2n^2 = 4k^2$$

or

$$n^2 = 2k^2$$

So n^2 must be even too. But this contradicts our supposition, that m and n are in lowest terms, with no common divisor. Hence, our supposition about $\sqrt{2}$ must be false. It is not, after all, a rational fraction.

There are various ways of expressing the underlying pattern of argument for reduction to absurdity. One is this:

$$P \to Q, P \to -Q \vdash -P.$$

That is, if P implies both Q and $-Q$, then we conclude that P is **(33)** T / F.

We can check the above argument form by deduction. It is perhaps simplest to start from the fact that **(34)** $Q \lor -Q$ / $Q \And -Q$ is a tautology. That is to say:

1. $\vdash Q \lor -Q.$

Now supply the rules of inference:

(35) _CONTRAPOSITION_.   2. $P \to Q, P \to -Q \vdash -Q \to -P$

(36) _CONTRAPOSITION_. 3. $P \to Q, P \to -Q \vdash --Q \to -P.$
(37) _Double Denial_. 4. „ $\vdash Q \to -P.$
(38) _Alternatives_. 5. „ $\vdash (Q \lor -Q) \to -P.$
(39) _Detachment_. 6. „ $\vdash -P.$

The form of the argument about $\sqrt{2}$ is a special case of reduction to absurdity. From the premise, or supposition, P, we deduced $-P$. Hence, P has as consequences both $-P$, and also (trivially) itself, namely, P. Since P implies both P and $-P$, we conclude that P itself is **(40)** T / F. **(41)** Draw a truth table to check that the following argument form is valid:

P	$-P$	$P \to -P$	$-P$
T	F	F	F
F	T	T	T

$P \to -P \quad \vdash -P.$

We conclude this chapter with a review of truth functional logic. It is useful if you are able to define, in your own words, key logical terms. On your own paper, answer those of the following questions that require definitions or explanations.

(42) What is a truth functional connective?
(43) Which of the following connectives are usually used in a strictly truth functional way? AND / OR / NEITHER, NOR / IF, THEN / ONLY IF / UNLESS / NOT / PROBABLY / IT IS NOT THE CASE THAT.
(44) What is the difference in meaning between *premise* and *antecedent*?
(45) What is a tautology?
(46) What is a contradiction?
(47) Are all statements either tautologies or contradictions? YES / NO.
(48) Explain why $P \to Q$ is a tautology whenever P is a contradiction.
(49) Explain why $P \to Q$ is a tautology whenever Q is a tautology.
(50) When is a set of statements inconsistent?
(51) If the premises of an argument are inconsistent, then the argument is valid. Explain why.
(52) How would you criticize an argument with inconsistent premises?
(53) What is a counterexample to an argument form?
(54) If R is a tautology, then for any statements P and $Q, P, Q \vdash R$. Why?
(55) Explain, using your own examples, why "if, then" is not strictly truth functional. (If in doubt, review Chapter 16.)
(56) What are De Morgan's laws of logical equivalence?
(57) Explain why if P and Q are logically equivalent, the biconditional $P \leftrightarrow Q$ is a tautology.
(58) If $P \vdash Q$ and $Q \vdash P$, then P and Q are logically equivalent. Explain why.
(59) Give an example of a valid argument with a false conclusion.
(60) Give an example of an invalid argument with a true conclusion.
(61) If P and Q are tautologies, then they are logically equivalent. Explain why.

(62) If P and Q are both contradictions, then the biconditional $P \leftrightarrow Q$ is a tautology. Explain why.

Match (leave no blanks):

(63) _H_ $P \to Q, P \vdash Q.$

(64) _J_ $-P \to Q \vdash -Q \to P.$

(65) _A_ $P \vdash P \lor Q.$

(66) _E_ $P, Q \vdash P \& Q.$

(67) _B_ $P \lor Q \vdash Q \lor P.$

(68) _K_ $(P \lor Q) \lor R \vdash P \lor (Q \lor R).$

(69) _E_ $P \& Q \vdash Q.$

(70) _I_ $P \lor -Q, -P \vdash -Q.$

(71) _C_ $-(P \lor Q) \vdash -P \& -Q.$

(72) _G_ $---P \vdash -P.$

(73) _K_ $P \& (Q \& R) \vdash (P \& Q) \& R.$

(74) _J_ $P \to Q \vdash -Q \to -P.$

(75) _F_ $P \to Q \vdash -P \lor Q.$

(76) _B_ $P \& Q \vdash Q \& P.$

(77) _D_ $P \to Q, R \to Q \vdash (P \lor R) \to Q.$

(78) _C_ $-P \& Q \vdash -(P \lor -Q).$

(a) Weakening.
(b) Permutation.
(c) De Morgan.
(d) Alternatives.
(e) Conjunction.
(f) Wedge-arrow.
(g) Double denial.
(h) Detachment of the consequent.
(i) Detachment of an alternative.
(j) Contraposition.
(k) Association.

Cross out the incorrect assertions.

(79) ~~$P \vdash P \& Q.$~~

(80) $-P \lor -Q \vdash -(P \& Q).$

(81) ~~$P \to Q, P \to R \vdash (P \lor Q) \to R.$~~

(82) $\vdash (P \to Q) \to (-Q \to -P).$

(83) $P \to Q, Q \to R \vdash P \to R.$

(84) $-P \lor Q, Q \to R \vdash -R \to -P.$

(85) ~~$P \to Q, -Q \lor R \vdash -R \to P.$~~

(86) $\vdash (P \to Q) \to ((Q \to R) \to (P \to R)).$

(87) ~~$\vdash ((P \to Q) \to (Q \to R)) \to (P \to R).$~~

(88) $P \to Q, -Q \vdash -P.$

(89) ~~$P \to Q, Q \vdash P.$~~

(90) ~~$-P \lor -Q \vdash P \& Q.$~~

Match (leave no blanks):

(91) _O_ P unless Q.

(92) _m_ P only if Q.

(93) _v_ If P, then − Q.

(94) _u_ − P if Q.

(95) _S_ Q if and only if P.

(96) _t_ If and only if − P, − Q.

(97) _n_ Unless − P, Q.

(98) _o_ Only if Q, − P.

(99) _v_ − P unless − Q.

(100) _r_ Only if − P, − Q.

(m) $P \to Q.$
(n) $Q \to P.$
(o) $-P \to Q.$
(p) $-Q \to P.$
(q) $-P \to -Q.$
(r) $-Q \to -P.$
(s) $Q \leftrightarrow P.$
(t) $-P \leftrightarrow -Q.$
(u) $Q \to -P.$
(v) $P \to -Q.$

Cross out the incorrect applications of conditional proof.

(101) If there is a deduction of $P, Q \vdash R$, then $Q \vdash P \to R.$
~~(102)~~ If there is a deduction of $P \vdash Q$, then $\vdash Q \to P.$
(103) If there is a deduction of $P, Q, R \vdash S$, then $P \vdash Q \to (R \to S).$
(104) If there is a deduction of $P, Q, R \vdash S$, then $R \vdash P \to (Q \to S).$
~~(105)~~ If there is a deduction of $P, Q, R \vdash S$, then $S \vdash P \to (Q \to R).$

Test for consistency:

(106) $P \lor Q.$ $-Q \lor R.$ $P \to R.$
(107) $Q \lor (P \lor R).$ $-(Q \& P).$ $-R.$
(108) $P \to (Q \to R).$ $-P.$ $-Q.$ $-R.$
(109) $P \to Q.$ $Q \to R.$ $-R.$ $-P.$

ALL ARE CONSISTENT.

22 / The Existential Quantifier

This chapter begins a more detailed analysis of statements and arguments that use words like "some" and "all."

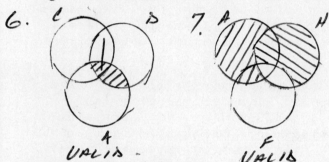

6. *c* *D*

VALID —

7. *A* *H*

VALID

Paraphrase this valid argument:

> Either Joseph cheats when he plays poker, or he is incredibly lucky. He does not cheat. So, he is incredibly lucky.

(1) *C V I, -C So I*. What are the statement connectives? (2) _EITHER OR_ and (3) ____NOT____. Since these connectives are the only elements that occur in the logical form of this argument, it is natural to say the argument form is valid in virtue of the properties of these (4) STATEMENT CONNECTIVES / LOGICAL DEDUCTIONS. In contrast, recall the kind of argument we studied using Venn diagrams. Such arguments are called (5) SYLLOGISMS / TRUTH FUNCTIONAL. Represent the logical forms of the following two syllogisms and draw diagrams to test their validity:

(6) Some cars have defective brakes.
Nothing with defective brakes is allowed on the highway.
So, some cars are not allowed on the highway.

(7) All anticyclones are weather systems accompanied by high barometric pressure.
Any weather system accompanied by high barometric pressure is relatively fine weather.
So, all anticyclones have relatively fine weather.

Which of these arguments are valid? (8) 6 / 7. What logical words in addition to "not" occur essentially in the argument forms of 6 and 7? (9) ALL / IF, THEN / SOME / NO / EITHER, OR / NOR.

It is natural to say that arguments 6 and 7 are **(10)** VALID / INVALID in virtue of the properties of the logical words you have just circled. Roughly speaking, each of these words has something to do with quantity: all, some, no, or none. Other words like "every" or "at least one" do a similar job. All are called "quantifiers." **(11)** Circle the four quantifiers in this passage:

Any reasonable man would have done the same thing, but after the legal and political problems of the *Pueblo* are over, everybody is still vaguely uneasy. The affair is out of the headlines, but some sensitive minds will not quickly forget it. For Commander Bucher, though he may have been a weak captain, has become a symbol of the helpless individual directed and even humiliated by the judgments and power of the state. None of us should forget that this is perhaps the central conflict in our society today.

We have learned how to test the validity of syllogisms using **(12)** VENN DIAGRAMS / TRUTH TABLES. Unfortunately, not all arguments using quantifiers can be tested for validity in this way. For one thing, we have no systematic way of combining the logic of the syllogism and the logic of truth functional connectives. Yet here is a valid argument that combines the two:

All people who are scared of the dark are neurotic. Hence, if everyone is scared of the dark, everyone is neurotic.

To test the validity of such arguments, we need an analysis that probes deeper than any developed so far in this book. We begin by looking more closely at some simple kinds of statement. For example:

Gandhi is a pacifist.

This says something about a particular individual, namely, **(13)** *GANDHI* . The statement says that this individual has a certain characteristic or property, namely, that of a pacifist. There are two parts to the statement: the name "Gandhi" is used to refer to a particular individual, and the words "is a pacifist" are used to say something about that individual. In traditional grammar, "is a pacifist" is called the "predicate." Notice that in the statement about Gandhi, the name "Gandhi" is taken to refer to **(14)** ONE / TWO / THREE definite thing. The words "is a pacifist," which constitute the **(15)** NAME / PREDICATE apply rather to a class of things, including Gandhi, Martin Luther King, and Thoreau. **(16)** Circle the name in this statement:

Washington is beautiful when the cherries bloom in the spring.

"Is beautiful when the cherries bloom in the spring" is the **(17)** *PREDICATE*
(18) Circle the name:

Lake Superior is navigable.

Lake Superior is an individual lake that can be referred to in many different ways; I could also say, for example, that:

The world's largest lake is navigable.

"The world's largest lake" is not, strictly speaking, a name like "Lake Superior," but it too singles out one definite thing we are talking about. It is called a *definite description*, because in context it describes one definite, unique thing, in contrast to the predicate of 18. **(19)** What is the predicate of 18? What is the definite description just used to refer to Lake Superior? **(20)** *'THE WORLDS LARGEST LAKE'* List all the things to which the definite description, "the world's largest lake" applies: **(21)** *IS NAVIGABLE* List a few of the things to which the predicate "is navigable" applies: **(22)** *MISTINKA, PACIFIC ETC.*

Circle the names or definite descriptions in the following:

(23) Rio de Janeiro is more beautiful than any other city.
(24) The world's most beautiful city is a port.
(25) Mendel began serious work in genetics.
(26) The great pioneer of genetics studied hereditary traits of peas.

Underline the predicates in the following:

(27) The Congo is rich in copper.
(28) Chicago is windy.
(29) The windy city is windy.
(30) Jim Ryun practically never needs more than four minutes to run a mile.

Logicians usually represent the logical form of such statements by letting small letters from the beginning of the alphabet stand for names:

$a, b, c, d \cdots$

Capital letters are used to stand for predicates:

$F, G, H \cdots$

(31) Circle the letters that would be used to stand for names: a G $/$ X $/$ d e E. The letter "H" would be used to stand for a **(32)** *PREDICATE*
In simple declarative English sentences, it is our custom to have the name come first, followed by the predicate:

Gandhi is a pacifist.

(33) Underline the name.   But this custom is not universal; one could say, with a rhetorical flourish:

A remarkable pacifist was G̲a̲n̲d̲h̲i̲, and a great leader of his people.

(34) Underline the name.   Does it come at the beginning?   **(35)** YES / NO̲.̲   In modern logic it is the custom to write the predicate first and then the name.   Thus, if we have:

F: is a father.
a: Abraham.

we represent the statement "Abraham is a father" by

$Fa.$

Let:

G: is a great lover.
b: Boaz.

Which of the following represents the statement "Boaz is a great lover"? **(36)** Fa / aF / Ga / aG / Fb / bF / $G̲b̲$ / bG.   We can form compound statements using the familiar connectives.   Thus the statement:

Abraham is a father and Boaz is a great lover.

would be schematized: **(37)** $Fa \lor Gb$ / $aF \& bG$ / $FG \& ab$ / $\underline{Fa \& Gb}$ / $Fb \& Ga$.   What statement is schematized by $Fa \lor Gb$?   **(38)** _____
ABRAHAM IS A FATHER OR BOAZ IS A GREAT LOVER
Schematize "If Abraham is a father, then Boaz is a great lover."   **(39)**
Fa → Gb.   What statement would be represented by $(Fa \& Ga) \rightarrow$ $(Fb \lor Gb)$?   **(40)** *IF ABRAHAM IS A FATHER AND ABRAHAM IS A GREAT LOVER, THEN, BOAZ IS A FATHER AND BOAZ* "$Fa \& Ga$" is the **(41)** PREMISE / ANTECEDENT.   Let: *IS A GREAT LOVER.*

P: was a great pacifist.
C: was a great leader of the American civil rights movement.
I: was a great Indian leader.
g: Gandhi.
k: Martin Luther King.

Schematize:

(42)   Martin Luther King was a great pacifist.

(43) Both King and Gandhi were great pacifists.

(44) Either Gandhi or Martin Luther King was a great leader of the American civil rights movement.

(45) Martin Luther King was a great leader of the American civil rights movement, and he was a great pacifist, but he was not a great Indian leader.

(46) If Gandhi was a great Indian leader, then Martin Luther King was a great leader of the American civil rights movement.

Let:

R: is run by Republicans.
D: is run by Democrats.
M: is mayor.
c: Chicago.
d: Daley.

42. Pk
43. Pk & Pg
44. Cg ∨ Ck
45. (Ck & Pk) & -Ik
46. Ig → Ck

Match:

(47) __c__ $Rc \rightarrow -Md$.

(48) __e__ $Dd \rightarrow Dc$.

(49) __a__ $Md \rightarrow Dc$.

(50) __b__ $-Dc \rightarrow Rc$.

(51) __d__ $-Md \rightarrow -Dc$.

(a) If Daley is mayor, then Chicago is run by Democrats.

(b) If Chicago is not run by Democrats, then it is run by Republicans.

(c) If Chicago is run by Republicans, then Daley is not mayor.

(d) If Daley is not mayor, then Chicago is not run by Democrats.

(e) If Daley is run by Democrats, then so is Chicago.

(52) Schematize the following, being careful to put brackets in the right places to avoid ambiguity: *(((Dc & Dd) & Md) ∨ -Dc) & (-Dc → -Md)*

Either Chicago is run by Democrats and Democrats run Daley, and also Daley is mayor, or else it is not run by Democrats; and if it is not run by Democrats, then Daley is not mayor.

In all of our examples so far, we have made elementary statements with sentences that have a name and a predicate, and then we have formed compounds out of these. Here is a different kind of statement:

There are philosophers.
Something is a philosopher.
There is at least one philosopher.
There are some philosophers.
Philosophers exist.

These statements express slightly different nuances of meaning. Despite this, they **(53)** _DO_ / DO NOT mean roughly the same. Does a name appear in any of them? **(54)** YES / _NO._

In order for such statements to be true, then at least one statement like the following must be true:

> Bertrand Russell is a philosopher.
> Jean-Paul Sartre is a philosopher.
> President Nixon is a philosopher.
> Plato's most famous teacher is a philosopher.

(55) Which of these are true? _Russell, Sartre, Plato's teacher_

Only the third statement is probably false. Since Russell, Sartre, and Socrates are philosophers, it is true that there are some philosophers. Thus there is some true way of filling in the blank in:

> _____ is a philosopher.

Give 3 true and 3 false ways of filling in the blank:

(56) True: 1. _Diehl_ . 2. _Kant_ . 3. _Russell_ .
(57) False: 1. _Botch_ . 2. _Bozo_ . 3. _Spiro_ .

There are plenty of ways to fill in the blank so as to get a true statement. That is why it is true to say that,

> There are some philosophers.

Not all statements of this form are true, for example,

> There are some men still alive who fought in the American War of Independence.

Is there any way of filling in the following blank:

> _____ is a man still alive who fought in the American War of Independence.

with a name or description, so as to get something true? **(58)** YES / _NO._ Because there is no true way to fill in the blank, the statement "there are some men still alive ..." is false. Thus we can analyze statements using "some" with the idea of filling in a blank.

The expression:

> _____ is a philosopher.

(59) IS / ~~IS NOT~~ in itself a sentence with which we could express a statement. It is only part of such a sentence; it has a blank in it. It is called an "open sentence." An open sentence is an expression that becomes a sentence capable of expressing a statement when the blanks are filled in by grammatically appropriate names or descriptions. Write out open sentences obtained by deleting the names in the following:

(60) Mt. Everest is the highest mountain.

——————— IS THE HIGHEST MOUNTAIN ———————.

(61) Washington was the first president.

——————— WAS THE FIRST PRESIDENT ———————.

(62) There is vegetation on Mars.

THERE IS VEGETATION ON ———————.———————.

Statements can have more than one name in them, for example,

There is life on Mars but none on Venus.

(63) Underline the two names. When there are two different names, it is natural to use different shaped blanks when writing the open sentence. For example:

There is life on ——————— but none on . . .

In contrast, a statement using one name twice will use the same kind of blank throughout, as in:

There is vegetation on Mars but Mars has no animal life.
There is vegetation on ———————, but ——————— has no animal life.

Write out an open sentence for:

Hannibal of Carthage nearly conquered Rome.

Since there are **(64)** ONE / TWO / THREE / FOUR names, you will need three kinds of blank.

(65) ——————— OF . . . . . NEARLY CONQUERED xxxxx

Write out an open sentence for:

Rome gave us law, Greece gave us philosophy, but Rome gave us no philosophy.

(66) ——————— GAVE US LAW . . . . . GAVE US

PHILOSOPHY, BUT ——————— ~~ROME~~

GAVE US NO PHILOSOPHY.

In the last example, you will have used the same blank twice for "Rome" and a different-shaped blank for "Greece." Here is an even more complex example:

> Not only was Thomas Jefferson a president of the United States, but also he wrote the Declaration of Independence and founded the University of Virginia.

In this statement we find names for: **(67)** A PERSON / A COUNTRY / A PLANET / A DOCUMENT / A UNIVERSITY. Circle all the names in the above statement. There is *one* error in the following open sentence corresponding to the statement about Jefferson. **(68)** Correct it. (Remember that since the pronoun "he" refers to Jefferson throughout, it should be replaced by the same kind of blank as replaces "Jefferson."):

> _____ was not only a president of . . . . but also _____ wrote _ _ _ _ _ _ _ _ _ _, and _____ founded * * * * * * *.

(69) Write out an open sentence for:

> Lincoln was president of the United States during the Civil War, and Lincoln was assassinated by Booth.

Obviously these different shaped blanks are cumbersome. It is easier to use different shaped letters instead. So logicians customarily use small letters from the end of the alphabet—x, y, z, w, v · · ·—for these different shaped blanks. So we could write out the open sentence about Lincoln as:

> x was president of y during z, and x was assassinated by w.

Just as it does not matter which shaped blank we use to replace which name, it does not matter which shaped letter we use to replace which name. Thus, one of the following is correct although the other is erroneous.

A. w was president of z during x, and x was assassinated by y.
B. w was president of z during x, and w was assassinated by y.

Which is wrong? **(70)** A / B. A is wrong because it uses the letter "x" to replace "The Civil War" and to replace the second occurrence of "Lincoln." But so long as we are consistent, as in B, it does not matter how we replace letters. Do not think of the "w" as being an abbreviation for "Lincoln": it simply marks a blank.

One way of replacing the blanks (letters) in B is the statement about Lincoln; but here is another statement with the same open sentence:

> J. F. Kennedy was president of the United States during the Cuba missile crisis, and Kennedy was assassinated by Oswald.

Our main reason for introducing open sentences is to provide an analysis of statements such as:

> There are some philosophers.

This statement is true if the open sentence:

> _____ is a philosopher.

or

> x is a philosopher.

can be filled in with a name or definite description in such a way as to get something true. Give two ways of filling in the blank "x" to get a true statement: **(71)** _DEWEY_ and **(72)** _KANT._

"There are some philosophers" means "There is some way of filling in the blank x in 'x is a philosopher' to get a true statement."

"There are some dictators" means "There is some way of filling in the blank x in **(73)** '_X IS A DICTATOR_'" to get a **(74)** _TRUE SENTENCE_

What does, "There are some unicorns" mean? **(75)** _THERE IS SOME WAY OF FILLING IN THE BLANK X IN ' X IS A UNICORN ' TO GET A TRUE SENTENCE._

In ordinary English, what is meant by, "There is some way of filling in the blank x in 'x is a baseball star' so as to get a true statement"? **(76)** _____
THERE ARE SOME BASEBALL STARS.

To save time, we shorten the long instruction "There is some way of filling in the blank x in ...." by writing a backward "E" for "exists." The statements:

> There exist baseball stars.

and,

> There are some baseball stars.

mean about the same. In all our examples we are concerned with *existence*, which we denote with "∃." Thus, we paraphrase:

> There are some baseball stars.

as:

> ($\exists x$)(x is a baseball star).

Now let:

> S: is a baseball star.
> b: Babe Ruth.

We schematize:

> Babe Ruth is a baseball star.

as (77) Sa / bS / Bs / SB / $\underline{Sb}$ / $Sabc$ / AS.   Hence:

> ($\exists x$)(x is a baseball star)

will be represented as (78) ($\exists x$)(Sb) / ($\exists x$)(Sx). The latter is correct and can be read as:

> There is an x such that x is a baseball star.

This means:

> There is some way of filling in the x in (79) " $\left(\exists x\right)\left(Sx\right)$ "   ~~X IS A BASEBALL STAR~~
> to get a true statement. X IS A BASEBALL STAR

Notice that since the letter "x" is just a mark for a blank, it does not matter what letter *from the end of the alphabet* we use, so long as we are consistent throughout.   Two of the following are incorrect; cross them out (80) ($\exists x$)(Sx) / ($\exists y$)(Sy) / ~~($\exists x$)(Sy)~~ / ($\exists w$)(Sw) / ~~($\exists b$)(Sb)~~.

Exactly the same holds for situations where the same blank occurs in several places.   Write out the open sentence for:

> Joseph made a million and he retired.

(81) X MADE A MILLION AND X RETIRED.

Now abbreviate it, letting M: made a million; R: retired.

(82) Mx & ~~M~~Rx.

"Someone made a million and retired" will thus be paraphrased (83) ($\exists x$)(Mx ∨ Rx) / ($\exists x$)(My & Ry) / ($\exists x$)(Mx & Rx) / ($\exists j$)(Mj & Rj).

Match (leave no blanks):

(84) _C_ _f_ (∃y)(y is a village).   (a) Something is a city.

(85) _b_ _e_ (∃w)(w is a town).   (b) There are towns.
                                       (c) Villages exist.
(86) _b_ _e_ (∃x)(x is a town).   (d) Cities exist.

(87) _C_ _f_ (∃x)(x is a village).   (e) There is at least one town.
                                       (f) There are some villages.
(88) _a_ _d_ (∃z)(z is a city).

(89) _a_ _d_ (∃v)(v is a city).

Here are several attempts to paraphrase:

Some poets come from the West.

letting *P*: is a poet; *W*: comes from the West.   Each of them is incorrect in one way or another.   Correct each error.

(90) $(\exists x)(Px \; Wx)$.
(91) $(\exists y)(Py \; \& \; Wy$.
(92) $(\exists z)(pz \; \& \; Wz)$.
(93) $(\exists x)(Py \; \& \; Wy)$.
(94) $(\exists x)(PX \; \& \; WX)$.
(95) $\exists y \; (Py \; \& \; Wy)$.
(96) $(\exists z)Pz \; \& \; Wz$.
(97) $(\exists v)Pv \; \& \; Wv)$.

Be careful to avoid each of these errors in future.
   Notice the difference between, for example:

A.   Some tall people are athletes.

and:

B.   Some people are tall and some people are athletes.

Which of these says that there is at least one person who is both tall and athletic?   **(98)** A / B.   Which says that there is at least one person who is tall, and at least one person, possibly a different person, who is an athlete?
(99) A / B.   Which is correctly paraphrased as the conjunction:

$$(\exists x)(Px \; \& \; Tx) \; \& \; (\exists x)(Px \; \& \; Ax)$$

(100) A / B.   Which is correctly paraphrased as the single existential statement:

$$(\exists x)((Px \; \& \; Tx) \; \& \; Ax)$$

(101) A / B.

Match (leave *two* blanks):

(102) __C__ $(\exists x)(Px \ \& \ Tx) \ \&$
$(\exists x)(Px \ \& \ -Ax).$

(103) _____ $(\exists y)(Py \ \& \ -(Ty \ \& \ Ay)).$

(104) __b__ $(\exists y)(Py \ \& \ -(Ty \ \& \ Ay)).$

(105) _____ $(\exists z)(Pz \ \& \ -Tz) \ \&$
$\exists z(Pz \ \& \ -Az).$

(106) __a__ $(\exists z)(Pz \ \& \ -Tz) \ \&$
$(\exists z)(Pz \ \& \ -Az).$

(107) __d__ $(\exists y)((Py \ \& \ Ay) \ \& \ -Ty).$

(a) Some people are not tall, and some people are not athletes.

(b) Some people are not tall athletes.

(c) There are some tall people, and some people who are not athletes.

(d) Some people who are athletes are not tall.

Statement (a) has been correctly paraphrased by 106; the blank "z" was used in both the first and second conjunct.   But of course we could have used any other blank in either conjunct.   Thus for example the first conjunct, "Some people are not tall," could have been paraphrased as "$(\exists x)(Px \ \& \ -Tx)$" whereas the second conjunct, "Some people are not athletes," could have been paraphrased as **(108)** $(\exists y)(Py \ -Ay)$ / $(\exists y)(Py \ \& \ -Ay)$ / $\exists y(Py \ \& \ -Ay)$. Hence, the whole conjunction, "Some people are not tall and some people are not athletes," could have been paraphrased:

$$(\exists x)(Px \ \& \ -Tx) \ \& \ (\exists y)(Py \ \& \ -Ay)$$

Cross out the incorrect paraphrases of the same thing:

~~(109)~~ $(w)(Py \ \& \ -Ty) \ \& \ (w)(Py \ \& \ -Ay).$
(110) $(\exists z)(Pz \ \& \ -Tz) \ \& \ (\exists w)(Pw \ \& \ -Aw).$
(111) $(\exists x)(Px \ \& \ -Tx) \ \& \ (\exists x)(Px \ \& \ -Ax).$
~~(112)~~ $(\exists y)(Px \ \& \ -Ty) \ \& \ (\exists x)(Py \ \& \ -Ax).$

Occasionally students feel something is wrong here.   The original statement says "Some people are not tall and some people are not athletes." That is, some people are not tall, and some possibly *different* people are not athletes.   So we should use *different* letters for the first conjunct than those used in the second.   If we adopted this convention, that would rule out, for example **(113)** 106 / 110 / 111.   However there is in fact nothing wrong with 106 or 111.   The first conjunct of 111 says "$(\exists x)(Px \ \& \ -Tx)$" or,

There is some way of filling in the blanks in "P _____ $\& \ -T$ _____" so as to get a true statement.

The second conjunct says "$(\exists x)(Px \& -Ax)$" or,

> There is some way of filling in the blanks in "P ____ & $-A$ ____" so as to get a true statement.

It does not matter what shape we draw the blanks, so long as we are consistent. But (112) above is wrong because it uses the letters x and y inconsistently.

Paraphrase:

(114) Some athletes are not people who are tall. $(\exists x)((Ax \& -(Px \& Tx))$

(115) Something that is tall is not an athletic person.
$(\exists x)(Tx \& -(Px \& Ax))$

(116) Some people are not tall athletes, and some athletes are not tall people. $(\exists x)(Px \& -(Tx \& Ax)) \& (\exists x)(Ax \& -(Tx \& Px))$

Let

G: is generous.
L: is a lout.
M: is a man.
P: is a policeman.
S: is sadistic.

What statements are paraphrased by the following? Two of the following are incorrect formulations, they paraphrase nothing correctly. Cross them out.

(117) $(\exists x)((Px \& Gx) \& -Lx)$. *Some generous policemen are not louts*

(118) $(\exists y)(Py \& Sy) \& (\exists z)(Pz \& -Sz)$. *Some policemen are generous and " " are not generous*

~~**(119)**~~ $(\exists z)(Lx \& -Px) \& (\exists x)(Px \& -Lx)$. *There are generous*

(120) $(\exists x)((Gx \& Px) \& (Lx \& -Sx))$. *policemen who are louts but not sadistic*

(121) $(\exists x)(Px \& -Lx) \& (\exists z)(Gz \& -Pz)$. *Some policemen are not louts and some generous things are*

~~**(122)**~~ $(\exists x)((Px \& Lx)(Sx \& -Gx))$. *not policemen*

The quantifier "$(\exists x)$" is read, "there exists an x such that," or, "there is some x such that," and so is called the *existential* quantifier. Our next step is to have a *universal* quantifier, which corresponds to, "all x are such that . . . ."

23 / The Universal Quantifier

The preceding chapter taught how to paraphrase existential statements featuring words like "some"; this chapter tells how to paraphrase universal statements using "all."

Paraphrase the following sentence, letting B: is beautiful:

> Something is beautiful.

(1) $(\exists x)(Bx.)$ This is an *existential* statement that says that there exist beautiful things. In contrast, a *universal* statement would say,

> Everything is beautiful.
> All things are beautiful.

If something is beautiful then there is some way of filling in the following blank to get a true statement:

> _____ is beautiful.

or

> x is beautiful.

But if everything is beautiful, then every way of filling in the blank must give the truth. If there is even one way of filling in the blank so as to get something false, then it **(2)** IS / ISN'T true that everything is beautiful. For example, if Do Hin Toc is a small boy who has just been severely burnt by napalm, then the statement,

> Do Hin Toc is beautiful.

is likely to be false. Because there are some such ways of filling in the blank so as to get something false, we know it is **(3)** T / <u>F</u> that everything is beautiful. But if every way of filling in the blank gave us a true statement, then we would conclude that **(4)** <u>EVERYTHING IS BEAUTIFUL</u> / NOT EVERYTHING IS BEAUTIFUL.

The clumsy phrase, "There is some way of filling in the blank marked by *x*," was abbreviated **(5)** ($\exists y$) / (<u>$\exists x$</u>) / $\exists x$. The backward "*E*" was to remind us of the word "exists." For the universal quantifier, we use an upside down "*A*" to remind us of "all." Thus while the statement that something is beautiful is paraphrased:

$$(\exists x)(Bx)$$

the statement that everything is beautiful, or that all things are beautiful, is paraphrased:

$$(\forall x)(Bx).$$

This is read, "For all *x*, *x* is beautiful." Let *W*: is wise. Paraphrase "Everything is wise." **(6)** ($\forall x$)(Bx) / ($\exists x$)(Wx) / (<u>$\forall x$</u>)(Wx) / (x)(Wx).

Paraphrase the following:

(7) Everything is not wise.   *($\forall x$) ($-Wx$)* .
(8) Something is not wise.   *($\exists x$) ($-Wx$)* .
(9) Not everything is wise.   *$-$ ($\forall x$) (Wx)* .

Now consider the statement:

Nothing is stupid.

This is equivalent to two of the three following statements. **(10)** Cross out the odd man out.

A. It is not true that something is stupid.
~~B.~~ It is false that something is not stupid.
C. Everything is not stupid.

To see why you should have crossed out B, imagine that there are just three things in the world, Adam, Boaz, and Cain. Now if nothing is stupid, is Adam stupid? **(11)** YES / <u>NO</u>. Is Boaz stupid? **(12)** YES / <u>NO</u>. Is Cain stupid? **(13)** YES / <u>NO</u>. Is anyone stupid, if there are just these three in the world? **(14)** YES / <u>NO</u>. Since Adam, Boaz, and Cain are not stupid, then, in this small world **(15)** EVERYTHING IS STUPID / <u>EVERYTHING IS NOT STUPID</u>. Thus, if nothing is stupid, everything is not stupid. And *vice versa*. So "Nothing is stupid" is logically equivalent to **(16)** B / <u>C</u> on the above list.

It is probably easier to see that if nothing is stupid, it is not true that something is stupid, and *vice versa*. So, "Nothing is stupid," is logically equivalent to **(17)** A / B / C. The odd man out must be **(18)** A / B / C. We have seen that these three are logically equivalent:

> Nothing is stupid.
> It is not true that something is stupid.
> Everything is not stupid.

Similarly, "Nothing is generous" would be equivalent to two of the following. Which two? **(19)** SOMETHING IS GENEROUS. / EVERYTHING IS UNGENEROUS. / IT IS FALSE THAT SOMETHING IS GENEROUS.

Let S: is stupid. Which is the correct paraphrase of A? **(20)** $(\exists x)(Sx)$ / $-(\exists x)(Sx)$. / $(\exists x)-(Sx)$. / $-(\forall x)(Sx)$. Which is the correct paraphrase of C? **(21)** $(\forall x)(Sx)$. / $-(\forall x)(Sx)$. / $(\forall x)-(Sx)$. / $(\exists x)-(Sx)$. But both A and C are equivalent to "Nothing is stupid." Hence, both must be equivalent to each other. That is:

$$-(\exists x)(Sx) \text{ and } (\forall x)-(Sx) \text{ are logically equivalent.}$$

Similarly, the two statements:

> Something is not stupid.

and

> Not everything is stupid.

must be logically equivalent. For if something is not stupid, there must be some individual, say Adam, who is not stupid. And in that event, not *everything* is stupid. Likewise, if not everything is stupid, there have got to be some things that are not stupid.

Paraphrase:

(22) Something is not stupid. $(\exists x)\sim(Sx)$.

(23) Not everything is stupid. $-(\forall x)(Sx)$.

$$-(\forall x)(Sx) \text{ and } (\exists x)-(Sx) \text{ are logically equivalent.}$$

Notice that it follows that $-(\forall x)-(Sx)$ is logically equivalent to $(\exists x)(Sx)$, for we have $-(\forall x)-(Sx)$ equivalent to $(\exists x)--(Sx)$, which is equivalent to $(\exists x)(Sx)$ by (24) DE MORGAN / DOUBLE DENIAL. Similarly, $-(\exists x)-(Sx)$ and $(\forall x)(Sx)$ are logically equivalent.

Rule of quantifier equivalence:	
$-(\exists x)$	$(\forall x)-$
$-(\forall x)$	$(\exists x)-$
$-(\exists x)-$	$(\forall x)$
$-(\forall x)-$	$(\exists x)$

Match each sentence in (a)–(d) opposite two logically equivalent forms below. But two of the ten forms below are incorrect. Leave them blank.

(25) __b__ $(\exists x)(Ox)$.

(26) __d__ $-(\forall x)(Ox)$.

(27) _____ $-\exists x-(Ox)$.

(28) __d__ $(\exists x)-(Ox)$.

(29) __c__ $(\forall x)(Ox)$.

(30) __c__ $-(\exists x)-(Ox)$.

(31) _____ $(\forall x)Ox$.

(32) __a__ $(\forall x)-(Ox)$.

(33) __b__ $-(\forall x)-(Ox)$.

(34) __a__ $-(\exists x)(Ox)$.

(a) Nothing is original.
(b) Something is original.
(c) Everything is original.
(d) Something is not original.

Letting C: is created by God, translate back into English:

(35) $(\forall x)(Cx)$. EVERYTHING IS CREATED BY GOD.
(36) $(\exists x)-(Cx)$ SOMETHING IS NOT CREATED BY GOD –
(37) $-(\forall x)-(Cx)$. SOMETHING IS CREATED BY GOD –
(38) $-(\exists x)(Cx)$. NOTHING IS CREATED BY GOD –

Now let C: is a company; B: is bankrupt. Paraphrase: Some companies are bankrupt. (39) $(\exists x)(Cx \& Bx)$
   It may seem a good guess to paraphrase:

   All companies are bankrupt.

as

$$(\forall x)(Cx \& Bx).$$

But this is wrong: this paraphrase says that for all *x*, *x* is both a company and bankrupt. Sticks and stones and broken bones—all, according to this paraphrase, are bankrupt companies. Thus,

Everything in the universe is a bankrupt company.

would be paraphrased correctly as,

$$(\forall x)(Cx \ \& \ Bx)$$

But this does *not* mean that all companies are bankrupt.
Take another example to reinforce this point:

All planets in the solar system go around the sun.

Let *P*: is a planet in the solar system; *S*: is something that goes around the sun. Then $(\forall x)(Px \ \& \ Sx)$ means that *everything* is a planet in the solar system and goes around the sun. This is certainly not true. Give an example of something that is not a planet in the solar system that goes around the sun. **(40)** ___*m a*___. Yet it is true that all planets in the solar system go around the sun. So $(\forall x)(Px \ \& \ Sx)$ must be an **(41)** CORRECT / INCORRECT paraphrase.

All F are G is not paraphrased $(\forall x)(Fx \ \& \ Gx)$.

But a paraphrase is easy to find. To say that all planets in the solar system go around the sun, is to say that *if* something is a planet in the solar system, *then* it goes around the sun. This suggests the paraphrase: **(42)** $(\forall x)(Px \lor Sx)$ / $(\forall x)(Px \to Sx)$ / $(\forall x)(Px \ \& \ Sx)$.

All F are G is paraphrased $(\forall x)(Fx \to Gx)$.

Some F are G is paraphrased $(\exists x)(Fx \ \& \ Gx)$.

(Memory aid: *All* with *arrow*. *Some* with *ampersand*.) There will be more explanation of this in a moment. First, teach yourself to make the correct paraphrases using this memory guide. Paraphrase the following statements.

(43)   Some people are cruel. $(\exists x)(Px \& Cx)$

(44)   Some wars are just. $(\exists x)(Wx \& Jx)$

(45)   All wars are just. $(\forall x)(Wx \to Jx)$

(46)   All mules are barren. $(\forall x)(Mx \to Bx)$

(47)   Some mares are fertile. $(\exists x)(Mx \& Fx)$

(48)   All actors are lecherous. $(\forall x)(Ax \to Lx)$

(49)   Some actresses are not promiscuous. $(\exists x)(Ax \& -Px)$

To help see why "all" goes with the **(50)** ARROW / AMPERSAND whereas "some" goes with the **(51)** ARROW / AMPERSAND, you might think of Venn diagrams. On a separate sheet of paper draw diagrams for statements 44 and 45.

(52) W

For the "some" statement 44 we used the device of **(53)** SCRATCHING OUT AN AREA / PUTTING IN A BAR. But for the "all" statement 45, we used the device of **(54)** *SCRATCHING OUT AN AREA* Thus we had to use different devices for drawing "some" and "all." We find the same thing is to some extent true in our new notation. The "all" statements require the **(55)** AMPERSAND / ARROW whereas the "some" statements require the **(56)** AMPERSAND / ARROW.

To get a deeper explanation of these facts, it will help to review De Morgan's laws. Apply De Morgan's laws to change the ampersand to the wedge in the following:

(57) $P \& Q.$ $-(-p \lor -q)$.

(58) $-P \& Q.$ $-(p \lor -q)$.

(59) $-P \& -Q.$ $-(p \lor q)$.

(60) $-(P \& Q).$ $-p \lor -q$.

(61) $-(-P \& Q).$ $p \lor -q$.

Also review wedge-arrow equivalence: Change the wedge to an arrow.

(62) $-(P \lor Q).$ $-(-p \to q)$.

(63) $-P \lor -Q.$ $p \to -q$.

(64) $P \lor -Q.$ $-p \to -q$.

(65) $-(-P \lor -Q).$ $-(p \to -q)$.

By combining De Morgan's laws and wedge-arrow equivalence, we can transform the ampersand to an arrow. Do it in two steps, first applying De Morgan, then wedge-arrow.

(66) *P & Q.*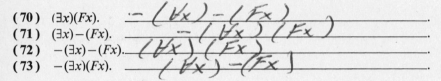

(67) −(*P & −Q*).

(68) −*P & −Q.*

(69) −(−*P & Q*).

Finally, review quantifier equivalences. In each case, change the existential quantifier into a universal quantifier.

(70) (∃x)(*Fx*).

(71) (∃x)−(*Fx*).

(72) −(∃x)−(*Fx*).

(73) −(∃x)(*Fx*).

Now consider the pair of statements:

A. All actors are lecherous.

B. It is not true that some actors are not lecherous.

These two have to be equivalent. For example, if every actor is lecherous, then there cannot be a single actor who is not lecherous, so it is not true that some actors are not lecherous.

Which of the following is the correct paraphrase of B? **(74)** −(∃x)−*Ax* & *Lx* / −(∃x)(*Ax & Lx*) / −(∃x)−(*Ax & Lx* / −(∃x)(*Ax & −Lx*). The correct answer is:

$$-(\exists x)(Ax \ \& \ -Lx)$$

Applying quantifier equivalence to this, we obtain **(75)** −(∀x)(*Ax & −Lx*) / −(∀x)−(*Ax & −Lx*) / (∀x)−(*Ax & −Lx*). The correct answer is:

$$(\forall x)-(Ax \ \& \ -Lx)$$

Now, applying De Morgan's laws to the matter in brackets, that is, to "(*Ax & −Lx*)," we obtain **(76)** (∀x)−(−*Ax* ∨ *Lx*) / (∀x)−−(−*Ax* ∨ *Lx*) / (∀x)−−(*Ax* ∨ −*Lx*). The correct answer is in the middle. Deleting double bars, we have:

$$(\forall x)(-Ax \ \vee \ Lx)$$

Now apply wedge-arrow equivalence to the matter in brackets, namely, "(−*Ax* ∨ *Lx*)": **(77)** (∀x)(*Ax* → *Lx*) You should have obtained **(78)** (∀x)(*Ax* → *Lx*) / (∀x)(*Lx* → *Ax*). Now, this is equivalent to the paraphrase of B above, with which we started. But A and B are equivalent. So this reasoning shows us that the correct paraphrase of:

A. All actors are lecherous.

must be **(79)** $(\forall x)(Ax \,\&\, Lx)$ / $(\forall x)(Ax \to Lx)$ / $(\forall x)(-Ax \to Lx)$. This reminds us that the correct paraphrase of "all" uses the **(80)** ARROW / AMPERSAND even though the correct paraphrase of "some" uses the **(81)** AMPERSAND

What English statements are expressed by the following paraphrases, if we continue to let A: is an actor; L: is lecherous?

(82) $-(\exists x)(Ax \,\&\, Lx)$. *No Actors are lecherous.*
(83) $(\exists x)(Ax \,\&\, Lx)$. *Some Actors are lecherous.*
(84) $(\forall x)(Ax \to Lx)$. *All Actors are lecherous*
(85) $(\forall x)(Ax \,\&\, Lx)$. *Everything is a lecherous actor.*
(86) $(\forall x)(-Ax \to -Lx)$. *All Non Actors are not lecherous.*
(87) $(\exists x)(Ax \,\&\, -Lx)$. *Some Actors are not lecherous.*
(88) $(\forall x)(-Lx \,\&\, Ax)$. *Everything is both Non lecherous and a actor*
(89) $(\forall x)(-Lx \to Ax)$. *Everything not lecherous is an actor*
(90) $-(\forall x)(-Lx \to Ax)$. *It is Not true that everything not lecherous is an actor.*

Many people have a tendency to paraphrase the statement that all actors are lecherous by "$(\forall x)(Ax \,\&\, Lx)$." You have learned not to do this, instead you write, **(91)** $(\forall x)(Ax \to Lx)$ But now you might start wondering why the statement that some actors are lecherous is not paraphrased with the arrow, too: $(\exists x)(Ax \to Lx)$. But apply wedge-arrow equivalence to $(\exists x)(Ax \to Lx)$. You get **(92)** $-(\exists x)(-Ax \lor Lx)$ / $(\exists x)(-Ax \lor Lx)$. This latter, which is correct, means there is something which is either not an actor, or is lecherous. For example, your left foot is not an actor, and so there is something, namely your left foot, that is not an actor, or is lecherous. But this does not mean that some actor is lecherous! Hence, we cannot paraphrase the "some" statement with the arrow.

24 / Monadic Predicate Logic

This chapter provides an opportunity for you to acquire more skill in paraphrasing and shows how the rules of inference developed for truth functions can be incorporated into the logic of predicates.

Our rule of thumb in paraphrasing says that the universal quantifier takes the **(1)** AMPERSAND / <u>ARROW</u> whereas the existential quantifier takes the **(2)** <u>AMPERSAND</u> / ARROW. Paraphrase:

(3) All students are hostile. $\quad (\forall x)(Sx \rightarrow Hx)$.
(4) Some students are hostile. $\quad (\exists x)(Sx \ \& \ Hx)$.
(5) No students are hostile. $\quad (\forall x)(Sx \rightarrow -Hx)$.
$\qquad\qquad\qquad\qquad\qquad\qquad -(\exists x)(Sx \ \& \ Hx)$ or

In the case of statement 5, there are two alternative paraphrases. You could paraphrase 5 as "It is not true that some students are hostile," namely, **(6)** $-(\exists x)(Sx \rightarrow Hx)$ / $\underline{-(\exists x)(Sx \ \& \ Hx)}$ / $(\exists x)-(Sx \ \& \ Hx)$ or as "All students are not hostile," namely, **(7)** $(\forall x)-(Sx \rightarrow Hx)$ / $(\forall x)-(Sx \ \& \ Hx)$ / $(\forall x)(Sx \rightarrow -Hx)$. Statements 6 and 7 are **(8)** VALID / <u>LOGICALLY EQUIVA-LENT</u>. Either 6 or 7 could be considered a correct paraphrase of 5; however, for brevity in the answer section, we shall usually give only one version, namely, 6. Thus we shall read "No F are G" as **(9)** SOME F ARE G / ALL F ARE NOT G / <u>NOT SOME F ARE G</u>.

Paraphrase:

(10) Nothing red all over is green all over. $\quad -(\exists x)(Rx \ \& \ Gx)$.
(11) Everything colored is extended. $\quad (\forall x)(Cx \rightarrow Ex)$.
(12) No irrational being is truly human. $\quad -(\exists x)(Ix \ \& \ Tx)$.
(13) Some men are irrational. $\quad (\exists x)(Mx \ \& \ Ix)$.

196

The statement "Some tedious speeches are ignored" says that there is something that is tedious, that is a speech, and is ignored. It would be paraphrased as **(14)** $(\exists x)(Sx \ \& \ Ix)$ / $\underline{(\exists x)((Sx \ \& \ Tx) \ \& \ Ix)}$ / $(\exists x)(Sx \rightarrow Tx)$. The statement "All tedious speeches are ignored" says that if something is a speech, and is tedious, then it is ignored. It would be paraphrased as **(15)** $(\forall x)((Sx \ \& \ Tx) \ \& \ Ix)$ / $\underline{(\forall x)((Sx \ \& \ Tx) \rightarrow Ix)}$ / $(\forall x)((Tx \rightarrow Sx) \rightarrow Ix)$. Notice that the statement "All speeches are tedious and ignored" says **(16)** THE SAME THING / SOMETHING ~~DIFFERENT~~, and is paraphrased as **(17)** $\underline{(\forall x)((Sx \ \& \ Tx) \rightarrow Ix)}$ / $(\forall x)(Sx \rightarrow (Tx \rightarrow Ix))$ / $\underline{(\forall x)(Sx \rightarrow (Tx \ \& \ Ix))}$. The correct answer is on the right. Notice that the answer in the middle means something different again. It says that **(18)** IF SOMETHING IS A SPEECH, THEN, IF IT IS TEDIOUS, IT IS IGNORED / EVERYTHING WHICH IS IGNORED IS A SPEECH IF IT IS TEDIOUS.

Notice also that "$(\forall x)((Sx \ \& \ Tx) \ \& \ Ix)$," though it **(19)** DOES / DOES NOT mean "All tedious speeches are ignored," is not ungrammatical or meaningless. It means **(20)** EVERYTHING IS A TEDIOUS SPEECH THAT IS IGNORED / EVERYTHING THAT IS A TEDIOUS SPEECH IS IGNORED. We call a sequence of symbols that doesn't paraphrase anything, perhaps because the brackets are in the wrong place, "ungrammatical." Which one of the following is grammatical? **(21)** $(\forall x)Sx \rightarrow Tx$ / $\underline{(\forall x)(Sx \rightarrow Tx)}$ / $(\forall x)(STx)$. Insert brackets in the following to make them grammatical. **(22)** $(\forall x)(Sx \rightarrow Tx)$ $(\forall x)(Sx \rightarrow Tx)$ $(\forall x)(Sx \rightarrow Tx)$

Translate the grammatical statements in the following list back into English, letting B: biased; W: witness; T: trustworthy. Do not paraphrase the ungrammatical sequences; cross them out.

(23) $(\forall x)((Bx \ \& \ Wx) \rightarrow -Tx)$. *ALL BIASED WITNESSES ARE NOT TRUSTWORTHY.*

(24) $(\exists x)((Bx \ \& \ Wx) \ \& \ Tx)$. *SOME BIASED WITNESSES ARE TRUSTWORTHY*

(25) $(\forall x)((Bx \ \& \ Wx) \ \& \ Tx)$. *EVERYTHING IS A BIASED WITNESS THAT IS TRUSTWORTHY.*

~~**(26)**~~ $(\forall x)(Bx \ \& \ Wx \rightarrow Tx)$.

(27) $(\forall x)(Wx \rightarrow (-Bx \ \lor \ -Tx))$. *ALL WITNESSES ARE UNBIASED OR UNTRUSTWORTHY.*

(28) $-(\exists x)((Bx \ \& \ Wx) \ \& \ Tx)$. *THERE ARE NO BIASED WITNESSES THAT ARE TRUSTWORTHY.*

~~**(29)**~~ $\forall x((Bx \ \& \ Wx) \rightarrow Tx)$. _____

~~**(30)**~~ $(\exists x)(Bx \ \& \ Wx)(\exists x)(Wx \ \& \ Tx)$. _____

~~**(31)**~~ $(\forall x)(Wx \rightarrow (-Bx \ \lor \ -Tx)$. _____

~~**(32)**~~ $(\forall x)((BxWx) \rightarrow Tx)$. _____

Paraphrase the following statements. Before checking in the answer section, be sure that you have made no grammatical errors:

(33) All research funds granted by military sources tend to subvert independent thought.

R: research funds; G: things granted by military sources; T: things that tend to subvert independent thought.

$(\forall x)((Rx \ \& \ Gx) \rightarrow Tx)$ _____

(34) No evidence for Freud's theory of taboos is found among the Kwakiutl Indians.

E: evidence for Freud's theory about taboos; K: evidence found among the Kwakiutl Indians.

$\sim (\exists x)(Ex \mathrel{\&} Kx)$

(35) Every society where marijuana and alcohol are freely available prefers marijuana and rejects alcohol.

S: societies where marijuana and alcohol are freely available; M: societies that prefer marijuana; A: societies that reject alcohol.

$(\forall x)(Sx \rightarrow (Mx \mathrel{\&} Ax))$

(36) Some deaf composers have written great music.

D: deaf; C: composers; M: people who have written great music.

$(\exists x)((Dx \mathrel{\&} Cx) \mathrel{\&} Mx)$

(37) Every voter is misinformed or ignorant.

$(\forall x)(Vx \rightarrow (Mx \lor Ix))$

(38) Some misinformed people are ignorant and are not voters.

$(\exists x)((Mx \mathrel{\&} Px) \mathrel{\&} (Ix \mathrel{\&} {-}Vx))$

Recall the use of "only" explained in Chapter 5. We found that "Only F are G" is logically equivalent to (39) ALL F ARE G / ALL G ARE F. On the other hand, "The only F are G," is logically equivalent to (40) ALL F ARE G / ALL G ARE F. If you do not recall this very well, review page 44; then paraphrase:

(41) Only unreliable loan companies would lend you money.

$(\forall x)(Lx \rightarrow (-Rx \mathrel{\&} Cx))$

(42) The only companies that would lend you money are unreliable.

$(\forall x)((Cx \mathrel{\&} Lx) \rightarrow -Rx)$

(43) Only people over 21 can vote; but some people over 21 cannot vote.

$(\forall x)(Cx \rightarrow (Px \mathrel{\&} Ox)) \mathrel{\&} (\exists x)((Px \mathrel{\&} Ox) \mathrel{\&} -Cx)$

(44) The only people who are drafted are males who are not younger than 18 and not older than 26.

$(\forall x)((Px \mathrel{\&} Dx) \rightarrow (Mx \mathrel{\&} (-Yx \mathrel{\&} -Ox)))$

The examples so far tend to have the quantifiers in front of the statement. But this is not a general rule. Take for example:

If all voters are misinformed, then none should vote.

The paraphrase of this "if, then" statement is a (45) CONJUNCTION / ALTERNATION / CONDITIONAL / COMPONENT / DENIAL. The (46) ANTECEDENT / PREMISE of this conditional is (47) SOME VOTERS ARE MISINFORMED / NO VOTERS SHOULD VOTE / ALL VOTERS ARE MISINFORMED / NO MISINFORMED PEOPLE SHOULD VOTE. What is the (48) CONCLUSION / CONSEQUENT of this conditional? (49) VOTERS ARE MISINFORMED / NONE SHOULD VOTE. Paraphrase the antecedent: (50) $(\forall x)(Vx \rightarrow M...$ Paraphrase the consequent: (51) $(\exists x)(Vx \mathrel{\&} Sx$

The whole compound statement would be correctly paraphrased by (52)
$(\forall x)(Vx \to Mx) \to -(\exists x)(Vx \& Sx)$ / $(\forall x)(Vx \to Mx) \to -(\exists x)(Sx)$.
   Paraphrase:

(53) Either some voters are misinformed, or some are ignorant.
   [handwritten: $(\exists x)(Vx \& Mx) \lor (\exists x)(Vx \& Ix)$]

In an example like the following, it may help you to bracket the parts before
paraphrasing: "If (some people over 21 are misinformed), then, (if (all
people over 21 are voters), (some voters are misinformed.))"

(54) If some people over 21 are misinformed, then if all people over 21 are
   voters, some voters are misinformed.
   [handwritten: $(\exists x)((Px \& Ox) \& Mx) \to$]
   [handwritten: $((Vx)((Px \& Ox) \to Vx) \to (\exists x)(Vx \& Mx))$]

In the following examples, obtain logically equivalent statements by
changing existential quantifiers into universal quantifiers, and vice versa.
Cross out the ungrammatical example.

(55) $(\forall x)(Fx \to Gx)$. *[handwritten: $-(\exists x) - (Fx \to Gx)$]*
(56) $(\forall x)(Fx) \to (\exists x)(Gx)$. *[handwritten: $-(\exists x) - (Fx) \to -(Fx) - (Gx)$]*
(57) $-(\forall x)(Fx) \lor (\exists x)(Gx)$. *[handwritten: $(\exists x) - (Fx) \lor -(Fx) - (Gx)$]*
(58) $-(\exists x) - Fx$. *[crossed out]*
(59) $-(\exists x) - (Fx) \& ((\forall x)(Gx) \to (\forall x)(Hx))$.
   [handwritten: $(Fx)(Fx) \& (-(\exists x) - (Gx) \to -(\exists x) - (Hx))$]

Apply De Morgan's law to change the wedge into an ampersand:
$(Fx \lor -Gx)$. (60) *[handwritten: $-(-Fx \& Gx)$]* You will have obtained $-(-Fx$
$\& Gx)$. The laws still hold if this component is inside a quantifier, thus,
$(\forall x)(Fx \lor -Gx)$ is logically equivalent to $(\forall x)-(Fx \& -Gx)$. Is this last
the same as $-(\forall x)(Fx \lor -Gx)$? (61) YES / NO. Which is $(\exists x)(Fx \&$
$Gx)$ logically equivalent to? (62) $(\exists x)-(-Fx \lor -Gx)$ / $-(\exists x)(-Fx \&$
$-Gx)$. Is $-(\forall x)(-Fx \lor -Gx)$ logically equivalent to $-(\forall x)-(Fx \&$
$Gx)$? (63) YES / NO.
   In these last examples, we have had a wedge or an ampersand "inside" a
quantifier. We can apply the laws of De Morgan even when the connective
comes between a quantifier. Thus, $(\exists x)(Fx) \lor (\forall x)(Gx)$ is logically equivalent to $-(-(\exists x)(Fx) \& -(\forall x)(Gx))$. The alternatives in the scheme we
start with are (circle two) (64) $(\forall x)(Fx)$ / $(\forall x)(Gx)$ / $(\exists x)(Fx)$ / $(\exists x)(Gx)$ /
$(\exists x)(Fx)$. To apply De Morgan's laws, we change the wedge to an amper-
sand, write bars in front of the alternatives, and write a bar in front of the
resulting compound, to obtain $-(-(\exists x)(Fx) \& -(\forall x)(Gx))$.
   One of the following pairs includes something ungrammatical. Put a big
circle around the error. Some of the other pairs are logically equivalent by
De Morgan. Cross out those that are not logically equivalent.

~~(65)~~ $(\forall x)(Fx \ \& \ -Gx)$. $(\forall x)(-Fx \lor Gx)$.
(66) $(\exists x)(Fx \lor -Gx)$. $(\exists x)-(-Fx \ \& \ Gx)$.
~~(67)~~ $(\exists x)(-Fx \lor -Gx)$. $-(\exists x)(Fx \ \& \ Gx)$.
(68) $(\exists x) \bigcirc (Fx \ \& \ -Gx)$. $(\exists x)-(Fx \lor Gx)$. *UNGRAMMATICAL*
~~(69)~~ $-(\forall x)-(Fx \lor Gx)$. $-(\forall x)(-Fx \ \& \ Gx)$.
~~(70)~~ $-(\forall x)-(Fx \ \& \ Gx)$. $(\forall x)(-Fx \lor Gx)$.

Naturally, we can combine different logical equivalences. For example, $-(\forall x)(-Fx \lor -Gx)$ is logically equivalent to **(71)** $-(\exists x)-(-Fx \lor -Gx)$ / $(\exists x)-(-Fx \lor -Gx)$ by quantifier equivalence. The second scheme is correct. It in turn is equivalent to **(72)** $(\exists x)-(Fx \ \& \ Gx)$ / $(\exists x)(Fx \ \& \ Gx)$ by De Morgan. Once again the second scheme is correct. Notice how much simpler it is than the scheme we began with.

Now using quantifier equivalence, or De Morgan, or both, simplify the following.

(73) $-(\forall x)(-Fx \ \& \ -Gx)$. $(\exists x)(Fx \lor Gx)$

(74) $-(\exists x)-(Fx \ \& \ Gx)$. $(\forall x)(Fx \ \& \ Gx)$

(75) $-((\forall x)-(Fx) \ \& \ (\exists x)-(Gx))$. $(\exists x)(Fx) \lor (\forall x)(Gx)$

Notice how the last cumbersome expression reduces to the simple $(\exists x)(Fx) \lor (\forall x)(Gx)$.

All the rules of deduction that you know can be applied to the logic of predicates. To review, match the following.

(76) _c_ Double denial.

(77) _a_ Contraposition.

(78) _j_ Quantifier equivalence.

(79) _f_ Alternatives.

(80) _d_ Detachment.

(81) _b_ De Morgan.

(82) _g_ Conjunction.

(83) _h_ Weakening.

(84) _e_ Wedge-arrow.

(85) _i_ Permutation.

(a) $(\forall x)(Fx) \rightarrow (\forall x)(Gx) \vdash$
        $-(\forall x)(Gx) \rightarrow -(\forall x)(Fx)$.

(b) $(\exists x)-(Fx \ \& \ Gx) \vdash$
        $(\exists x)(-Fx \lor -Gx)$.

(c) $--(\forall x)--(Fx) \vdash (\forall x)(Fx)$.

(d) $(\exists x)(Fx) \rightarrow (\forall x)(Gx)$,
        $(\exists x)(Fx) \vdash (\forall x)(Gx)$.

(e) $(\exists x)(Fx) \rightarrow (\exists x)(Gx) \vdash$
        $-(\exists x)(Fx) \lor (\exists x)(Gx)$.

(f) $(\forall x)(Fx) \rightarrow (\exists x)(Hx)$,
        $(\forall x)(Gx) \rightarrow (\exists x)(Hx) \vdash$
        $((\forall x)(Fx) \lor (\forall x)(Gx))$
        $\rightarrow (\exists x)(Hx)$.

(g) $(\forall x)(Fx) \ \& \ (\exists x)(Gx) \vdash (\exists x)(Gx)$.

(h) $(\exists x)(Fx) \vdash (\forall x)(Gx) \lor (\exists x)(Fx)$.

(i) $(\exists x)(Fx) \lor (\exists x)(Gx) \vdash$
        $(\exists x)(Gx) \lor (\exists x)(Fx)$.

(j) $-(\forall x)-(Gx) \vdash (\exists x)(Gx)$.

(86)–(91) is a list of assertions about inference. Some of them are ungrammatical. Cross them out. Some are correct. These are based on

exactly *two* of the rules in 76–85.   Put a check (√) in front of these.   Others
are incorrect, they represent invalid inferences.   Put a cross (×) in front of
these.

(86) _____ $(\forall x)(Fx \lor Gx) \vdash -(\exists x)(-Fx \;\&\; -Gx)$.

(87) __×__ $(\exists x)(Fx \;\&\; Gx) \vdash -(\forall x)-(-Fx \lor Gx)$. *INCORRECT* -

(88) _____ $(\forall x)Fx \to (\exists x)Gx \vdash (\forall x)-Gx \to (\exists x)-Fx$. *UNGRAMMATICAL*

(89) _____ $(\forall x)(Fx) \to (\exists x)(Gx) \vdash (\forall x)-(Gx) \to (\exists x)-(Fx)$.

(90) _____ $-(\forall x)-(Fx) \vdash (\exists x)(Fx) \;\&\; (\forall x(Gx)$. *UNGRAMMATICAL*

(91) _____ $-(\exists x) - (Fx) \vdash (\forall x)(Fx) \lor (\forall x)(Gx)$.

25 / Deductions and Counterexamples

This chapter gives some more rules of deduction for predicate logic and begins to show how to construct counterexamples.

If an argument has the form of a syllogism with two premises and a conclusion, there **(1)** IS / IS NOT a mechanical system for deciding whether or not the argument form is valid. This is the system of Venn **(2)** DIAGRAMS . Drawing a diagram is not the only way to tell whether an argument is valid. In the case of syllogisms, we used counterexamples to show that various argument forms were **(3)** VALID / INVALID. A counterexample is an **(4)** INTERPRETATION / DEDUCTION of an argument form in which all of the premises are evidently **(5)** T / F whereas the conclusion is evidently **(6)** T / F. A favorable example of an argument form would be an interpretation in which the premises and conclusion were both T. Does finding a favorable example show that an argument form is valid? **(7)** YES / NO. For an argument might have true premises and true conclusion, and yet still be invalid. Give an example. **(8)** Some cars are Fords .
    Some Fords go .
    So, Some cars go .
Hence, finding a "favorable" example does not prove much about validity.

Counterexamples provide *negative* answers to the question of validity. They show that an argument form **(9)** IS / IS NOT valid. But no number of favorable examples can show that an argument form is **(10)** VALID . In contrast, drawing a Venn diagram settles the question of validity. If we get a negative result, we know the argument is **(11)** VALID / INVALID. If we get a positive result and see that the conclusion has been diagramed as soon as the premises have been diagramed, we know the argument is **(12)** VALID / INVALID. Venn diagrams are a definite procedure for settling the question of validity in a positive or negative way. This is called a *decision procedure* for validity.

Is there a decision procedure for truth functional arguments? **(13)** YES / NO. This procedure is called the method of truth **(14)** _TABLES_. If we find a row in the truth table where all premises are T and the conclusion is F, we know the argument form in question is **(15)** _INVALID_. Thus the question of validity is answered in a **(16)** NEGATIVE / POSITIVE way. On the other hand, if there is no row in the truth table where all premises are **(17)** T / F and the conclusion is **(18)** T / F, we know the argument form is valid. Thus the question of validity is answered in a **(19)** NEGATIVE / POSITIVE way.

Truth tables and Venn diagrams give decision **(20)** _PROCEDURES_ appropriate kinds of argument forms. They offer mechanical procedures which are bound to settle the question of validity in a positive or negative way. But looking for examples to form counterexamples can at best settle the question in a **(21)** POSITIVE / NEGATIVE way. A counterexample can show an argument form is **(22)** VALID / INVALID. Can favorable examples ever show that an argument form is valid? **(23)** YES / NO.

We have also introduced the method of deduction. In this method, we single out a small number of valid argument forms that we call rules of inference. A long chain of inferences, each in accord with a valid rule of inference, will provide a **(24)** VALID / INVALID argument. If we are given some premises, and an alleged conclusion, we can show the argument to be **(25)** VALID / INVALID by finding a deduction passing from the premises to the conclusion. But suppose we try very hard to find a deduction and do not succeed; can we conclude that for sure the argument is not valid? **(26)** YES / NO. If we find a deduction, we know the argument is **(27)** VALID / INVALID. Thus, the question of validity is answered in a **(28)** POSITIVE / NEGATIVE way. If we fail to find a deduction, can we conclude that the argument is not valid? **(29)** YES / NO. Thus, deductions can, in general, provide only **(30)** POSITIVE / NEGATIVE answers to the question of validity. In contrast, counterexamples can provide only **(31)** POSITIVE / NEGATIVE answers to the question of validity. Thus deduction and counterexamples are, as it were, opposite sides of validity. To show that an argument is valid, we construct a **(32)** DEDUCTION / COUNTEREXAMPLE. To show that an argument is invalid, we construct a **(33)** DEDUCTION / COUNTEREXAMPLE. Can deductions, in general, show argument forms to be invalid? **(34)** YES / NO. Can counterexamples show argument forms to be valid? **(35)** YES / NO.

If there is a decision procedure for some kind of argument form, we have a technique that is **(36)** ONLY NEGATIVE / ONLY POSITIVE / BOTH POSITIVE AND NEGATIVE. That is, we can show both validity and invalidity for argument forms of the appropriate kind. A decision procedure may be very long, as for a truth table with, say, 14 components (which would have 16,384 rows!), but it is sure and steady and is guaranteed to answer our questions if we are faithful to the method. Deductions may be short and sweet, and simplify things very much, but if we set out looking for a deduction or a counter-

example, is there any guarantee that we will succeed? **(37)** YES / NO.
There are some famous problems in arithmetic that have been around for
three centuries; many mathematicians have tried to deduce a positive answer
or construct a counterexample, but so far, all attempts have failed. This is
because there is no decision procedure for the kind of arithmetical problem in
question.

In studying syllogisms and truth functional arguments, we are not obliged
to use deduction or counterexamples, because we have decision **(38)**
~~Procedures~~ in the case of the syllogism decision a procedure is **(39)**
Venn Diagrams ; in the case of truth functional logic it is
(40) _Truth Tables_ .

One of the most profound results of modern logic is that there is no
decision procedure for predicate logic. This was discovered by the American
logician Alonzo Church in 1936, as a corollary of an even more important
discovery by Kurt Gödel in 1931. It is a consequence of Gödel's theorem
that there *cannot* be a decision procedure for predicate logic. It is not just
that logicians have not been lucky enough to hit on some device like truth
tables or Venn diagrams. We know now that there **(41)** CAN / CANNOT be
such a device.

This means we are forced to use deductions and counterexamples to study
validity in predicate logic. Since there **(42)** IS A / IS NO decision procedure
for predicate logic we must try to find a deduction if we think the argument
form of interest is **(43)** VALID / INVALID whereas if we think it is invalid, we
must try to find a **(44** counter ex., Of course we may fail at both of
these endeavors. Predicate logic requires more skill—and perhaps more
luck—than anything we have studied so far.

For review, remember that we have been representing predicates by **(45)**
LOWER CASE LETTERS FROM THE END OF THE ALPHABET / CAPITAL LETTERS /
LOWER CASE LETTERS FROM THE BEGINNING OF THE ALPHABET; we have been
representing the quantified "blanks" by **(46)** _lower case_
letters from end of alphabet ;
and in Chapter 22 names were represented by **(47)** _lower case_
letters from beginning of alphabet.
Thus we would expect "*x*" to be a **(48)** _blank_ , and we would
expect "*a*" to stand for a **(49)** _name_ .

Now suppose we know that Bertrand Russell is a philosopher. We
know at once that **(50)** THERE ARE SOME PHILOSOPHERS / THERE ARE NO
PHILOSOPHERS. That is to say, the argument:

> Bertrand Russell is a philosopher,
> So, there are some philosophers,

is **(51)** VALID / INVALID. Letting *F*: is a philosopher; *b*: Bertrand Russell,
paraphrase this argument: **(52)** _Fb so $(\exists x)(Fx)$_ . The
argument form "*Fb*, so $(\exists x)(Fx)$" is valid. This rule is called the rule of

existential conclusion, for the conclusion is a general statement, beginning with the existential quantifier.

Existential conclusion: $Fb \vdash (\exists x)(Fx)$

Put a check ($\checkmark$) in front of those of the following statements that are correct, grammatical, applications of this rule.

(53) $\underline{\quad\checkmark\quad}$ $Fa \vdash (\exists x)(Fx)$.

(54) $\underline{\quad\quad}$ $Fb \vdash (\exists x)(Fy)$.

(55) $\underline{\quad\quad}$ $(\exists x)(Fx) \vdash Fa$.

(56) $\underline{\quad\quad}$ $Fx \vdash (\exists x)(Fx)$.

(57) $\underline{\quad\quad}$ $Fa \vdash (\forall w)(Fw)$.

(58) $\underline{\quad\quad}$ $Fa \vdash (\exists x)(Fa)$.

(59) $\underline{\quad\quad}$ $Fa \vdash (\exists u)Fu)$.

(60) $\underline{\quad\quad}$ $Hb \vdash (\exists x)(Fx)$.

(61) $\underline{\quad\checkmark\quad}$ $Hc \vdash (\exists x)(Hx)$.

(62) $\underline{\quad\quad}$ $Ha \vdash \exists y(Hy)$.

Now suppose that you believe that all logicians are philosophers. You would have to conclude that if Kurt Gödel is a logician, then Kurt Gödel is a philosopher. That is, the argument:

All logicians are philosophers.
So, if Kurt Gödel is a logician, he is a **(63)** *PHILOSOPHER* .

must be **(64)** VALID / INVALID. Let L: is a logician; P: is a philosopher; g: Kurt Gödel and paraphrase this argument: **(65)** $(\forall x)(Lx \rightarrow Px)$
$\underline{\qquad\qquad So, \quad Lg \rightarrow Pg \qquad\qquad}$.

This is an example of the more general form:

$$(\forall x)(Fx) \vdash Fa$$

Let F: is ferocious; a: Abraham and write out an argument of this form:
(66) $\underline{\quad EVERYTHING \; IS \; FEROCIOUS \quad}$.
$\underline{\quad So, \quad ABRAHAM \; is \; FEROCIOUS \quad}$.

This is a case of what we call "instantiation." We call it instantiation because the conclusion is an *instance* of what the premise says:

Instantiation: $(\forall x)(Fx) \vdash Fb$

Cross out all of the following that are not grammatical instances of either instantiation or existential conclusion:

(67) $(\forall x)(Gx) \vdash Fb.$
(68) $(\forall x)Gx \vdash Ga.$
(69) $(\exists x)(Gx) \vdash Gc.$
(70) $(\forall x)(Hy) \vdash Ha.$
(71) $Fx \vdash (\exists x)(Fx).$
(72) $Fa \vdash (\forall x)(Fx).$
(73) $(\exists x)(Sx) \vdash (\forall x)(Sx).$
(74) $aF \vdash (\exists x)(Fx).$

Both our rules need to be stated more exactly to attain full and correct generality. The following, though incomplete, will suffice for our purposes.

Rule of existential conclusion
Take any statement scheme in which there is a name. Replace one or more occurrences of this name by a letter, which does not occur in the statement scheme, from the end of the alphabet and write the corresponding existential quantifier in front of the resulting scheme. Taking the opening scheme as premise and the changed scheme as conclusion, we have a valid argument form.

Cross out the incorrect or ungrammatical applications of this rule:

(75) $(\exists x)(Fx \ \& \ Gx) \vdash Fa \ \& \ Ga.$
(76) $(Fa \lor Ga) \ \& \ Gb \vdash (\exists x)((Fx \lor Gx) \ \& \ Gb).$
(77) $(Fa \lor Ga) \ \& \ Gb \vdash (\exists x)((Fx \lor Ga) \ \& \ Gb).$
(78) $(Fa \lor Ga) \ \& \ Gb \vdash (\exists x)((Fa \lor Ga) \ \& \ Gx).$
(79) $(Fa \lor Ga) \ \& \ Gb \vdash (\exists x)((Fa \lor Ga) \ \& \ Gb).$
(80) $(Fa \lor Ga) \ \& \ Gb \vdash (\exists x)((Fx \lor Gx) \ \& \ Gx).$

Notice that only one of the following is incorrect; cross it out:

(81) Fa & $Ga \vdash (\exists x)(Fx$ & $Gx)$.
(82) Fa & $Ga \vdash (\exists x)(Fx$ & $Ga)$.
(83) Fa & $Ga \vdash (\exists x)(Fa$ & $Gx)$.
(84) Fa & $Ga \vdash (\exists x)(Fx$ & $Gb)$.

The instantiation rule is equally generally applicable:

Rule of instantiation
Take any statement scheme starting with a universal quantifier.
Replace every blank governed by this quantifier by one and the
same name. Delete the universal quantifier. Taking the open-
ing scheme as premise and the resulting scheme as conclusion,
we have a valid argument form.

Cross out incorrect applications of this rule.

(85) $(\forall x)(Fx \rightarrow Gx) \vdash Fc \rightarrow Gc$.
(86) $(\forall x)(Fx \rightarrow Gx) \vdash Fa \rightarrow Gb$.
(87) $(\forall x)(Fx \rightarrow Gx) \vdash Fx \rightarrow Gx$.
(88) $(\forall z)(Fz \rightarrow Gz) \vdash Fc \rightarrow Gz$.
(89) $(\forall z)(\forall x)(Fx \rightarrow Gz) \vdash (\forall x)(Fz \rightarrow Ga)$.

Now we can combine our rules into various deductions. For example:

$$(\forall x)(Fx) \vdash (\exists x)(Fx)$$

Explain the steps that are taken:

1. $(\forall x)(Fx) \vdash Fa$.   **(90)** _INSTANTIATION_
2.   „ $\vdash (\exists x)(Fx)$.   **(91)** _EXISTENTIAL CONCLUSION_

Naturally, we have as well:

$$(\forall x)(Fx) \vdash (\exists y)(Fy).$$

Prove it:

(92) $(\forall x)(Fx) \vdash Fa$ _INSTANTIATION_
            „ $\vdash (\exists y)(Fy)$ _EXISTENTIAL CONCLUSION_

Is it true that $(\forall x)(Fx) \vdash (\exists x)(Gx)$?   **(93)** YES / NO.

What about $(\exists x)(Fx) \vdash (\forall x)(Fx)$? This is **(94)** VALID / INVALID. To show that an argument form is invalid, we need a **(95)** DEDUCTION / COUNTER-EXAMPLE: that is to say, an **(96)** INTERPRETATION in which the premises are all **(97)** T / F and the conclusion is **(98)** T / F. Here it is easy to invent one. The argument is of the form "**(99)** SOMETHING / EVERYTHING is F, so **(100)** SOMETHING / EVERYTHING is F." Take F as, say, "is a fish." We get the argument.

Something is a fish, so everything is a fish.

Is the premise true? **(101)** YES / NO. Is the conclusion true? **(102)** YES / NO. Hence, we have provided a **(103)** DEDUCTION / COUNTEREXAMPLE, and the argument form is **(104)** VALID / INVALID.

Provide another interpretation that gives a counterexample: **(105)** F: IS A FEMALE.

Here are some assertions. In the case of the correct assertions, deductions can be found using the rules of quantifier equivalence, existential conclusion, and instantiation, plus rules of truth functional logic. None of the deductions needs more than three or four steps. On your own paper, *provide deductions for the correct assertions and counterexamples for the incorrect ones.*

(106) $Fa \vdash -(\forall x)-(Fx)$.
(107) $-(\exists x)-(Fx) \vdash Fb$.
(108) $-(Fc) \vdash -(\exists x)(Fx)$.
(109) $-(\exists x)(Fx \lor Gx) \vdash (\forall x)(-Fx \;\&\; -Gx)$.
(110) $-(\exists x)(Fx \lor Gx) \vdash -Fb \;\&\; -Gb$.
(111) $-(\exists x)(Fx \;\&\; Gx) \vdash -Fa \lor -Gb$.

06. $Fa \vdash (\exists x)(Fx)$

$Fa \vdash -(\forall x) - (Fx)$

07. $-(\exists x) - (Fx) \vdash (\forall x)(Fx)$

$\vdash Fb$

08. INVALID –

$Ex.$

$F:$ PRESIDENT OF U.S.

$c:$ BERTRAND RUSSELL

09. $-(\exists x)(Fx \lor Gx) \vdash$

$(\forall x) - (Fx \lor Gx)$

$\vdash (\forall x)(-Fx \,\&\, -Gx)$

10. $-(\exists x)(Fx \lor Gx) \vdash$

$(\forall x) - (Fx \lor Gx)$

$\vdash (\forall x)(-Fx \,\&\, -Gx)$

$\vdash -Fb \,\&\, -Gb$

11. INVALID.

$F.$ WOMEN

$G.$ MEN.

$a.$ MRS. NIXON

$b.$ MR. NIXON.

26 / More Deductions

This chapter provides two final rules for predicate logic. They are, unfortunately, perhaps the two most troublesome rules we have come across.

We have not used conditional proof for some time, and it should be reviewed. The rule says that you can take the premise of a valid argument and move it over to become the antecedent of a conditional. In the following assertion, underline the only antecedent of a conditional, and circle the only premise: **(1)** (P) ⊢ Q → P. Do the same for this assertion: **(2)** ((∀x)(Fx) ⊢ (∃x)(Gx) → (∀x)(Fx). Which of the following are correct applications of conditional proof? *CROSS OUT INCORRECT*

(3) If P ⊢ Q, then ⊢ P → Q.
~~**(4)**~~ If P, Q ⊢ R, then P, R ⊢ Q.
~~**(5)**~~ If P, −Q ⊢ −R, then P ⊢ −R → −Q.
(6) If P, Q, R ⊢ S, then P, R ⊢ Q → S.
(7) If (∀x)(Fx) ⊢ (∃x)(Gx), then ⊢ (∀x)(Fx) → (∃x)(Gx).
(8) If (∀x)(Fx → Gx) ⊢ (∀x)(Fx → Hx), then
⊢ (∀x)(Fx → Gx) → (∀x)(Fx → Hx).

Circle those of the following that can correctly be inferred by instantiation from (∀x)(Fx → Gx). **(9)** (∀x)(Fx) | Fa → Gb | Ga | Fa → Ga | Fx → Gx | Fb | (∀x)(Gx) | (∀y)(Fy → Gy) | −Ga → −Fa. Notice that although the last two do not follow by instantiation only, they do follow from (∀x)(Fx → Gx). For example, from it we can derive Fa → Ga by instantiation, and then −Ga → −Fa by **(10)** *CONTRAPOSITION*

(∀x)(Fx → Gx) has other consequences too. For example, take the premise,

All frankfurters are good to eat.

If this is true, then, if *everything* were a frankfurter, everything would be (11~~Goes to Eat~~ That is to say, the following pattern of inference seems appropriate:

$$(\forall x)(Fx \rightarrow Gx), (\forall x)(Fx) \vdash (\forall x)(Gx).$$

Complete the following patterns of the same form.

(12) $(\forall x)(Gx \rightarrow Hx), (\forall x)(Gx) \vdash$ *(Vx)(Hx)*
(13) $(\forall y)(Hy \rightarrow Fy),$ *(Vy)(Hy)* $\vdash (\forall y)(Fy).$

We would like to be able to deduce the conclusion $(\forall x)(Gx)$ from the premises $(\forall x)(Fx \rightarrow Gx)$ and $(\forall x)(Fx)$. Unfortunately, the rules of inference so far stated do not justify this pattern. We can only go this far. Justify each step.

1. $(\forall x)(Fx \rightarrow Gx), (\forall x)(Fx) \vdash Fa.$ (14) *INSTANTIATION*.
2.   „ $\vdash Fa \rightarrow Ga.$ (15) *INSTANTIATION*
3.   „ $\vdash Ga.$ (16) *DETACHMENT*.

What is the conclusion we would like to reach? (17) *(Vx)(Gx)*. We have no rule telling us to pass from Ga to $(\forall x)(Gx)$. In fact such a move looks invalid. Is it a case of instantiation? (18) YES / NO. Instantiation tells us that from $(\forall x)(Gx)$ we can infer (19) *Ga*, but not the other way around. Provide a counterexample to this argument form:

Ga, so $(\forall x)(Gx).$

(20)   Counterexample: *G*: *IS GAY* .
        a: *ARNOLD* .

Now steps 1, 2, 3 above lead us from the premises to the conclusion of line 3, namely (21) *Ga* Since it is not true that $Ga \vdash (\forall x)(Gx)$, steps 1–3 look like a bad road to the conclusion we are after, namely, (22) *(Vx)(Gx)*. However, look again at the sequence of inferences 1, 2, and 3. At 3 we arrived at the conclusion Ga. But we could equally well have arrived at Gb, or Gc, or "G" *followed by any name we choose*. That is, this argument form is *generally* applicable to anything we can name or describe. From the premises in 1, construct an argument to the conclusion Ge:

(23)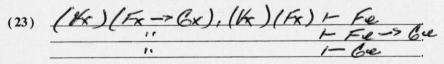

Thus, from these premises we can prove that the predicate "G" applies to anything whatsoever we care to name.   In 1, 2, and 3, there is nothing special about the name "*a*."   It does not occur in the premises.   If it did, then probably it would be special to the argument, but since it does not occur there, we can draw not just the particular conclusions Ga, Gb, Gc, Gd, Ge, or whatever, but we can also conclude that the predicate G applies to everything.   This is a legitimate place to *generalize*.

Rule of Generalization
If we have derived a deduction of

PREMISES $\vdash Fa$

and the name "a" does not occur in the premises, we can assert (for some letter x not in FA):

PREMISES $\vdash (\forall x)(Fx)$.

Thus at step 3 above we had:

3. $(\forall x)(Fx \rightarrow Gx)$, $(\forall x)(Fx) \vdash$ **(24)** Ga.

We finish the deduction by applying generalization:

4. $(\forall x)(Fx \rightarrow Gx)$, $(\forall x)(Fx) \vdash (\forall x)(Gx)$.

Notice that the "*a*" in the conclusion of step 3 **(25)** DOES / <u>DOES NOT</u> occur in the premises of step 3. Would step 4 be correct if there were an "*a*" in the premises? (26) YES / <u>NO</u>. Would a "*b*" in the premises matter? (27) <u>YES</u> / NO. Is step 4 as it stands correct? (28) <u>YES</u> / NO.

Below on the left are some assertions.   *Suppose* that we have deductions for each.   Whenever you can generalize on the conclusion, write the result in the blank on the right.   If you cannot generalize, leave the blank blank.

(29) $(\forall x)(Fx) \vdash Fc.$ __$(\forall x)(Fx)$__
(30) $(\forall y)(Gy) \vdash Gb.$ ___$(\forall x)(Fx)$ or $(\forall y)(Fy)$ ETC.___
(31) $(\exists z)(Gz \,\&\, Fa) \vdash Ga.$ ___
(32) $(\forall z)(Gz \,\&\, Fa) \vdash Gb.$ ___$(\forall x)(Gx)$ or $(\forall z)(Gz)$ ETC___
(33) $(\exists x)(Fx)$, $(\forall x)(Gx)$, $Ha \vdash Gb \rightarrow Fb.$ __$(\forall x)(Gx \rightarrow Fx)$___
(34) $(\exists x)(Fx)$, $(\forall x)(Gx)$, $Ha \vdash Ga \rightarrow Fa.$ ___.

One of the two following deductions is fallacious.   Cross it out.

(35) $(\forall x)(Fx), (\exists x)(Gx), Fa \vdash Gb \rightarrow Fc$ by some valid deduction.
        ,, $\vdash (\forall x)(Gb \rightarrow Fx)$.
        ,, $\vdash (\forall y)(\forall x)(Gy \rightarrow Fx)$.

~~(36)~~   SAME PREMISES $\vdash Gb \rightarrow Fa$ by some valid deduction.
        ,, $\vdash (\forall x)(Gb \rightarrow Fx)$.
        ,, $\vdash (\forall y)(\forall x)(Gy \rightarrow Fx)$.

Although the rule of generalization may seem strange, it is familiar to anyone who has had a basic course in Euclidean geometry.   Many of the proofs go like this.   "In the triangle ABC we see that . . . ., hence in the triangle ABC it must be true that _____; therefore, for any triangle with the property . . . ., it must also have the property _____."   The argument is couched in terms of a particular figure, but if the argument is correct, it would apply to any other figure satisfying certain conditions, and so we conclude with a general proposition.   Our rule provides a formal equivalent to this intuitive procedure.

Here are some deductions.   Justify each step.

$(\forall x)(\forall y)(Fx \ \& \ Gy) \vdash (\forall y)(\forall x)(Fx \ \& \ Gy)$.

Deduction:

1.	$(\forall x)(\forall y)(Fx \ \& \ Gy) \vdash (\forall y)(Fa \ \& \ Gy)$	(37) _INSTANTIATION_
2.	,, $\vdash Fa \ \& \ Gb$	(38) _____
3.	,, $\vdash (\forall x)(Fx \ \& \ Gb)$	(39) _GENERALIZATION_
4.	,, $\vdash (\forall y)(\forall x)(Fx \ \& \ Gy)$	(40) _____

$\vdash (\forall x)(Fx \rightarrow Gx) \rightarrow ((\forall x)(Fx) \rightarrow (\forall x)(Gx))$.

Deduction:

1.	$(\forall x)(Fx \rightarrow Gx), (\forall x)(Fx) \vdash Fb \rightarrow Gb$	(41) _INSTANTIATION_
2.	,, $\vdash Fb$	(42) _INSTANTIATION_
3.	,, $\vdash Gb$	(43) _DETACHMENT_
4.	,, $\vdash (\forall x)(Gx)$	(44) _GENERALIZATION_
5.	$(\forall x)(Fx \rightarrow Gx) \vdash (\forall x)(Fx) \rightarrow (\forall x)(Gx)$	(45) _CONDITIONAL PROOF_
6.	$\vdash (\forall x)(Fx \rightarrow Gx) \rightarrow ((\forall x)(Fx) \rightarrow (\forall x)(Gx))$	(46) _CONDITIONAL PROOF_

The conclusion of step 6 is like the tautologies of Chapter 20.   It is asserted on the basis of (47) TWO / ONE / NO premises.

Give correct examples of the following rules:

(48)   Quantifier equivalence. _$-(\forall x)(Fx) \vdash (\exists x)-(Fx)$_ .
(49)   Existential conclusion. _$Fa \vdash (\exists x)(Fx)$_ .
(50)   Instantiation. _$(\forall x)(Fx) \vdash Fa$_ .

We now have the rule of generalization for getting a universal quantifier into the conclusion. What we still need is a rule for getting the existential quantifier into the premise. This rule, which is the very last rule, is very much like the rule of generalization. Suppose that from some premise *Fa* we can derive a conclusion and that the name *a* does not occur in the conclusion. Then to infer this conclusion, all we need to know is that something or other is *F*. That is to say, the conclusion would also follow from $(\exists x)(Fx)$.

Rule of existential premise
If we have derived a deduction of

$$Fa, \text{ maybe more premises} \vdash \text{conclusion}$$

and the name "a" does not occur anywhere in the other premises or in the conclusion, we can assert (for some letter x not in Fa)

$$(\exists x)(Fx), \text{ the other premises} \vdash \text{conclusion}$$

Which of the following are correct applications of this rule?
CROSS OUT THE INCORRECT

(51) If $Fa \vdash Gb$, then $(\exists x)(Fx) \vdash Gb$.
(52) If $Fb \vdash Gb$, then $(\exists x)(Fx) \vdash Gb$.
(53) If $(\exists x)(Fx \,\&\, Ga) \vdash (\exists x)(Fx)$, then $(\exists y)(\exists x)(Fx \,\&\, Gy) \vdash (\exists x)(Fx)$.
(54) If $(\exists x)(Fx \,\&\, Ga) \vdash (\exists x)(Fx \,\&\, Ga)$, then $(\exists y)(\exists x)(Fx \,\&\, Gy) \vdash$
$$(\exists x)(Fx \,\&\, Ga).$$

Summary of Quantifier Rules

In addition to quantifier equivalences, we now have ONE / TWO / THREE / FOUR / FIVE / SIX quantifier rules. Two of these are easy; two more difficult. Here we state them in rough schematic form for ready reference. Let "*F*" be any predicate and "*a*" be any name.

INSTANTIATION

$$(\forall x)(Fx) \vdash Fa$$

(where "*Fa*" is got by replacing *every* "*x*" in "*Fx*" by "*a*").

EXISTENTIAL CONCLUSION. Let "x" be any letter from the end of the alphabet not found in "Fa":

$$Fa \vdash (\exists x)(Fx)$$

(where "Fx" is got by replacing *one or more* occurrences of "a" in "Fa" by "x").

GENERALIZATION. Let "x" be any letter from the end of the alphabet not found in "Fa":

If PREMISES $\vdash Fa$ and "a" does not occur in the premises, then PREMISES $\vdash (\forall x)(Fx)$.

EXISTENTIAL PREMISE. Let "x" be any letter from the end of the alphabet not found in "Fa":

If Fa, PREMISES $\vdash$ CONCLUSION and "a" does not occur in the other premises or the conclusion, then $(\exists x)(Fx)$, PREMISES $\vdash$ CONCLUSION.

In the following exercise, some assertions are ungrammatical. Cross them out. Others are correct; state what rule is applied. Others still are incorrect: write an × in front of these. State the rule used for correct, grammatical assertions.

(56) _____ $(\forall x)(Fx) \vdash Fa$. *INSTANTIATION* .

(57) ✗ $(\exists x)(Fx) \vdash Fa$. _____ .

(~~58~~) _____ $(\forall x)(Fx \rightarrow Gx \vdash Fa \rightarrow Ga$. _____ .

(59) _____ $(\forall x)(Fx \rightarrow Gx) \vdash Fb \rightarrow Gb$. *INSTANTIATION* .

(~~60~~) _____ $(\forall x)(Fx \rightarrow Gx) \vdash Fx \rightarrow Gx$. _____ .

(61) ✗ $(\exists x)(Gx) \vee (\exists x)(Fx) \vdash Ga \vee Fb$. _____ .

(62) _____ $Fa \vdash (\exists x)(Fx)$. *EXISTENTIAL CONCLUSION* .

(63) ✗ $Fa \vdash (\exists x)(Fx \& Gx)$. _____ .

(~~64~~) _____ $Gb \vdash \exists y(Gy)$. _____ .

(65) _____ $Gb \vdash (\exists y)(Gy)$. *EXISTENTIAL CONCLUSION* .

(66) ✗ $Ha \& Gb \vdash (\forall x)(Hx \& Gb)$. _____ .

(67) _____ If $Fa, Gb \vdash Hc$ then $(\exists x)(Fx), Gb \vdash Hc$. *EXISTENTIAL PREMISE*

(68) ✗ If $Fa, Gb \vdash Ha$, then $(\exists x)(Fx), Gb \vdash Ha$. _____ .

(69) __X__ If $Fa, Gb \vdash Ha$; then $Fa, Gb \vdash (\forall x)(Hx)$. _____.

(70) _____ If $Fa, Gb \vdash Hc$, then $Fa, Gb \vdash (\forall x)(Hx)$. *GENERALIZATION*

Construct deductions for the following:

(71) $(\forall x)(Fx) \vdash (\forall y)(Fy)$.

$(\forall x)(Fx) \vdash Fa$ *INSTANTIATION*

$\vdash (\forall y)(Fy)$ *GENERALIZATION*

(72) $(\exists x)(Fx) \vdash (\exists y)(Fy)$.

$Fa \vdash (\exists y)(Fy)$ *EXISTENTIAL CONCLUSION*

$(\exists x)(Fx) \vdash (\exists y)(Fy)$ *EXISTENTIAL PREMISE*

(73) $(\forall x)(\forall y)(Fx \ \& \ Gy) \vdash (\forall y)(\forall x)(Fx \ \& \ Gy)$.

1. *INSTANTIATION*   3. *GENERALIZATION*

2. *INSTANTIATION*   4. *GENERALIZATION*

(74) $(\exists x)(\exists y)(Fx \ \& \ Gy) \vdash (\exists y)(\exists x)(Fx \ \& \ Gy)$.

1. *EXISTENTIAL CONCLUSION* 3. *EXISTENTIAL PREMISE*

2. *EXISTENTIAL CONCLUSION* 4. *EXISTENTIAL PREMISE*

1.
2.
3.
4.

73. $(\forall x)(\forall y)(Fx \ \& \ Gy) \vdash (\forall y)(Fa \ \& \ Gy)$

$\vdash Fa \ \& \ Gb$

$\vdash (\forall x)(Fx \ \& \ Gb)$

$\vdash (\forall y)(\forall x)(Fx \ \& \ Gy)$

74. 1. $Fa \ \& \ Gb \vdash (\exists x)(Fx \ \& \ Gb)$

2. $Fa \ \& \ Gb \vdash (\exists y)(\exists x)(Fx \ \& \ Gy)$

3. $(\exists y)(Fa \ \& \ Gy) \vdash$ ''

4. $(\exists x)(\exists y)(Fx \ \& \ Gy) \vdash$ ''

27 / Relations

This chapter shows how to paraphrase statements that express relations.

So far we have been concerned with statements that say something about one individual, or with quantified versions of the same. For example, in the statement:

Anne is lovely.

the name is **(1)** <u>*ANNE*</u> and the predicate is **(2)** *IS LOVELY*.
(3) Underline the name and circle the predicate in:

<u>Anne</u> (is a woman.)

From these two statements we can build up compounds like:

If Anne is a woman, then she is lovely.

(4) Write out the open sentence corresponding to this statement.
IF X IS A WOMAN, THEN X IS LOVELY.
Remember that to get an open sentence we replace the names (and only names) by letters x, y, z.
Finally we can form a quantified statement:

$(\forall x)(x$ is a woman $\rightarrow x$ is lovely$)$

which would commonly be expressed in English by, **(5)** ALL ANNES ARE LOVELY / NO WOMEN ARE LOVELY / <u>ALL WOMEN ARE LOVELY</u>.

Now consider the statement:

Anne is the mother of Rachel.

How many names are there? **(6)** ONE / _TWO_ / THREE / FOUR. This statement expresses the relation between Anne and Rachel, namely the relation
of being the mother of. The corresponding open sentence is **(7)** x IS THE
MOTHER OF x / _x IS THE MOTHER OF y_ / y IS THE MOTHER OF y.
Write out an open sentence corresponding to,

(8) Rachel is a sister _X IS A SISTER_
(9) Daniel is a brother. _X IS A BROTHER_
(10) Rachel is the sister of Daniel. _X IS THE SISTER OF y_
(11) Circle the names in the statement:

~~Adam~~ is the father of ~~Cain~~

The relation expressed is **(12)** ADAM / BOAZ / CAIN / IS THE FATHER OF / IS
THE MOTHER OF. The open sentence is:

x is the father of y.

We shall abbreviate this as "xFy." Hence, the statement that Adam is the
father of Cain would be abbreviated **(13)** xFy / _aFc_ / Fac / cFa / xFc
aFy. Abbreviate:

Boaz is the father of Adam.

(14) _bFa_ .
Match:

(15) _b_ bMa.   (a) Anne is the mother of Daniel.
(16) _d_ aMb.   (b) Beth is the mother of Anne.
(17) _a_ aMd.   (c) Anne is Calvin's mother.
(18) _e_ bMc.   (d) Beth's mother is Anne.
(19) _c_ aMc.   (e) Beth is Calvin's mother.

Obviously the "direction" of the relation matters. Is saying that Anne is
the mother of Beth, the same as saying that Beth is the mother of Anne?
(20) YES / _NO_. Notice also that we have various ways of expressing the same
relation. Paul is the father of Timothy if and only if **(21)** TIMOTHY IS PAUL'S
FATHER / PAUL IS TIMOTHY'S FATHER.
Statements involving relations can be quantified. The statement that

someone is Daniel's father means there is some true way of filling in the blank marked by x in:

x is the father of Daniel.

Hence, we can paraphrase the statement:

Someone is the father of Daniel.

by **(22)** $(\exists x)(xFy)$ / $(\exists x)(xFd)$ / $(\exists x)(dFx)$. On the other hand, if we want to say that Daniel has a child, we could say:

Daniel is the father of someone.

This would be paraphrased as **(23)** $(\exists x)(xFy)$ / $(\exists x)(xFd)$ / $(\exists x)(dFx)$. Do "$(\exists x)(dFx)$" and "$(\exists x)(xFd)$" signify the same thing? **(24)** YES / NO.
Match:

(25) __e__ $(\exists x)(xFd)$.   (a)   Someone is the father of Adam.

(26) __b__ $(\exists x)(aFx)$.   (b)   Adam is someone's father.

(27) __g__ $(\exists x)(bFx)$.   (c)   Someone is the father of Calvin.

(28) __f__ $(\exists x)(dFx)$.   (d)   Calvin is the father of someone.

(29) __d__ $(\exists x)(cFx)$.   (e)   Someone is the father of Daniel.

(30) __c__ $(\exists x)(xFc)$.   (f)   Someone is Daniel's child.

(31) __a__ $(\exists x)(xFa)$.   (g)   Barth is someone's father.

(32) __h__ $(\exists x)(xFb)$.   (h)   Someone is Barth's father.

Let L: is larger than; j: Jupiter; e: Earth. What is "jLe" short for? **(33)** _JUPITER IS LARGER THAN EARTH_. Abbreviate "Earth is larger than Jupiter." **(34)** _eLj_. What does "$(\exists x)(xLe)$" mean? **(35)** _SOMETHING IS LARGER THAN EARTH_. What does "$(\exists x)(jLx)$" mean? **(36)** _JUPITER IS LARGER THAN SOMETHING_.
We have just had paraphrases of the statements:

Something is larger than Earth.

and

Jupiter is larger than something.

We can also say:

Something is larger than something.

We express this by first forming the open sentence from:

Jupiter is larger than Earth.

namely **(37)** x IS LARGER THAN x / x IS LARGER THAN y. To say "something is larger than something," is to say that the blanks x and y can be replaced so as to obtain a true statement. Hence, the paraphrase must be **(38)** $(\forall x)(xLy)$ / $(\exists x)(\exists y)(xLy)$ / $(\exists x)(xLx)$ / $(\exists x)(jLe)$. Which is the paraphrase of "Someone is the father of someone"? **(39)** $(\exists x)(Fxx)$ / $(\exists x)(xFx)$ / $(\exists x)(\exists y)(xFy)$ / $(\exists x)(\exists x)(xFy)$. All of the following attempt to paraphrase "Someone is the mother of someone." But some of these attempts are ungrammatical; cross them out. **(40)** $(\exists x)(\exists y)(xMy)$ / $(\exists z)(\exists w)(zMw)$ / ~~$(\exists w \exists x)(wMx)$~~ / $(\exists y)(\exists x)(yMx)$ / ~~$(\exists w)(\exists z)(Mwz)$~~ / ~~$(\exists y)(\exists w)yMw$~~ / ~~$(\exists x)(\exists y)$~~ ~~$xyM$~~ / ~~$(\exists a)(\exists b)(aMb)$~~.

Paraphrase:

Everything is larger than Jupiter.

(41) $(\forall x)(jLx)$ / $(\forall x)(jLe)$ / $(\forall x)xLj$ / $\forall x(xLj)$ / $\underline{(\forall x)(xLj)}$.

Jupiter is larger than everything.

(42) $\underline{(\forall x)(jLx)}$ / $(\forall x)(jLe)$ / $(\forall x)(Ljx)$ / $\underline{(\forall x)(jLx)}$.

Everything is larger than Earth. **(43)** $(\forall x)(xLe)$
Earth is larger than everything. **(44)** $(\forall x)(eLx)$

"Everything is larger than everything," a statement that is certainly false, may be paraphrased as (circle two) **(45)** $(\forall x \forall y)(xLy)$ / $\underline{(\forall z)(\forall w)(zLw)}$ / $(xy)(xLy)$ / $(\forall x)(\forall y)xLy$ / $\underline{(\forall x)(\forall y)(xLy)}$ / $(\forall x)(\forall y)xLy$.

Match: Cross out the ungrammatical entries.

(46) _d_ $(\exists z)(zLj)$.   (a) Jupiter is larger than Earth.

(47) _L_ $(\exists x)(\exists y)(xLy)$.   (b) Earth is larger than Jupiter.

(48) _X_ $(\exists x)eLx$.   (c) Something is larger than Earth.

(49) _c_ $(\exists x)(xLe)$.   (d) Something is larger than Jupiter.

(50) _X_ $(\exists e)(eLj)$.   (e) Earth is larger than something.

(51) _K_ $(\forall x)(\forall y)(xLy)$.   (f) Jupiter is larger than something.

(52) _b_ eLj.   (g) Everything is larger than Earth.

(53) _X_ $\forall x \forall y(xLy)$.   (h) Everything is larger than Jupiter.

(54) _f_ $(\exists w)(jLw)$.   (i) Jupiter is larger than everything.

(55) _a_ jLe.   (j) Earth is larger than everything.

(56) _X_ $(\forall e)(\forall j)(eLj)$.   (k)   Everything is larger than everything.

(57) _e_ $(\exists y)(eLy)$.   (l)   Something is larger than something.

(58) _J_ $(\forall x)(eLx)$.

(59) _g_ $(\forall x)(xLe)$.

(60) _X_ $(\forall x \forall y)(xLy)$.

(61) _l_ $(\forall y)(jLy)$.

(62) _K_ $(\forall z)(zLj)$.

Letting S: is the same size as, paraphrase:

(63)   Jupiter is the same size as Earth. _j'Se_____.
(64)   Something is the same size as Jupiter. _(∃x)(xSj)_____.
(65)   Something is the same size as something. _(∃x)(∃y)(xSy.)_
(66)   Jupiter is the same size as Jupiter. _jSj_ ;_c_____.
(67)   Jupiter is the same size as itself. _____jSj_____.

You will have paraphrased statements 66 and 67 as jSj. Hence, "something is the same size as itself" becomes (68) $(\exists x)(\exists y)(xSy)$ / $(\exists x)((xSx)$ / $\underline{(\exists x)(xSx)}$. Notice that the scheme on the left in 68 corresponds to "Something is the same size as something or other" whereas the correct scheme at the end corresponds to "Something is the same size as itself." Paraphrase "Everything is the same size as itself." (69) _(∀x)(xSx.)_

Now consider the statement:

Everything is larger than something.

It is best to paraphrase double quantifiers step by step. The two quantifiers are (70) EVERYTHING / NOTHING / SOMETHING / ANYONE / NO ONE. Which comes first? (71) _EVERYTHING_ We paraphrase it first. (72) Cross out the *wrong* paraphrase:

~~$(\forall x)$(something is larger than x).~~
$(\forall x)(x$ is larger than something).

The lower paraphrase is correct. Now we paraphrase the material in brackets. How would you paraphrase "Jupiter is larger than something"? (73) _(∃x)(j Lx.)_ We do the same for "x is larger than something," *leaving the outside quantifier unchanged on the outside.* Since we already have an "x" quantifier we move to a new letter, say "y." Which of the following schemes is correct? (74) Cross out the wrong one:

$(\forall x)(\exists y)(x$ is larger than $y)$.
~~$(\exists y)(\forall x)(x$ is larger than $y)$.~~

This time the top one is correct.   Now we replace "is larger than" by "L."
(75) Cross out the incorrect scheme:

~~$(\forall x)(\exists y)(yLx)$.~~
$(\forall x)(\exists y)(xLy)$.

Summary of Steps Paraphrasing Statements

To paraphrase "Everything is larger than something":

STEP 1   Paraphrase outer quantifier:

$(\forall x)(x$ is larger than something).

STEP 2   Paraphrase inner quantifier.   Leave outer quantifier untouched.
In this case "$(\forall x)$" is left untouched and we have to paraphrase, "... (x is
larger than something)."   We get: "... $(\exists y)(x$ is larger than $y)$," or, with
$(\forall x)$, "$(\forall x)(\exists y)(x$ is larger than $y)$."

STEP 3

$$(\forall x)(\exists y)(xLy)$$

Now try your hand at:

Something is larger than everything.

We offer two choices at each step.   Cross out each incorrect choice.

STEP 1   **(76)** $(\exists x)(x$ is larger than everything) / ~~$(\exists x)(\text{everything is larger than } x)$.~~

STEP 2   **(77)** $(\exists x)(\forall y)(x$ is larger than $y)$ / ~~$(\forall y)(\exists x)(x \text{ is larger than } y)$.~~

STEP 3   **(78)** $(\exists x)(\forall y)(xLy)$ / ~~$(\exists x)(\forall y)(yLx)$.~~

Some people have trouble seeing the difference between:

A.   Something is larger than everything.

and:

B.   Everything is larger than something or other.

So let us take some other examples:

C.   Someone voted for everyone.
D.   Everyone voted for someone or other.

In an election where there are three candidates, statement C says that some voter voted for all three candidates.   But statement D says only that everyone actually voted.   Contrast again with:

E.   There is someone for whom everyone voted.

This is saying that there is one definite person who got all the votes.   Is this the same as the second statement, that everyone voted for someone or other?
(79) YES _/_ NO.

To get even clearer about these differences, let us take some stories illustrating these points.   Three students called Peter, Rachel, and Sugar stage a small demonstration.   They are evicted by three policemen called Purtill, Riley, and O'Neill.   Now look at these statements.

F.   There is a student who shouts at every policeman.
G.   There is a policeman at whom every student shouts.
H.   Every student shouts at some policeman or other.
I.   Every policeman is shouted at by some student or other.

Indicate which of these four statements are true in the following stories.

(80) _HI_ Peter shouts at Purtill, Rachel at Riley, and Sugar shouts at
O'Neill.   That is all the shouting there is.

(81) _FI_ Peter shouts at Purtill, Riley, and O'Neill.   Sugar and Rachel
stay quiet.

(82) _GH_ All three shout at Riley, and at no one else.

Now consider the following four statements:

J.   There is a policeman who hits every student.
K.   There is a student whom every policeman hits.
L.   Every policeman hits some student or other.
M.   Every student is hit by some policeman or other.

(83)   Tell a story in which K is T, but J and M are F.
Riley, O'Neill & Purtill hit Peter and no one else.

(84)   Tell a story in which J is T, but K and L are F.
Riley hit Peter, Sugar, & Rachel, O'Neill & Purtill hit No One.

(85)   Tell a story in which L and M are T, but J and K are F.
Riley hits Peter, Purtill hits Sugar, O'Neill hits Rachel -

(86)   Tell a story in which only L is T.
Riley & Purtill hit Peter and O'Neill Hit Sug

(87) Tell a story in which only M is T.

Ricky Hits Peter & Sugar AND Partill Hit Rachel

Could there be a story in which K is T but L is F? **(88)** YES / <u>NO</u>. Could there be a story in which J is T but M is F? **(89)** YES / <u>NO</u>. Could there be a story in which M is T but J is F? **(90)** <u>YES</u> / NO. Which of your stories above is an example of 90? **(91)** *07 (+86)*

Paraphrasing these statements is not easy. Let us start with statement F:

F. There is a student who shouts at every policeman.

We begin with the **(92)** INSIDE / <u>OUTSIDE</u> quantifier, which is **(93)** SOME / <u>THERE IS A</u> / EVERY / NONE / ALL.

STEP 1 $(\exists x)(x$ is a student & x shouts at every policeman). Inside the brackets we have:

x is a student & x shouts at every policeman.

This is a **(94)** CONDITIONAL / <u>CONJUNCTION</u> / ALTERNATION. Are there any quantifiers in the first conjunct? **(95)** YES / <u>NO</u>. Hence, we can leave the first conjunct alone, so far as quantifiers are concerned, because it has none. What quantifier is in the second conjunct? **(96)** ALL / SOME / THERE IS A / <u>EVERY</u> / NONE. This is an **(97)** <u>UNIVERSAL</u> / EXISTENTIAL quantifier. The universal quantifier is typically paraphrased using the **(98)** <u>ARROW</u> / AMPERSAND. The second conjunct is **(99)** <u>x SHOUTS AT EVERY POLICEMAN</u> / x IS A POLICEMAN. This conjunct means that for anyone you choose, if he is a policeman, then x shouts at him. So the correct paraphrase is **(100)** $(\forall y)(x$ IS A POLICEMAN $\rightarrow x$ SHOUTS AT $y)$ / <u>$(\forall y)(y$ IS A POLICEMAN $\rightarrow x$ SHOUTS AT $y)$</u> / $(\exists y)(y$ IS A POLICEMAN $\rightarrow x$ SHOUTS AT $y)$. This is the paraphrase of the **(101)** FIRST / <u>SECOND</u> conjunct. We are now ready to paraphrase the result of Step 1, arriving at Step 2.

STEP 1 $(\exists x)(x$ is a student & x shouts at every policeman).

STEP 2 $(\exists x)(x$ is a student & $(\forall y)(y$ is a policeman $\rightarrow x$ shouts at $y))$.

STEP 3 $(\exists x)(Sx$ & $(\forall y)(Py \rightarrow xOy))$.

We have set "O: shouts at" because the first letter "S" was taken for "student."

Notice that the second step is the hardest. A few people can do these paraphrases in their head, but most people need to go step by step. Unless you have absolutely no difficulty, use the step-by-step method. If you do proceed step by step, *don't* try to save time by skimming thoughtlessly over the second step. It is the hardest. Do it best.

In the following examples, you are offered three choices at each step. Only one is correct. Cross out the other two. Work through the steps for paraphrasing statement F once more before proceeding.

G.   There is a policeman at whom every student shouts.

STEP 1

(102) $(\exists x)(x$ is a policeman & every student shouts at $x)$.
~~$(\exists x)(x$ is a policeman & x shouts at every student).~~
~~$(\exists x)(x$ is a policeman whom every student shouts at).~~

STEP 2

(103) $(\exists x)(x$ is a policeman & $(\forall y)(y$ is a student $\to y$ shouts at $x))$.
~~$(\exists x)(x$ is a policeman & $(\forall y)(y$ is a student & y shouts at $x))$.~~
~~$(\exists x)(x$ is a policeman & $(\forall y)(y$ is a policeman & y shouts at $x))$.~~

STEP 3

(104) $(\exists x)(Px$ & $(\forall y)(Sy \to yOx))$.
~~$(\exists x)(Px$ & $(\forall y)Sy \to yOx))$.~~
~~$(\exists x)(Px$ & $(\forall y)(Sx \to xOy))$.~~

H.   Every student shouts at some policeman or other.

STEP 1

(105)   ~~$(\forall x)(x$ is a student & x shouts at some policeman or other).~~
~~$(\forall x)(x$ is a student who shouts at some policeman or other).~~
$(\forall x)(x$ is a student $\to x$ shouts at some policeman or other).

STEP 2

(106)   ~~$(\forall x)(x$ is a student & $(\exists y)(x$ shouts at y & y is a policeman)).~~
~~$(\forall y)(x$ is a student $\to (\exists y)(x$ shouts at $y \to y$ is a policeman)).~~
$(\forall y)(x$ is a student $\to (\exists y)(x$ shouts at y & y is a policeman)).

STEP 3   *Should be $(\forall x)$*

(107)   ~~$(\forall x)(Sx \to (\exists y)(Py$ & $Oxy))$.~~
~~$(\forall x)(Sx(\exists y)(Py$ & $xOy))$.~~
$(\forall x)(Sx \to (\exists y)(Py$ & $xOy))$.

I.   Every policeman is shouted at by some student or other.

STEP 1

(108) $(\forall x)(x$ is a student & x shouts at every policeman).
$(\forall x)(x$ is a policeman who is shouted at by some student or other).
$(\forall x)(x$ is a policeman $\rightarrow x$ is shouted at by some student or other).

STEP 2

(109) $(\forall x)(x$ is a policeman $\rightarrow (\exists y)(y$ is a student & x shouts at $y))$.
$(\forall x)(x$ is a policeman $\rightarrow (\exists y)(y$ is a student & x is shouted at by $y))$.
$(\forall x)(x$ is a policeman $\rightarrow (\forall y)(y$ is a student $\rightarrow x$ is shouted at by $y))$.

STEP 3

(110) $(\forall x)(Px \rightarrow (\exists y)(Sy$ & $yOx))$.
$(\forall x)(Px \rightarrow (\exists y)(Sy$ & $xOy))$.
$(\forall x)(Px \rightarrow (\exists y)(Sx$ & $xOy))$.

J.   There is a policeman who hits every student.

STEP 1

(111) $(\forall x)(x$ is a policeman who hits every student).
$(\exists x)(x$ is a policeman $\rightarrow x$ hits every student).
$(\exists x)(x$ is a policeman & x hits every student).

STEP 2

(112) $(\exists x)(x$ is a policeman & $(\forall y)(x$ hits $y \rightarrow y$ is a student)).
$(\exists x)(\forall y)(x$ is a policeman & x hits y & x is a student)).
$(\exists x)(x$ is a policeman & $(\forall y)(y$ is a student $\rightarrow x$ hits $y))$.

STEP 3

(113) $(\exists x)(Sx$ & $(\forall y)(Py \rightarrow xHy))$.
$(\exists x)(Px$ & $(\forall y)(Sy \rightarrow xHy))$.
$(\exists x)(Px$ & $(\forall y)(Sy \ xHy))$.

Which of the following was the correct paraphrase of "There is a student who shouts at every policeman"? (See step 3 in the example for paraphrasing statement F). **(114)** $(\exists x)(Sx \rightarrow (\forall y)(Py$ & $xOy))$ / $(\exists x)(Sx$ & $(\forall y)(Py \rightarrow xOy))$. Which of the following is the correct paraphrase of J: "There is a policeman who hits every student"? **(115)** $(\exists x)(Px$ & $(\forall y)(Sx \rightarrow xHy))$ / $(\exists x)(Px$ & $(\forall y)(Sy \rightarrow xHy))$. In each case, you should have chosen the second scheme.   Different letters occur in these schemes.   However, do they have the same basic form?   **(116)** YES / NO.   They have the same form, as can be seen by replacing "*S*" in 114 by "*P*", "*P*" in 114 by "*S*", and "*O*" in 114 by the letter **(117)** _H_.

The fact that these two have the same basic form is to be expected from the formal similarity between F and J:

E.   There is a student who shouts at every policeman.
J.   **(118)** _THERE IS A POLICEMAN WHO HITS EVERY STUDENT._

In either case, we have a statement of the form "There is a . . . that has such-and-such a relation to every _ _ _."

What is the paraphrase of:

G.   There is a policeman at whom every student shouts.

If necessary, look back at your answer to 104, and copy your answer exactly.

(119)   Paraphrase of G: $(\exists x)(Px \& (y)(Sy \rightarrow yOx))$.

What is the paraphrase of:

K.   There is a student whom every policeman hits.

If necessary, look at your answer to 119, and imitate it.   Or on your own paper, paraphrase step by step.

(120)   Paraphrase of K: $(\exists x)(Sx \& (y)(Py \rightarrow yHx))$

What is the paraphrase of:

H.   Every student shouts at some policeman or other.

Check with your answer to 107, if you want.

(121)   Paraphrase of H: $(x)(Sx \rightarrow (\exists y)(Py \& xOy))$

What is the paraphrase of the similar statement:

L.   Every policeman hits some student or other.

(122)   Paraphrase of L: $(x)(Px \rightarrow (\exists y)(Sy \& xHy))$.

What is the paraphrase of:

I.   Every policeman is shouted at by some student or other.

Check with your answer to 110, if you want.

(123)   Paraphrase of I: $(Vx)(Px \rightarrow (\exists y)(Sy \& y Ox))$.
What is the paraphrase of:

M.   Every student is hit by some policeman or other?

(124)   Paraphrase of M: $(Vx)(Sx \rightarrow (\exists y)(Py \& y Hx))$.
Let: A: admires; H: hates; P: is a person.   Note that "somebody" = "some person."   Match:

(125) _d_ $(\exists x)(Px \& xHx)$.

      (a)   Every person admires something or other.

(126) _a_ $(\forall x)(Px \rightarrow (\exists y)(xAy))$.

      (b)   Each person admires himself.

(127) _f_ $(\exists x)(Px \& (\forall y)(Py \rightarrow xAy))$.

      (c)   Somebody hates everything.

(128) _i_ $(\forall x)(Px \rightarrow (\exists y)(Py \& xHy))$.

      (d)   Some people hate themselves.

(129) _j_ $(\forall x)(Px \rightarrow ((\exists y)(Py \& yAx) \& (\exists z)(Pz \& zHx)))$.

      (e)   Some person is admired by every person.

(130) _e_ $(\exists x)(Px \& (\forall y)(Py \rightarrow yAx))$.

      (f)   Somebody admires everybody.

(131) _g_ $-(\exists x)((Px \& (\forall y)(xHy))$.

      (g)   Nobody hates everything.

(132) _c_ $(\exists x)(Px \& (\forall y)(xHy))$.

      (h)   Everybody hates something.

(133) _b_ $(\forall x)(Px \rightarrow xAx)$.

      (i)   Everybody hates someone or other.

(134) _h_ $(\forall x)(Px \rightarrow (\exists y)(xHy))$.

      (j)   Everyone is admired by someone and hated by someone.

What English statements correspond to the following, if we let: S: supports; V: voter; C: candidate; N: newspaper.

(135) $(\forall x)(Nx \rightarrow (\exists y)(Cy \& xSy))$. _Every newspaper supports some candidate or other._

(136) $(\forall x)(Cx \rightarrow (\exists y)(Ny \& ySx))$. _Every candidate is supported by some newspaper or other._

(137) $(\exists x)(Cx \& (\forall y)(Ny \rightarrow -ySx))$. _There is a candidate not supported by any newspaper._

(138) $-(\exists x)(Nx \& (\forall y)(Cy \rightarrow xSy))$. _No newspaper supports every candidate._

Paraphrase the following:

(139)   Some newspaper supports every candidate. _____

$$(\exists x)(Nx \;\&\; (\forall y)(Cy \rightarrow xSy))$$

(140)   There is a voter who does not support any candidate. _____.

$$(\exists x)(Vx \;\&\; -(\exists y)(Cy \;\&\; xSy))$$

(141)   Some voters support every candidate supported by a newspaper. _____.

$$(\exists x)(Vx \;\&\; (\forall y)((Cy \;\&\; (\exists z)(Nz \;\&\; zSy)) \rightarrow xSy))$$

28 / Kinds of Relation

This chapter provides a little of the elementary theory of relations and shows how to construct counterexamples to some
argument forms.

Do Venn diagrams provide a decision procedure for the syllogism? **(1)**
YES / NO. Name a decision procedure for truth functional logic. **(2)**
Truth Tables. Is there a decision procedure for predicate logic?
(3) YES / _NO_. Counterexamples can show an argument form is **(4)** VALID /
INVALID but favorable examples can never show that an argument form is
(5) _VALID_. Finding a deduction of the conclusion from the
premises can show that an argument is **(6)** _VALID_. If you fail to
find a deduction, does that show that an argument is invalid? **(7)** YES / _NO_.
A counterexample to an argument form is an interpretation in which all the
premises are **(8)** _T_ and the conclusion is **(9)** _F_.

It is possible to make the notion of an interpretation more flexible. Suppose we consider the relation S: smaller than. What does the following
mean: $(\forall x)(\exists y)(xSy)$? **(10)** EVERYTHING IS LARGER THAN SOMETHING OR
OTHER / SOMETHING IS SMALLER THAN EVERYTHING / _EVERYTHING IS SMALLER
THAN SOMETHING OR OTHER_.

The statement that everything is smaller than something or other is
probably false. Is the whole universe smaller than anything else that exists?
(11) YES / _NO_. The *universe* is not smaller than anything else. But now
suppose we restrict ourselves to the domain of whole numbers—1, 2, 3,
4 . . ., and so on, unendingly. Is any number in this domain greater than 1?
(12) _YES_ / NO. Is any greater than 2? **(13)** _YES_ / NO. In fact no matter
what number we pick, we can always find a greater number, simply by
adding 1. There is a number greater than a million, for example, 1,000,001.
In this domain, is it true that everything is smaller than something or other?
(14) _YES_ / NO.

But now consider the domain of the numbers 1, 2, and 3 only.   Is 1 smaller than a number in this domain?   **(15)** YES / NO.   Is 2?   **(16)** YES / NO. However, 3 is not smaller than any number in this domain because 3 is not smaller than 1, 2, or 3.   In this domain, is it true that *everything* is smaller than something or other?   **(17)** No.

Thus we see that the interpretation alone may not be enough to settle whether a statement is true or false; we must also consider the domain of the interpretation.

To sum up this example, we take the scheme,

$$(\forall x)(\exists y)(xSy)$$

Is this true under the interpretation letting S: smaller than, and within the domain of the universe and everything in it?   **(18)** YES / NO.   Is it true under the interpretation S: smaller than, and within the domain of the whole numbers?   **(19)** YES / NO.   Is it true under the interpretation S: smaller than, and within the domain of the set of the numbers 1, 2, and 3? **(20)** YES / NO.   Is it true under the interpretation S: younger than, and within the domain of the set of children born to one woman (say, Martha Washington)?   **(21)** YES / NO.   Is it true under the interpretation S: younger than or equal in age to, in the domain of human beings?   **(22)** YES / NO.   Notice that the answer to 21 is no, so long as the woman has any children, for the oldest child is not younger than any child in the domain. The answer to 22 is yes, for the interpretation is:

Everything is younger than or equal in age to something or other.

Since every human is younger than or equal in age to himself, this is certainly true!

Examine more closely the relations:

O: older than.
E: exactly as old as.

in the domain of human beings.   Under this interpretation, write out the meanings of the following:

(23) $(\forall x)(xOx)$. EVERY HUMAN IS OLDER THAN HIMSELF
(24) $(\forall x)(xEx)$. Every Human is EXACTLY AS OLD AS HIMSELF.

Which of these two is true in the domain of human beings, given this interpretation?   **(25)** 23 / 24.   Obviously 23 is F: nobody is older than himself. But 24 is T, for each person is exactly as old as himself.   A relation like "exactly as old as" in the domain of human beings is a bit like a mirror: we have xEx holding for all x; the "x" on the left is reflected on the right.   Such a relation is called reflexive.

A relation, R, is reflexive in a domain if and only if
$$(\forall x)(xRx)$$
is true in that domain.

Write "R" in front of the following relations that are reflexive.

(handwritten: T) (26) _____ North of, in the domain of points on the surface of the earth.

(handwritten: S) (27) _R_ Equals, in the domain of whole numbers.

(28) _____ Loves, in the domain of people.

(handwritten: S) (29) _R_ Born within five days of the birthday of, in the domain of people.

(handwritten: T) (30) _R_ No richer than, in the domain of people.

(handwritten: T) (31) _____ Taller than, in the domain of people.

(handwritten: T) (32) _R_ Taller than or equal in height to, in the domain of people.

(33) _____ Ancestor of, in the domain of people, living or dead.

(34) _____ Brother of, in the domain of people.

(handwritten: S) (35) _____ Different from, in *any* domain with two or more things in it, say the domain of airplanes.

(36) _____ Knowing the name of, in the domain of people, including people who have amnesia.

(37) _R_ Knowing the name of, in the domain of people who know their own names.

Notice that 36 is *not* reflexive, for we require that for *all x, xRx.* There are some people with amnesia who do not know their own names. But 37 is reflexive.

Returning to *O*: older than, and *E*: exactly as old as, in the domain of people, what are the meanings of the following?

(handwritten: GIVEN ANY TWO HUMANS: IF ONE IS OLDER THAN THE OTHER; THEN THE LATTER IS OLDER THAN THE FORMER.)

(38) $(\forall x)(\forall y)(xOy \rightarrow yOx)$.

(39) $(\forall x)(\forall y)(xEy \rightarrow yEx)$. *(handwritten: GIVEN ANY TWO HUMANS; IF ONE IS EXACTLY AS OLD AS THE OTHER THEN THE LATTER IS EXACTLY AS OLD AS THE FORMER)*

Which of these is true in the domain of human beings? **(40)** 38 / 39. Expression 38 is F; it says that for any two people you choose, if the first is older than the second, then the second is older than the first. Expression 39 is T: for any two people you pick, if the first is exactly the same age as the second, then the second is the same as the first. Expression 39 **(41)** DOES / DOES NOT say that everyone is the same age.

In this domain, the relation *E* is in a certain sense symmetric. For any *x* and *y* you choose, *E* looks the same in either direction: if you have *xEy*, you also have *yEx*. Hence this relation is called *symmetric*.

A relation R is symmetric in a domain if and only if in that domain

$$(\forall x)(\forall y)(xRy \rightarrow yRx).$$

(42) Write "S" in front of those relations among 26–37 that are symmetric. Notice that "loves" is, unfortunately, not symmetric outside a paradise of true lovers. "Different from," in contrast, is certainly symmetric; if that is different from this, then this is different from that. Finally, "brother" is not symmetric, for John is brother of Mary, but Mary is *sister* of John, not brother.

Returning to O and E in the domain of people what do these two schemes mean? *FOR ANY THREE (NOT NECESSARILY DIFFERENT) PEOPLE YOU CHOOSE*

(43) $(\forall x)(\forall y)(\forall z)((xOy \ \& \ yOz) \rightarrow xOz).$ *IF THE FIRST IS OLDER THAN THE SECOND AND THE SECOND OLDER THAN THE THIRD THEN THE FIRST IS OLDER THAN THE THIRD*

(44) $(\forall x)(\forall y)(\forall z)((xEy \ \& \ yEz) \rightarrow xEz).$ *IF THE FIRST IS EXACTLY AS OLD AS THE SECOND AND THE SECOND EXACTLY AS OLD AS THE THIRD THEN THE FIRST IS EXACTLY AS OLD AS THE THIRD.*
It is hard to express these in concise English. If one person is older than a second, and a second is older than a third, then the first is older than the third. Is that true? **(45)** YES / NO. Likewise, 44 is true.

In these relations, if we go from x to y, that is, (xRy), and from y to z, that is, (yRz), then we can go from x to z, (xRz). Thus, we can, in a sense, go across R, from x to y to z. Hence, such relations are called *transitive*, for "trans" means "across," as in "transatlantic."

A relation R is transitive in a domain if and only if in that domain

$$(\forall x)(\forall y)(\forall z)((xRy \ \& \ yRz) \rightarrow xRz)$$

(46) Write "T" in front of those relations in the list 26–37 that are transitive. Notice that "North of" is certainly transitive. But "East of" in the domain of points on the equator is not transitive. This is because "East of" means something like, "East of by the shortest route." In the following picture of the earth, we see three cities, A, B, and C.

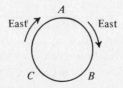

A is east of C, and B is east of A, but is B east of C by the shortest route?
(47) YES / NO.

Notice that "ancestor of" is transitive in the domain of people, but "father of" is not. Why not?

(48) <u>THE FATHER OF THE FATHER OF X</u>
<u>IS THE GRANDFATHER OF X</u>.

"Different from" may give trouble. It may look transitive. But taking D: different from, we require that for every x, y, and z:

$$(xDy \ \& \ yDz) \rightarrow xDz$$

That is, no matter how we fill in the blanks x, y, and z, we must get something true. Do we have to fill in each occurrence of the blank x with the same name? **(49)** YES / NO. However, *there is no requirement that we fill in the blanks x and z with different names.* So fill in the "x" with "Louis Pasteur" and the "y" with "Madam Curie" and the "z" with "Louis Pasteur." You obtain (fill in) **(50)** *Louis Pasteur* is different from *Madam Curie* and *Madam Curie* is different from *Louis Pasteur* → *Louis Pasteur* is different from *Louis Pasteur* Is the antecedent true? **(51)** YES / NO. Is the consequent true? **(52)** YES / NO. Is the whole conditional true? **(53)** YES / NO. Is "different from" transitive in the domain of people? **(54)** YES / NO.

Using the list 26–37 draw up a list of relations satisfying the following combinations.

		Relation	Domain
(55)	Not reflexive Not symmetric Not transitive.	*Look back to page 231* 28, 34, 36	
(56)	Reflexive only.	37	
(57)	Symmetric only.	35	
(58)	Transitive only.	26, 31, 33	
(59)	Reflexive Symmetric Not transitive.	29	
(60)	Reflexive Transitive Not symmetric.	30, 32	
(61)	Reflexive Symmetric Transitive.	27	

We can use this new list in constructing counterexamples to some argument forms.   Take for instance,

$$(\forall x)(\forall y)(\forall z)((xRy \text{ \& } yRz) \to xRz), \text{ so } (\forall x)(xRx).$$

To show that this is invalid, we need to find a counterexample.   This is an interpretation and a domain in which the premise takes the value **(62)** T / F and the conclusion takes the value **(63)** F / T.

A relation R for which the premise is true is **(64)** TRANSITIVE / REFLEXIVE / SYMMETRIC.   A relation R for which the conclusion takes the value F is **(65)** NOT TRANSITIVE / NOT SYMMETRIC / NOT REFLEXIVE.

Hence, a counterexample will be provided by finding a transitive relation that is not reflexive.   This is provided by 33, for example.   Thus a counter-example is given by:

> Interpretation: ancestor.
> Domain: people.

Using the same method, find counterexamples for the following argument forms.

(66) $(\forall x)(xRx), (\forall x)(\forall y)(xRy \to yRx)$.   *BORN WITHIN FIVE DAY*
So, $(\forall x)(\forall y)(\forall z)((xRy \text{ \& } yRz) \to xRz)$.   *OF THE BIRTHDAY OF.*
Interpretation: ~~different from~~
Domain: ~~objects~~ *(at least two)* *PEOPLE*

(67) $(\forall x)(xRx), (\forall x)(\forall y)(\forall z)((xRy \text{ \& } yRz) \to xRz)$.
So, $(\forall x)(\forall y)(xRy \to yRx)$.
Interpretation: *NO RICHER THAN.*
Domain: *PEOPLE*

Here are some special cases.   At 34 you found that "brother of" is not transitive in the domain of people.   Abel is the brother of Cain, and Cain is the brother of Abel.   If being a brother were transitive, then we require **(68)** ABEL IS THE BROTHER OF ABEL / ABEL IS NOT THE BROTHER OF ABEL.   The first choice is what transitivity requires.   But Abel is not the brother of Abel.   So brotherhood is not transitive *in the domain of people*.   Is it transitive among the domain of the sons of Adam?   **(69)** YES / NO.   However, consider the domain of only sons, that is, sons with no brothers or sisters. Is anyone in this domain the brother of anyone else?   **(70)** YES / NO. Notice, however, that the relation "brother of" is transitive in this domain! Transitivity says that for any x, y, and z **(71)** xRy / $(xRy \text{ \& } yRz) \to xRz$ / $xRy \to yRx$.   What is the antecedent?   **(72)** $(xRy \text{ \& } yRz)$ What is the consequent?   **(73)** xRz .   If R: brother, and the domain is the domain of only sons, is there any way of filling in the blanks in

$$xRy$$

so as to get a true statement? **(74)** YES / NO. Is there any way of filling in the blanks in the antecedent $(xRy \\& yRz)$ so as to get a true statement? **(75)** YES / NO. If the antecedent of a conditional is F, what is the truth value of the conditional? **(76)** T / F. Is there any way of filling in the blanks in

$$(xRy \\& yRz) \to xRz$$

so as to get a false statement, when R: brother and the domain is the domain of only sons? **(77)** YES / NO. Is "brother of" transitive in the domain of only sons? **(78)** YES / NO.

Explain why "brother of" is symmetric in the domain of only sons. The explanation is very similar to our explanation of the fact that this relation is transitive in the domain of only sons. **(79)** _Since the premisses can never be true you can't go from true premisses to false conclusion._

Is "brother of" reflexive in the domain of only sons? **(80)** YES / NO. Give an example of a relation that is transitive and symmetric, but not reflexive.

(81) Interpretation: R: _Brother of_.
(82) Domain: _only sons._

Give an example of a relation which is transitive in one domain but not in another. **(83)** R: _Brother_. Domain where R is transitive: **(84)** _only sons_. Domain where R is not transitive: **(85)** _People_.
Provide a counterexample to the following argument form:

$$(\forall x)(\forall y)(\forall z)((xRy \\& yRz) \to xRz),$$
$$(\forall x)(\forall y)(xRy \to yRz),$$
so, $(\forall x)(xRx).$

(86) Interpretation. R: _Brother of_
(87) Domain: _only sons_

You have just shown that transitivity and symmetry do not imply reflexivity.

29 / Prenex Forms

This chapter obtains some standard results in predicate logic to give more practice in making deductions and to increase your understanding of how quantifiers work.

Check the following assertions that are correct.

(1) _✓_ $Fa \vdash (\exists x)(Fx)$.
(2) _____ $(\exists x)(Fx) \vdash Fa$.
(3) _✓_ $(\forall x)(Fx) \vdash Fa$.
(4) _____ $Fa \vdash (\forall x)(Fx)$.

Provide counterexamples (with interpretation and domain) for the incorrect assertions.

(5) For (2): Interpretation:_F PRESIDENT OF USA_.
PEOPLE Domain:_a BERTRAND RUSSELL_
(6) For (4): Interpretation:_F PRESIDENT OF USA_.
PEOPLE Domain:_a RICHARD NIXON_.

Check the following arguments that are valid.

(7) _✓_ Every logician is a philosopher. Kurt Gödel is a logician. Hence, he is a philosopher.

(8) _____ Some logicians are philosophers. Kurt Gödel is a logician. Hence, he is a philosopher.

(9) _✓_ Kurt Gödel is a logician and a philosopher. So some philosophers are logicians.

(10) _____ Kurt Gödel is a logician and a philosopher.   So every logician is a philosopher.

If there is a deduction of

$$Premises \vdash Fa$$

Then we can assert,

$$Premises \vdash (\forall x)(Fx)$$

where "Fx" is arrived at from "Fa" by replacing every occurrence of "a" by "x," and "x" is a letter not occurring in "F."

The above rule of inference is incorrect.   However, it is correct if a certain restriction is made.   Write out the necessary restriction:

(11) Restriction: _a Doesn't occur in the premises_

(Refer to page 211 if in doubt.)   This restricted rule is called the rule of (12) EXISTENTIAL PREMISE / INSTANTIATION / <u>GENERALIZATION</u> / EXISTENTIAL CONCLUSION.

Write out the restriction needed to make the following rule correct.

If there is a deduction of

$$Fa, Premises \vdash Conclusion$$

Then we can assert,

$$(\exists x)(Fx), Premises \vdash Conclusion$$

where "Fx" is obtained from "Fa" by replacing all occurrences of "a" by "x," and "x" is a letter that does not occur in "Fa."

---

(13) Restriction: _a Doesn't occur in the other premises or conclusion_

The name of this restricted rule is (14) _Existential Premise_

Paraphrase the following statements step by step.

(15) All pacifists despise every general.

$~~~~~~(\forall x)(Px \rightarrow (\forall y)(Gy \rightarrow xDy)).$

(16) Every general despises some pacifist.

$~~~~~~(\forall x)(Gx \rightarrow (\exists y)(Py \,\&\, xDy)).$

You will have obtained:

$$(\forall x)(Px \rightarrow (\forall y)(Gy \rightarrow xDy))$$

and

$$(\forall x)(Gx \rightarrow (\exists y)(Py \,\&\, xDy))$$

A question might arise whether the inside quantifiers "$(\forall y)$" and "$(\exists y)$" could be moved outside the brackets. They can. To see how, it is easiest to change the arrow into a wedge using wedge-arrow equivalence. The basic point is this. Let Q be any statement in which y does not occur, and F any predicate. Then:

$$Q \rightarrow (\exists y)(Fy) \vdash (\exists y)(Q \rightarrow Fy)$$

Deduction:

Let b be some letter not found in Q.

1. $-Q \vdash -Q \vee Fb.$ **(17)** WEAKENING.
2. $~~,,~~ \vdash (\exists y)(-Q \vee Fy).$ **(18)** EXISTENTIAL CONEL.
3. $\vdash -Q \rightarrow (\exists y)(-Q \vee Fy).$ **(19)** CONDITIONAL PROOF
4. $Fb \vdash -Q \vee Fb.$ **(20)** WEAKENING.
5. $~~,,~~ \vdash (\exists y)(-Q \vee Fy).$ **(21)** EXISTENTIAL CONEL.
6. $(\exists y)(Fy) \vdash (\exists y)(-Q \vee Fy).$ **(22)** EXISTENTIAL PREMISE
7. $\vdash (\exists y)(Fy) \rightarrow (\exists y)(-Q \vee Fy).$ **(23)** CONDITIONAL PROOF
8. $\vdash (-Q \vee (\exists y)(Fy)) \rightarrow (\exists y)(-Q \vee Fy).$ Rule of alternatives on 3 and 7.
9. $Q \rightarrow (\exists y)(Fy) \vdash -Q \vee (\exists y)(Fy).$ **(24)** WEDGE ARROW.
10. $~~,,~~ \vdash (\exists y)(-Q \vee Fy).$ Detachment, 8, 9.
11. $~~,,~~ \vdash (\exists y)(Q \rightarrow Fy).$ **(25)** WEDGE ARROW

We use almost exactly the same pattern of deduction to show that

$$(\forall x)(Gx \rightarrow (\exists y)(Py \,\&\, xDy)) \vdash (\forall x)(\exists y)(Gx \rightarrow (Py \,\&\, xDy))$$

The only difference is that we need a few more steps because of the second quantifier "$(\forall x)$." Furnish the reasons for 26–36 and compare with 17–25:

Deduction:

1. $-Ga \vdash -Ga \lor (Pb \,\&\, aDb)$. **(26)** *WEAKENING*.

2. „ $\vdash (\exists y)(-Ga \lor (Py \,\&\, aDy))$. **(27)** *EXISTENTIAL CONCLUSION*

3. $\vdash -Ga \to (\exists y)(-Ga \lor (Py \,\&\, aDy))$. **(28)** *CONDITIONAL PROOF*

4. $Pb \,\&\, aDb \vdash -Ga \lor (Pb \,\&\, aDb)$. **(29)** *WEAKENING*.

5. „ $\vdash (\exists y)(-Ga \lor (Py \,\&\, aDy))$. **(30)** *EXISTENTIAL CONCLUSION*

6. $(\exists y)(Py \,\&\, aDy) \vdash (\exists y)(-Ga \lor (Py \,\&\, aDy))$. **(31)** *EXISTENTIAL PROMISE*

7. $\vdash (\exists y)(Py \,\&\, aDy \to (\exists y)(-Ga \lor (Py \,\&\, aDy))$. **(32)** *CONDITIONAL PROOF*

8. $\vdash (-Ga \lor (\exists y)(Py \,\&\, aDy)) \to (\exists y)(-Ga \lor (Py \,\&\, aDy))$.
   By the rule of alternatives applied to 3 and 7.

9. $(\forall x)(Gx \to (\exists y)(Py \,\&\, xDy)) \vdash Ga \to (\exists y)(Py \,\&\, aDy)$. **(33)** *INSTANTIATION*.

10. „ $\vdash -Ga \lor (\exists y)(Py \,\&\, aDy)$. **(34)** *WEDGE ARROW*.

11. „ $\vdash (\exists y)(-Ga \lor (Py \,\&\, aDy))$.
    Detachment, 8, 10.

12. „ $\vdash (\forall x)(\exists y)(-Gx \lor (Py \,\&\, xDy))$. **(35)** *GENERALIZATION*

13. „ $\vdash (\forall x)(\exists y)(Gx \to (Py \,\&\, xDy))$. **(36)** *WEDGE ARROW*.

(37) Compare 17–25 with 26–36. *SAME EXCEPT FOR STEPS 33 & 35 IN THE LATTER –*

We have seen that so long as y does not occur in Q:

$$Q \to (\exists y)(Fy) \vdash (\exists y)(Q \to Fy).$$

One might guess that if y does not occur in Q:

$$Q \to (\forall y)(Fy) \vdash (\forall y)(Q \to Fy).$$

If we try to imitate steps 17–25 we make fallacious steps. Indicate the mistaken steps in this nondeduction.

1. $-Q \vdash -Q \vee Fb$.   Weakening.
2. „ $\vdash (\forall y)(-Q \vee Fy)$.   Generalization.
3. $\vdash -Q \rightarrow (\forall y)(-Q \vee Fy)$.   Conditional proof.
4. $Fb \vdash -Q \vee Fb$.   Weakening.
5. „ $\vdash (\forall y)(-Q \vee Fy)$.   Generalization.
6. $(\forall y)(Fy) \vdash (\forall y)(-Q \vee Fy)$.   From 5.
7. $\vdash (\forall y)(Fy) \rightarrow (\forall y)(-Q \vee Fy)$.   Conditional proof.
8. $\vdash (-Q \vee (\forall y)(Fy)) \rightarrow (\forall y)(-Q \vee Fy)$.
                                                             From 3 and 7.
9. $Q \rightarrow (\forall y)(Fy) \vdash -Q \vee (\forall y)(Fy)$.   Wedge-arrow.
10. „ $\vdash (\forall y)(-Q \vee Fy)$.   Detachment.
11. „ $\vdash (\forall y)(Q \rightarrow Fy)$.   Wedge-arrow. *5-6 OCCURS IN THE PREMIS*

Which steps are incorrect in the above nondeduction? **(38)** *5-6 - NOT AUTHORIZED*
Does this show that the conclusion is incorrect? **(39)** YES / NO. In
general, we can establish the positive result, that an argument is valid, only
by finding a **(40)** COUNTEREXAMPLE / DEDUCTION, whereas to show that an
argument is invalid we require a **(41)** COUNTEREXAMPLE / DEDUCTION. The
mistakes in proving 11 do not show that 11 is incorrect. Instead of the
incorrect step 5 we can proceed as follows:

4+. $(\forall y)(Fy) \vdash Fb$.   **(42)** *INSTANTIATION*.
5+. „ $\vdash -Q \vee Fb$.   **(43)** *WEAKENING*.
6. „ $\vdash (\forall y)(-Q \vee Fy)$.   **(44)** *GENERALIZATION*.

Is this the same as 6 above? **(45)** YES / NO. Hence, we obtained 6 by 4+
and 5+ instead of by 4 and 5 and the rest of the deduction is correct. We
have corrected the error and achieved a correct deduction.

We saw that if y does not occur in Q:

$$Q \rightarrow (\exists y)(Fy) \vdash (\exists y)(Q \rightarrow Fy).$$

We now show that if y does not occur in Q:

$$(\exists y)(Q \rightarrow Fy) \vdash Q \rightarrow (\exists y)(Fy).$$

In other words the left and right hand sides are **(46)** COUNTEREXAMPLES /
DEDUCTIONS / LOGICALLY EQUIVALENT. As before, let b be any letter not
in Q.

1. $Fb \vdash (\exists y)(Fy)$.   **(47)** *EXISTENTIAL CONCL*
2. „ $\vdash -Q \vee (\exists y)(Fy)$.   **(48)** *WEAKENING*.
3. $\vdash Fb \rightarrow (-Q \vee (\exists y)(Fy))$.   **(49)** *CONDITIONAL PROOF*
4. $-Q \vdash -Q \vee (\exists y)(Fy)$.   **(50)** *WEAKENING*
5. $\vdash -Q \rightarrow (-Q \vee (\exists y)(Fy))$.   **(51)** *CONDITIONAL PROOF*

6. $\vdash (-Q \lor Fb) \to (-Q \lor (\exists y)(Fy))$.   **(52)** ~~ALTERNATIVES 3 & 5~~

7. $Q \to Fb \vdash -Q \lor Fb$.   **(53)** ~~WEDGE ARROW~~

8.   ,, $\vdash -Q \lor (\exists y)(Fy)$.   **(54)** ~~DETACHMENT 6 & 7~~

9. $(\exists y)(Q \to Fy) \vdash -Q \lor (\exists y)(Fy)$.   **(55)** ~~EXISTENTIAL PREMISE~~

10.   ,, $\vdash Q \to (\exists y)(Fy)$.   **(56)** ~~WEDGE ARROW~~

In a similar way we can show that, if y does not occur in **(57)** $F|Q$

$$(\forall y)(Q \to Fy) \vdash Q \to (\forall y)(Fy)$$

Since we have already shown that the right-hand side implies the left-hand side, we conclude that these two are logically **(58)** ~~EQUIVALENT~~ $Q \to (\exists y)(Fy)$ is logically equivalent to **(59)** ~~$(\exists y)(Q \to Fy)$~~ / $(\exists y)(Q \to (\exists y)(Fy))$. So we can bring the quantifier which is directly after the arrow, (and in front of the **(60)** ~~CONSEQUENT~~ / ANTECEDENT / PREMISE / CONCLUSION) out in front of the whole statement. What is $Q \to (\forall y)(Fy)$ equivalent to? **(61)** ~~$(Fy)(Q \to Fy)$~~

Paraphrase:

If every person suffers, then God is evil.
P: person S: suffers Q: God is evil.

(62) ~~$(\forall x)(Px \to Sx) \to Q$~~

Here we obtain a statement of the form;

$$(\forall x)(Fx) \to Q$$

where "Fx" is in turn "$Px \to Sx$." In a statement of the form:

$$(\forall x)(Fx) \to Q$$

the universal quantifier qualifies the **(63)** CONSEQUENT / CONCLUSION / WHOLE STATEMENT / PREMISE / ~~ANTECEDENT.~~ However, we cannot take it out to modify the whole of the statement. That is, we do *not* have a logical equivalence with:

$$(\forall x)(Fx \to Q).$$

To show this, we need to find a counterexample to the argument form:

$$(\forall x)(Fx) \to Q, \text{ so } (\forall x)(Fx \to Q).$$

We want a / an **(64)** DEDUCTION / ~~INTERPRETATION~~ in which the **(65)** ANTECEDENT / ~~PREMISE~~ takes the value **(66)** ~~T~~ and the **(67)** CONSEQUENT / ~~CONCLUSION~~ takes the value **(68)** ~~F~~.

In order to make the premise true, we can, for example, choose an interpretation where the antecedent "$(\forall x)(Fx)$" is (69) TRUE / FALSE, for a conditional is always true when the (70) *ANTECEDENT* is false.

In order to make the conclusion false, we shall require that Q is false. So we could construct an interpretation as follows:

Interpretation: F: fish. Q: The oceans cannot support life.
Domain: The Universe.

Under this interpretation, the premise is:

Everything is a fish → the oceans cannot support life.

This is (71) TRUE / FALSE simply because the antecedent is false.   What is the conclusion $(\forall x)(Fx \to Q)$, under this interpretation?   (72) *IT IS TRUE OF ANYTHING WHAT-SO-EVER, THAT, IF IT IS A FISH, THEN the OCEANS CANNOT SUPPORT LIFE.* We see that the conclusion is false.   For the conclusion of the form "$(\forall x)(x$ is a fish → the oceans cannot support life)" says that any way of filling in the blank marked by "x" with a name or description must be true.   If we replace "x" by "The salmon I had for dinner last night" (which is a description that does, on the day of writing these pages, apply to a definite fish), we get:

The salmon I had for dinner last night is a fish → the oceans cannot support life.

Is this true?   (73) YES / NO.
Here is another counterexample to the invalid argument form:

$(\forall x)(Fx) \to Q$, so $(\forall x)(Fx \to Q)$.

Interpretation: F: is smaller than 15; Q: $2 + 2 = 6$.
Domain: Whole numbers.

Explain why this is a counterexample to the above argument form.

(74) *PREMISE IS TRUE CAUSE ANTECEDENT IS FALSE. BUT CONCLUSION IS FALSE*.

Would this still be a counterexample if the domain consisted of even numbers only?   (75) YES / NO.
Now on your own paper compose your own counterexample.   Notice that the key feature of our examples is that $(\forall x)(Fx)$ comes out false and Q is false, but there is some x for which Fx is true.

Are $(\forall x)(Q \to Fx)$ and $Q \to (\forall x)(Fx)$ logically equivalent?   (76) YES / NO.
Are $(\forall x)(Fx \to Q)$ and $(\forall x)(Fx) \to Q$ logically equivalent?   (77) YES / NO.

Although the answer to the last question is no, we can find a way of putting the quantifier in "$(\forall x)(Fx) \to Q$" out in front. Apply contraposition to:

$$(\forall x)(Fx) \to Q.$$

You arrive at **(78)** $-(\forall x)(Fx) \to -Q$ / $-Q \to (\forall x)(Fx)$ / $\underline{-Q \to -(\forall x)}$ $\underline{(Fx)}$. The last choice is correct. Now apply quantifier equivalence to this answer. You get **(79)** $-Q \to -(\exists x)(Fx)$ / $Q \to (\exists x)-(Fx)$ / $\underline{-Q \to}$ $\underline{(\exists x)-(Fx)}$. Once again the last choice is correct. Now we have a quantifier after an arrow and before **(80)** Fx / Q / $-Fx$ / $\underline{-(Fx)}$. The statement "$-Q \to (\exists x)-(Fx)$" is logically equivalent to **(81)** $(\exists x)(-Q \to Fx)$ / $\underline{(\exists x)(-Q \to -Fx)}$ / $(\forall x)(-Q \to -Fx)$. The choice in the middle is correct. Conclude by applying contraposition again. We obtain:

$$(\exists x)(Fx \to Q)$$

as logically equivalent to $(\forall x)(Fx) \to Q$. When the quantifier is before the antecedent, the "opposite" quantifier qualifies the whole statement!

The reasoning in 78–81 is informal but it is the kind of tinkering that you should be able to do instinctively if you want to understand quantifiers or do more advanced predicate logic. Constructing formal deductions is less important. For the record, however, we should work through a deduction of the above result. For variety, we will prove the corresponding result for the existential quantifier. So long as x does not occur in Q:

$$(\exists x)(Fx) \to Q \vdash (\forall x)(Fx \to Q)$$

Let b be some letter not found in Q.

Deduction:

1.	$-(\exists x)(Fx) \vdash (\forall x)-(Fx).$	**(82)**	*QUANTIFIER EQUIVALENCE*
2.	„ $\vdash -Fb.$	**(83)**	*INSTANTIATION*.
3.	„ $\vdash -Fb \lor Q.$	**(84)**	*WEAKENING*.
4.	$\vdash -(\exists x)(Fx) \to (-Fb \lor Q).$	**(85)**	*CONDITIONAL PROOF*
5.	$Q \vdash -Fb \lor Q.$	**(86)**	*WEAKENING*.
6.	$\vdash Q \to (-Fb \lor Q).$	**(87)**	*CONDITIONAL PROOF*
7.	$\vdash (-(\exists x)(Fx) \lor Q) \to (-Fb \lor Q).$	**(88)**	*ALTERNATIVES*.
8.	$(\exists x)(Fx) \to Q \vdash -(\exists x)(Fx) \lor Q.$	**(89)**	*WEDGE ARROW*.
9.	„ $\vdash -Fb \lor Q.$	**(90)**	*DETACHMENT 7 & 8*
10.	„ $\vdash (\forall x)(-Fx \lor Q).$	**(91)**	*GENERALIZATION*.
11.	„ $\vdash (\forall x)(Fx \to Q).$	**(92)**	*WEDGE ARROW*.

We can also show that:

$$(\forall x)(Fx \to Q) \vdash (\exists x)(Fx) \to Q$$

An expression with *all* the quantifiers in front is said to be in "prenex" form. Thus in the assertion just made, the expression on the **(93)** LEFT / RIGHT of the "⊢" is in prenex form. Is $(\forall x)(Fx \to (\exists x)(Gx))$ in prenex form? **(94)** YES / NO. Give logically equivalent expressions in prenex form for the following, assuming that x does not occur in P or Q.

(95) $(\forall x)(Gx) \to P.$ _(∃x)(Gx → P)_ .
(96) $(\exists x)(Gx) \to (P \lor Q).$ _(∀x)(Gx → (p ∨ q))_ .
(97) $P \to (\exists x)(Fx).$ _(∃x)(p → Fx)_ .
(98) $(P \& Q) \to (\forall x)(Gx).$ _(∀x)((p ∧ q) → Gx)_ .

We can apply the same technique if there are several quantifiers. For example:

$$(\forall x)(Fx) \to (\exists y)(Gy)$$

is equivalent to:

$$(\exists x)(Fx \to (\exists y)(Gy))$$

which is equivalent to:

$$(\exists x)(\exists y)(Fx \to Gy)$$

Find a prenex form for $(\exists x)(Fx) \to (\forall y)(Gy)$:

(99) _(∀x)(∀y)(Fx → Gy)_ .

Warning: Be careful of forms where the same quantifier letter occurs in different places, such as:

$$(\forall x)(Fx) \to (\exists x)(Gx)$$

It would be absurd to change this to

$$(\exists x)(\exists x)(Fx \to Gx).$$

Instead, remember that, for example, $(\exists x)(Gx)$ is equivalent to **(100)** $(\exists x)(Fx)$ / $(\exists y)(Gy)$ / $(\forall x)(Gx)$ and first change $(\forall x)(Fx) \to (\exists x)(Gx)$ to:

$$(\forall x)(Fx) \to (\exists y)(Gy)$$

and then to:

$$(\exists x)(\exists y)(Fx \to Gy)$$

(101) Find a prenex form for: $(\exists x)(Fx) \to (\forall x)(Gx).$ _(∀x)(∀y)(Fx → Gy)_

(102) A really hard exercise: find a prenex form for:

$$(\forall x)(Fx \to Gx) \to ((\forall x)(Fx) \to (\forall x)(Gx)).$$ _(∃x)(∃y)(∀z)(Fx → Gx) → (Fy → Gz)_

30 / Arranging Quantifiers

This final chapter completes your practice in operating with quantifiers and finding counterexamples to invalid arguments.

Usually the order of quantifiers matters. Compare these two statements:

A. Everyone voted for someone or other.
B. There is someone for whom everyone voted.

Do these mean the same? **(1)** YES / NO. The basic difference is the difference in the order of quantifiers:

C. $(\forall x)(\exists y)(xVy)$.
D. $(\exists y)(\forall x)(xVy)$.

In the domain of people, or citizens, or whatever, statement A is an interpretation of **(2)** C / D and B is an interpretation of D. If there is someone for whom everyone voted, did everyone vote for someone or other? **(3)** YES / NO. If everyone voted for someone or other, does it follow that there is someone whom everyone voted for? **(4)** YES / NO.

Hence, **(5)** A IMPLIES B BUT B DOES NOT IMPLY A / B IMPLIES A BUT A DOES NOT IMPLY B. This leads one to expect that one of the following argument forms is valid, and the other is invalid. Cross out the invalid one.

~~**(6)** $(\forall x)(\exists y)(xVy)$ so $(\exists y)(\forall x)(xVy)$.~~
(7) $(\exists y)(\forall x)(xVy)$ so $(\forall x)(\exists y)(xVy)$.

Statement 7 is correct, that is, $(\exists y)(\forall x)(xVy) \vdash (\forall x)(\exists y)(xVy)$.

245

Deduction:

1. $(\forall x)(xVb) \vdash aVb$.
2.   „ $\vdash (\exists y)(aVy)$.
3.   „ $\vdash (\forall x)(\exists y)(xVy)$.
4. $(\exists y)(\forall x)(xVy) \vdash (\forall x)(\exists y)(xVy)$.

(8) *INSTANTIATION* .
(9) *EXISTENTIAL CONCLUSION*
(10) *GENERALIZATION* .
(11) *EXISTENTIAL PREMISE*

One might try to find a deduction for the incorrect assertion:

$$(\forall x)(\exists y)(xVy) \vdash (\exists y)(\forall x)(xVy)$$

(12) Indicate the errors in this nondeduction:

1. $(\forall x)(\exists y)(xVy) \vdash (\exists y)(aVy)$.   Instantiation.
2.   „ $\vdash (\exists y)(\forall x)(xVy)$.   Generalization on 1. ✔

QUANTIFYER SHOULD $(\forall x)(\exists y)(xVy)$
BE OUTSIDE

(13) Indicate the errors in this nondeduction:

1. $aVb \vdash (\forall x)(xVb)$.   Generalization. ✔ (*A IS IN THE PREMISES*)
2.   „ $\vdash (\exists y)(\forall x)(xVy)$.   Existential conclusion, 1.
3. $(\exists y)(aVy) \vdash (\exists y)(\forall x)(xVy)$.   Existential premise, 2.
4. $\vdash (\exists y)(aVy) \rightarrow (\exists y)(\forall x)(xVy)$.   Conditional proof, 3.
5. $(\forall x)(\exists y)(xVy) \vdash (\exists y)(aVy)$.   Instantiation.
6. $\vdash (\exists y)(\forall x)(xVy)$.   Detachment, 4, 5.

Although there are errors in the nondeductions above, does our failure to find a correct deduction show that the assertion:

$$(\forall x)(\exists y)(xVy) \vdash (\exists y)(\forall x)(xVy)$$

is false? **(14)** YES / NO.   In order to refute this assertion we need to invent a **(15)** *COUNTER EX.* .   This is easy.

Interpretation: V: voted for.
Domain: all persons who voted for a candidate in the last presidential election.

In this domain, it is true that everyone voted for someone or other, but false that there is any one person for whom everyone voted.   So in this domain, under this interpretation, we have a premise that is **(16)** T / F and a conclusion that is **(17)** T / F.   Hence, the argument form is **(18)** VALID / INVALID.

Another interpretation will remind us of the importance of the domain in the counterexample.

Interpretation: V: equals.
Domain: Whole numbers.

In this domain, the premise is true; for any whole number, we can find a whole number (namely, itself) that it equals.   But there is no whole number equal to every whole number, so the conclusion is **(19)** TRUE / FALSE.

However, suppose that the domain was the whole number 2 only.   In this domain, is the premise true?   **(20)** YES / NO.   In this domain, is the conclusion true?   **(21)** YES / NO.   Hence, using the interpretation, V: equals, and the domain consisting of the number 2 only, we **(22)** WOULD / WOULD NOT get a counterexample.   The domain matters.

When we were studying truth tables, we said that two expressions were *consistent* if **(23)** THEY WERE BOTH TRUE UNDER EVERY COMBINATION OF TRUTH VALUES / THEY TOOK THE VALUE T IN EVERY ROW IN THE TRUTH TABLE / THEY BOTH TOOK THE VALUE T AT SOME ROW IN THE TRUTH TABLE.

Statements are consistent if they can all be true at once.   We can use the same idea in predicate logic: we have consistency if we can find some interpretation, and some domain, where all the statements in question are true.

Take for example the statement schemes we have just looked at:

$$(\forall x)(\exists y)(xVy)$$

and

$$(\exists y)(\forall x)(xVy)$$

To show these are consistent, we need an interpretation and domain in which

(24) ONE IS TRUE / BOTH ARE TRUE / BOTH ARE FALSE.

Can you find such an interpretation and domain?   (If necessary, refer back to 21 and 22 above.)

(25)   Interpretation: ___*V - EQUALS*___.
   Domain: ___*THE NUMBER 2*___.

Show that the following pairs or triplets of statement schemes are consistent.   If necessary, refresh your memory by looking back at Chapter 28.

$$(\forall x)(xRx). \quad (\forall x)(\forall y)(xRy \rightarrow yRx)$$

(26)   Interpretation: ___*R = EQUALS*___.
   Domain: ___*WHOLE NUMBERS —*___.

$$-(\forall x)(xRx). \quad -(\forall x)(\forall y)(\forall z)((xRy \ \& \ yRz) \rightarrow xRz)$$

(27)   Interpretation: *R = LOOKS*___.
   Domain: ___*PEOPLE —*___.

$(\forall x)(\forall y)(\forall z)((xRy \,\&\, yRz) \rightarrow xRz).$ $(\forall x)(xRx).$ $-(\forall x)(\forall y)(xRy \rightarrow yRx)$

(28) Interpretation: _Taller Than or Equal Height_
Domain: _People ._

Statements that are not consistent are called *inconsistent*. If we find an interpretation and domain in which some statement schemes are all true, we know these schemes are **(29)** CONSISTENT / INCONSISTENT. But suppose we do not hit on any such interpretation. Can we infer that the schemes are inconsistent? **(30)** YES / NO.

The situation here is like testing for validity. When we have no decision procedure, a positive proof of validity is given by a **(31)** COUNTEREXAMPLE / DEDUCTION whereas the negative result of invalidity is given by a **(32)** _Counter Example_ In testing for consistency we have the reverse situation. If we can get an example where all statements are true, we have the positive result of consistency. But if we fail to find such an interpretation, we cannot infer inconsistency. Inconsistency can in general only be shown *by deducing a contradiction*.

We deduce a contradiction from some set of statements or statement schemes when we can deduce both P and $-P$ from this set, for some statement P. For a simple example, take the pair:

$$(\forall x)(Fx), \; (\exists x)-(Fx)$$

We have:

$$(\exists x)-(Fx) \vdash -(\forall x)(Fx)$$

by quantifier equivalence. Hence, we have both:

$$(\forall x)(Fx), \; (\exists x)-(Fx) \vdash (\forall x)(Fx)$$

and

$$(\forall x)(Fx), \; (\exists x)-(Fx) \vdash -(\forall x)(Fx)$$

So there is some statement, namely, "$(\forall x)(Fx)$" such that we can deduce both it and its negation from this pair. Hence, the pair is **(33)** CONSISTENT / INCONSISTENT.

Here is another inconsistent pair:

$$(\exists y)(\forall x)(xVy)$$
$$-(\forall x)(\exists y)(xVy)$$

We know these are inconsistent, because at 8–11 we deduced:

$$(\exists y)(\forall x)(xVy) \vdash (\forall x)(\exists y)(xVy)$$

Hence, we have both:

$$(\exists y)(\forall x)(xVy), \; -(\forall x)(\exists y)(xVy) \vdash (\forall x)(\exists y)(xVy)$$

and

$$(\exists y)(\forall x)(xVy), \; -(\forall x)(\exists y)(xVy) \vdash \; -(\forall x)(\exists y)(xVy)$$

Thus whereas validity is shown by **(34)** COUNTEREXAMPLE / DEDUCTION and invalidity is shown by **(35)** _Counterexample,_ consistency is shown by giving an interpretation in which all members of the consistent set are **(36)** _True_, and inconsistency is shown by **(37)** _Deducing a contra-diction_. Validity and consistency are thus closely related. Two statements P and Q are inconsistent if we can deduce $-Q$ from P. If the argument, P so $-Q$, is valid, the pair **(38)** "P, Q" / "$-P, Q$" / "$P, -Q$" is inconsistent.

The relation between consistency and validity turns up even in truth tables. If the argument P so $-Q$ is truth functionally valid, then there is no row in the truth table where P is **(39)** _T_ and $-Q$ is **(40)** _F_. Hence, there is no row where P is **(41)** _T_ and Q is **(42)** _T_. Hence the pair (P, Q) is inconsistent.

Answers

Chapter 1 *Statements and Arguments*

1–5. Use your own judgment to answer. "T" or "F" or "T or F."
6. Neither true nor false.
7. No.
8. No.
9. Either true or false.
10. Statement.
11. Neither true nor false.
12–16. Numbers 12 and 15 are statements.
17. T.
18. F.
19. T.
20. F.
21. Argue.
22. Reasons.
23. One.
24. No. (Or so most people would say.)
25. Reason.
26. Conclusion.
27. Premises.
28. Premises.
29. Conclusion.
30. The Oakley reservoir is not the best choice.
31. So.
32. We should hurry to accept the alternative.
33. Yes.
34. So.
35. Many black citizens . . . community.
36. Therefore.
37. No.
38. After.
39. End.
40. The last first-rate president this country had was Calvin Coolidge.
41. For.
42. The Russians . . . missiles.
43. Because.
44. Since.
45. There is a difference between the two substances.
46. End.
47. C.
48. P.

49. P.
50. P.
51. C.
52. C.
53. Conclusion.
54. The valor . . . debacle.
55. Statement.
56. No.
57. The pay . . . work.
58. Yes.
59. The bottom lands are not valuable.
60. Yes.
61. It is important . . . and not to flood them.
62. Yes.
63. No conclusion.
64. No.
65. No conclusion.
66. No.
67. The decision . . . surveillance.
68. Yes.
69. There seems . . . births.
70. Yes.
71. Beginning.

Chapter 2   *Criticizing Arguments*

1. Would not.
2. Making a request.
3. Giving an order.
4. Would not.
5. Statement.
6. False.
7. Are not.
8. Statement.
9. Reason.
10. Conclusion.
11. Premise.
12. A, B.
13. C.
14. B.
15. C.
16. A. F.; B. T.; C. F.
17. Yes.   A is F.
18. At least one of the premises is F.
19. A. F.; D. T.; E. T.
20. A.
21. At least one premise is F.
22. F.

23. T.
24. Kennedy.
25. False.
26. Unconvincing.
27. Statements.
28. True, false.
29. True, false.
30. False.
31. True.
32. False.
33. Criticizing.
34. A. T.; B. T.; C. F.
35. No.
36. Cannot.
37. Unconvincing.
38. True.
39. Does not.
40. Would not.
41. Cannot.
42. False.
43. Follow from.
44. False.
45. Does not.
46. A.
47. B.
48. The second premise is false, and the conclusion does not follow from the premises.
49. Bad.
50. True.
51. True.
52. Yes.
53. No.
54. No.
55. Yes (in the opinion of most people).
56. Yes.
57. Yes.
58. Yes.
59. No.
60. No.
61. Beginning.
62. Yes.
63. No.
64. No.
65. Circle A and D.
66. A. T, T, T.
     B. T, T, T.
     C. F, T, F.
     D. F, T, F.
67. Yes.

68. True.
69. Does not.
70. True.
71. True.
72. True.
73. C, D.
74. B, C.
75. A, B.
76. A.
77. Two.
78. One.
79. Can.
80. Did not.
81. Did.
82. Need.
83. Don't need.
84. Is not.
85. Do.
86. Do not.
87. Logic.
88. Follows.
89. False.
90. Isn't.
91. Premises.
92. Valid.
93. Is.
94. Beginning.
95. T.
96. T.
97. Does.
98. Astronomy.
99. Do not.
100. Beginning.
101. T.
102. Do.
103. Could.
104. Logic.

Chapter 3 *Logical Form*

1. Statements.
2. True or false.
3. Valid or invalid.
4. Follows from.
5. Imply.
6. Imply.
7. Follows from.

8. Infer.
9. Follows from.
10. Imply.
11. Infer.
12. Beginning.
13–21. Put an × in front of 13, 14, 16, 19, 20.
22. Imply.
23. Infer.
24. True.
25. Valid.
26. Premises.
27. Conclusion.
28. False.
29. Religion.
30. Astronomy.
31. American social problems.
32. Imply.
33. Logic.
34. Yes.
35. Infer.
36. (You know best.)
37. (You know best.)
38. Yes.
39. A long-necked animal.
40. Mammals.
41. Catholic priests, unmarried men
42. Bertrand Russell, philosopher who lived to be over 97.
43. E.
44. Bertrand Russell.
45. Monkey, mammal.
46. Giraffe, long-necked animal.
47. Name: Bertrand Russell.
    Terms: Philosopher jailed in World War I for pacifism, logician.
48. *a, d, c, b.*
49. Monkeys.
50. Mammals.
51. Athens.
52. Plato, Descartes, Confucius, etc.
53. All farmers are greedy.
    Adolph is a farmer.
    So, Adolph is greedy.
54. Yes.
55–61. Check: 57, 60, 61.
62. Is not.
63. Do.
64. For example: All managers of this company are despicable people.
65. For example: All sodium salts are substances that burn with a yellow flame.
66. For example: All the consultants are courageous people.
67. For example: All candidates are liars.

68. For example: All people who know him are people who like him.

69. For example: All actions as courageous as that are actions that deserve some sort of reward.

70. All exercises are things that bore me.

Chapter 4 *Some Forms of Argument*

1. All far away hot bodies are galaxies.
Arcturus is a far away hot body.
So, Arcturus is a galaxy.

2. Yes.

3. Planets of the sun.

4. Planets that are at least as big as the earth.

5. Mars.

6. No.

7. No.

8. Yes.

9. No.

10. Imply.

11. No.

12. No.

13. Invalid.

14. Cannot.

15. Can.

16. Interpretation.

17. Invalid.

18. False.

19. Invalid.

20. D.

21. For example, take: F: men, G: women, a: Hefner.

22. For example, take: F: people, G: men, a: Hefner.

23. Counterexample.

24. Some large cities are cities where shooting seldom occurs.
Chicago is a large city.
So, Chicago is a city where shooting seldom occurs.

25. False.

26. Counterexample.

27. For example: F: women, G: men, a: Hefner.

28. For example: F: men, G: women, a: Hefner.

29. For example: F: men, G: people, a: Hefner.

30. F.

31. T.

32. T.

33. T.

34. T.

35. F.

36. T.

37. F.
38. T.
39. F.
40. Truth.
41. Falsehood.
42. "*F*" and "*G*" are interchanged in one premise and the conclusion.
43. A.
44. All Wall Street stockbrokers are people with offices in New York.
    U Thant is a person with offices in New York.
    So, U Thant is a Wall Street stockbroker.
45. True.
46. False.
47. Counterexample.
48. True.
49. False.
50. For example: All women are people. Hugh Hefner is a person. So, Hugh Hefner is a woman.
51. Anarchists in Cleveland.
52. Members of the *ad hoc* committee on urban reform.
53. J. B. Baxter.
54. The last two are invalid.
55. Middle.
56. Statements made in Russian newspapers.
57. Statements that are false and asserted only for propaganda.
58. The statement in question.
59. Valid.
60. All *F* are *G*.
    a is *F*.
    So, *a* is *G*.
61. Follow from.
62. Invalid.
63. True.
64. Invalid argument.
65. Premise D is false.
66. True.
67. Invalid.
68. All *F* are *G*.
    a is *F*.
    So, *a* is *G*.
69. Valid.
70. No.
71. For example, *F*: American astronauts, *G*: Men, *H*: Women, *a*: The Queen of England.
72. In the example given in (71) All American astronauts are men. The Queen of England is a woman. So, the Queen of England is a man.
73. False.
74. Valid.
75. True.
76. Invalid.

Chapter 5 *Drawing Statements (I)*

1. Interpretation.
2. True.
3. False.
4. Invalid.
5. No.
6. False.
7. Is not.
8. Farmers.
9. Greedy.
10. Greedy people who are *not* farmers.
11. Farmers.
12. Greedy.
13. 2.
14. 3.
15. Empty.
16. 2.
17. 3.
18. 2.
19. No.
20. No.
21. 1.
22. 3.
23. More.
24. 2.
25. C.   No greedy people are farmers.
26. No.
27. Information.
28. Information.
29. 2.
30. Yes.
31. C.
32. The same.
33. Information.
34. Logically equivalent.
35. Logically equivalent.
36. G.
37. I.
38. II.
39. III.
40. I.
41. III.
42. II.
43. II.
44. I.
45. II.
46. I.
47. Good to eat.

48. Fresh meat.
49. II.
50. All *G* are *F*.
51. Logically equivalent.
52. All faithful husbands are gullible people.
53. All gullible people are faithful husbands.
54. (b), (c).
55. (a), (d).
56. (e), (f).
57. (e), (f).
58.

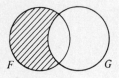

59. All *F* are *G*.
60. Deserving.
61. Members of this church, communicants.
62. Good leaders, decisive.
63. A.
64. Is not.
65. All people whom he trusts are people under 30.
66. All people eligible for this scholarship are children of missionaries.
67. All masters of yoga are relaxed.
68. All children rejected by their mothers are children who develop neurotic traits during adolescence.
69. All vehicles allowed on this path are bicycles.
70. The same as 69.
71. The same as 69.
72. All rock bands are audible things.
73.

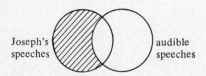

74. All Joseph's speeches are audible.
75. No.
76. False.
77. All trustworthy people are responsible people.
78. F.
79. T.
80. F.
81. F.

Chapter 6   *Drawing Statements (II)*

1.

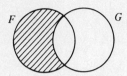

2.

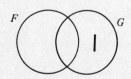

3. No.
4. Crossed out.
5. Empty.
6. Empty.
7. Empty.
8. No *F* are *G*.
9. Some *F* are *G*.
10. Nothing.
11. Something.
12. Different.
13. *G*.
14. Information.
15. *F*.
16. *G*.
17. *G*.
18. Equivalent.
19. Is not.
20. Some *G* are not *F*.
21. Putting a bar in.
22.

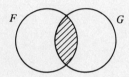

23. Some students will fail.
24. No.
25. Are.

26. Putting a bar in.

27–39. Cross out 31 and 34.

40.

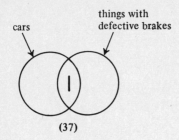

(37)

41.

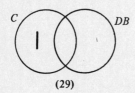

(29)

42.

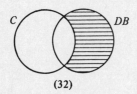

(32)

43. VI.

44. I.

45. IV.

46. V.

47. VI.

48. V.

49. III.

50. IV.

51. V.

52. III.

53. II.

54. IV.

55. II.

56. I, IV.

57. Some cooperative people are not teachers.

58. Some teachers are cooperative people, or some cooperative people are teachers.

59.

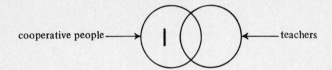

cooperative people ⟶ teachers

60. No.
61. Information.
62.

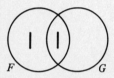

F G

63.

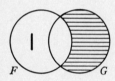

F G

64. Is.
65. Nothing.
66. Cannot.
67. Cannot.
68. Inconsistent.
69.

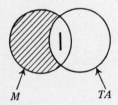

M TA

70. Yes.
71.

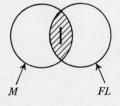

M FL

72. No.

73.

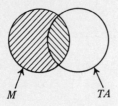

M   TA

74. Yes.
75. Mice.
76. There are no mice.
77. Can.
78. Unicorns.
79. Not any.
80. Consistent.
81. *F.*
82. Inconsistent.
83. Is not.
84. Does not.

Chapter 7   *Venn Diagrams*

1. False.
2. Invalid.
3. False.
4. Invalid.
5. Is.
6. Follows.
7. True.
8. Yes.
9. Yes.
10. Yes.
11. Yes.
12. Yes.
13. Yes.
14. No.
15. Interpretation.
16. Premises.
17. Conclusion.
18. Counterexample.
19. Invalid.
20. No.

21. A, C, and D are invalid.
22. Two.
23. Farmers.
24. Greedy people.
25. Two.
26. Greedy people.
27. Hungry people.
28. Three.
29. Farmers.
30. Greedy people.
31. Hungry people.
32. Two.
33. Three.
34. Information.
35. Eight.
36. Four.
37. Twice as many.
38. C.
39. 2, 5.
40. D.
41. Greedy people.
42. Greedy people who are not farmers.
43. Hungry.
44. Inside.
45. Inside.
46. Outside.
47. Greedy.
48. Hungry.
49. 5.
50. 2.
51. 4.
52. 1.
53. 6.
54. 3.
55. 7.
56. 8.
57. Eight.
58–63. Cross out 58, 61, 62, 63.
64.

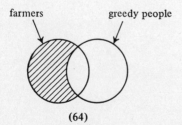

(64)

65.

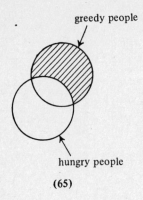

greedy people

hungry people

(65)

66.

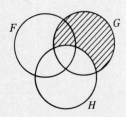

67. The left-hand diagram should be:

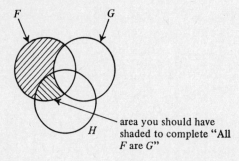

area you should have
shaded to complete "All
F are *G*"

68. II.
69. I.
70.

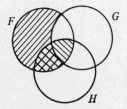

71.

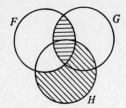

72.

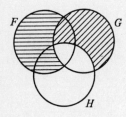

73. 1, 2, 3, and 4.
74. Empty.
75. Empty.
76. 1.
77. 2.
78. Already.
79. Already.
80. Valid.
81. Valid.
82. 2, 5, 6, 7.
83. Failures, guaranteed success, but not heart transplants.
84. Failures, guaranteed success and heart transplants.
85. Guaranteed success, heart transplants, but not failures.
86. Heart transplants, not failures, and not guaranteed success.
87. Empty.
88. 5.
89. 6.
90. Already.
91. Valid.
92.

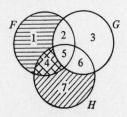

93. 1.
94. 2.
95. No.
96. 1, 4, 7.
97. 2.
98. Invalid.
99. Valid.

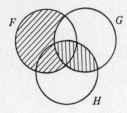

100. Invalid.

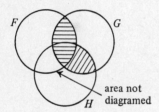

101. Valid.

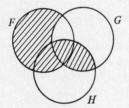

102. Valid.

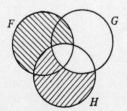

103. Valid.

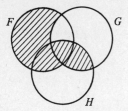

104. Invalid.

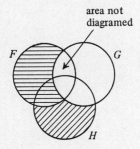

Chapter 8   *Valid Syllogisms*

1. Three.
2. Diagrams.
3. Valid.
4. Invalid.
5. Blank.
6. No.
7. Information.
8. Information.
9. Premises.
10. No more.
11. Contained in.
12. True.
13. True.
14. Valid.
15. False.
16. Contained in.
17. Contained in.
18. True.
19. Information.
20. Interpretation.
21. True.
22. False.
23. Invalid.

24. Is not.
25. Counterexample.
26.

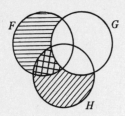

27. No.
28. 6.
29. 7.
30. 7.
31. 6.
32. Yes.
33. No.
34. Counterexample.
35. Invalid.
36. Conclusion.
37. Premises.
38. Incorrect.
39. True.
40. False.
41. Invalid.
42. Invalid.
43. No.
44. Procedure.
45. Decision procedure.
46. Decision procedure.
47. All *F* are *G.*
48. Some *F* are *G.*
49. No *F* are *G.*
50. Some *F* are not *G.*
} in any order.
51. More than.
52. Incorrect.
53. Valid.
54. F.
55. T.
56. T.
57. F.
58. F.
59. T.
60. V.
61. II.
62. III.

63. I.
64. VIII.
65. V.
66. VIII.
67. IV.
68. No.
69. No.
70. Yes.
71. *G*.
72. *F*.
73. *G*.
74. *H*.
75. Wrong.
76. 5.
77. *F*.
78. *G*.
79. *H*.
80. Some *F* are *G*.
81. More.
82. Is not.
83. Some *F* are *G* and *H*.
84.

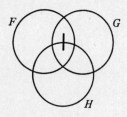

85. Yes.
86. Yes.
87. Cuts.
88. 1.
89. 4.
90. No.
91. *H*.
92. IV.
93. I.
94. II.
95. III.
96. I.
97. II.
98. III.
99. I.
100. II.
101. I.

102. 4.

103. 5.

104. 4.

105. Either 4 or 5.

106. There is nothing in 4.

107. 5.

108. 4.

109. 5.

110. 5.

111. 5.

112. 6.

113. 5.

114. Valid.

115. 4.

116. 5.

117. 4.

118. No.

119. Invalid.

120. 1.

121. 2.

122. 2.

123. 5.

124. 5.

125. 2.

126. Valid.

127. 4.

128. 7.

129. 6.

130. 7.

131. Is not.

132. Invalid.

133. Invalid, because we cannot be sure there is anything common to F and H. We know there is something in 5 *or* 6, but do not know there is something in 5.

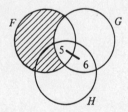

Counterexample.   Let F: husbands; G: men; H: bachelors.

    All husbands are men.

    Some men are bachelors.

    So, some husbands are bachelors.

The premises are T, the conclusion F.

134. Valid.

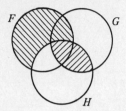

135. Invalid.   To get a counterexample, you could use the *F*, *G*, and *H* of 133 again.

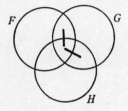

136. Invalid.   Same as 135.

137. Invalid.   Counterexample.   Let *F*: husbands; *G*: married people; *H*: men.

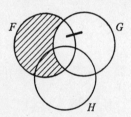

Chapter 9   *Review with Applications*

  1. False.
  2. Valid.
  3. Invalid.
  4. Can.
  5. True.
  6. True.
  7. False.
  8. True.
  9. True.
10. False.
11. Invalid.
12. Interpretation.
13. True.

14. False.
15. Does not.
16. Venn diagrams.
17. Conclusion.
18. Diagramed.
19. Contained in.
20. Premises.
21. Correct.
22. All *G* are *F*.
23. (c).
24. (b).
25. (e).
26. (a).
27. (c).
28. (a).
29. (a).
30. (a).
31. (a).
32. (b).
33. Conclusion.
34. Invalid.

      All *M* are *P*.
      No *M* are *C*.
      So, no *P* are *C*.

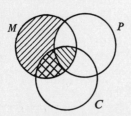

      Counterexample: Let *M*: Men, *P*: People, and *C*: Women, obtaining,
      All men are people.
      No men are women.
      So, no people are women.

35. Valid.

      Only *B* are *C* = All *C* are *B*.
      Some *R* are not *B*.
      So, some *R* are not *C*.

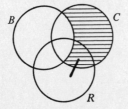

36. Valid.

   All *G* are *C*.
   All *C* are *P*.
   So, all *G* are *P*.

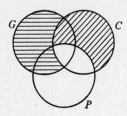

37. Invalid.

   Some *T* are not *P*.
   Some not *P* are D = Some *D* are not *P*.
   So, some *T* are *D*.

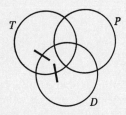

Counterexample: *T*: Men, *P*: Teachers, *D*: Women.
   Some men are not teachers.
   Some people who are not teachers are women.
   So, some men are women.

38. Invalid.

   No *A* are *E*.
   Some *M* are *A*.
   So, no *M* are *E*.

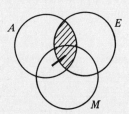

Counterexample: Let *A*: Cats, *E*: Dogs, *M*: Pets.

Chapter 10   *Compound Statements*

1. The conclusions are:
   A. This newspaper is lying.
   B. That many people were slaughtered at that time.
   C. He is at home.
   D. Lydia is in Lincoln Park.
2. C.
3. D.
4. B.
5. A.
6. Yes.
7. Yes.
8. Yes.
9. Yes.
10. All the premises.
11. Invalid.
12. False.
13. True.
14. Different from.
15. Statements.
16. Something different from.
17. G.
18. either . . . or.
19. E, F.
20. The ministers were obviously wary about the North Atlantic Alliance taking on the task of creating better human environments, ⟨and⟩ some ministers feared that Mr. Nixon's other two ideas might undercut the Permanent Council.
21. Compound.
22. Compound.
23. Check: b, d.
24. The communique reflects some of the President's thoughts on Nato's future, ⟨but⟩ it does not immediately accept any of his three ideas for additional alliance machinery.
25. ⟨If⟩ the faculty refuses to speak out plainly on this issue of the original humiliation of the university, ⟨then⟩ it will be forever unable to defend the principle of the peaceful settlement of disputes.
26+. Our lives will be terminated by attack from outside ⟨or⟩ our lives will be terminated by revolution from within.
27. Is not.
28. Check: a, g.
29. The Army has an overriding concern for the preservation of discipline, ⟨but⟩ the employment of McCarthy-type tactics will command no respect.
30. The blacks in this country have many grievances that are not removed by peaceful debate, ⟨and⟩ even at Columbia there were appalling stupidities that no amount of polite discourse seemed to change.
31. Only ⟨if⟩ the government is responsive to citizen protest will such discussions have any effect.   The other component is: "Such discussions will have any

effect." (Remember, everything you call a component must be a statement capable of standing on its own. The expression, "will such discussions have any effect" is *not* a statement.)

32. For decades men have used the oceans ⟨and⟩ the navigable waters as free dumping grounds. The other component is: "For decades men have used the navigable waters as free dumping grounds."

33. The bill makes the owner or operator liable for up to $10 million. The other component is: "The bill makes the operator liable for up to $10 million."

34. Connective.

35. Compound.

36. Component.

37. Statement.

38. Compound.

39. Component.

40. Component.

41. Connective.

42. Component.

43. Statement.

44. The first has "not" in it and says the opposite of the second.

45. Denials.

46. Compound.

47. The imposition of Neanderthal disciplinary practices is going to command the respect of the educated young men needed to man a modern army.

48. Compound.

49. Shall.

50. Yes.

51. G.

52. E.

53. G.

54. Isn't.

55. No.

56. Yes.

57. It is not true that there are military programs . . . (or, there are no military programs . . .)

58. Base components.

59. Connectives: but, not.
    Components: The army . . . discipline.
    The imposition . . . is going to . . . army.

60. Connectives: It is not true that, or.
    Components: He can complain of lack of freedom at Harvard.
    He can complain of abuse . . . at Harvard.

61. Connectives: if, not.
    Components: Every organic species naturally procreates its kind at so high a rate that the earth would soon be covered by the progeny of a single pair.
    Second component: Most of its members were destroyed.

62. Connectives: and, not, even, literally.

Components: Slow breeding man has doubled in 25 years. At this rate, in less
than 1,000 years there would be standing room for his progeny.

Chapter 11 *"And," "Or," and "Not"*

1. Or.
2. Joseph is at home.
3. Joseph is in his office.
4. Not.
5. Joseph is at home.
6. In Lincoln Park.
7. The same as.
8. He will spend 5 years in jail or he will pay $10,000 fine.
   He will not spend 5 years in jail.
   So, he will pay $10,000 fine.
9. Or, not.
10. False.
11. True.
12. Truth value.
13. F.
14. T.
15. Opposite to.
16. F.
17. F.
18. T.
19. F.
20. T.
21. $-Q$.
22.

P	$-P$
T	F
F	T

23. Or.
24. Yes.
25. Yes.
26. Yes.
27. No.
28. P or Q but not both.
29. No.
30. Two.
31. P or Q but not both.
32. Includes.
33. Excludes.
34. Exclusive.
35. P or Q or both.
36. P or Q or both.
37. Vel.
38. P or Q or both.
39. Not.

40. Wedge.
41. Inclusive sense of "or."
42. Or.
43. Joseph is a swimmer.
    Joseph is a runner.
44. Yes.
45. Yes.
46. Yes.
47. No.
48. Inclusive.
49. Four.
50. True.
51. Both.
52. Yes.
53. Yes.
54. Yes.
55. No.
56. F.
57. F.
58. Fourth.
59. F.
60. F.
61. T.
62. T.
63. T.
64. F.
65. T.
66. F.
67. T.
68. T.
69. F.
70. F.
71. F.
72. Only.
73. The builders will use reinforced concrete, or the building will collapse during the earthquake.
74. Does not.
75. Possibility.
76. F.
77. T.
78. Do not.
79. Does.
80. Possibility.
81. F.
82. F.
83. Does not.
84. Four.
85. Joseph has a good job.
    Joseph has a pretty wife.

86. No.
87. No.
88. Yes.
89. F.
90. 1.
91. F.
92. Or.
93. Not.
94. And.
95. 1.
96. T.
97. Only.
98. T.
99. F.
100. F.
101. F.
102. T.
103. F.
104. Does not.
105. Does.
106. F.
107. T.
108. F.
109. T.
110. F.
111. F.
112. T.
113. F.

114.

P	Q	$P \vee Q$	$P \& Q$	$-P$	$-Q$
T	T	T	T	F	F
T	F	T	F	F	T
F	T	T	F	T	F
F	F	F	F	T	T

115. He is rich or strong.

116. He is rich and strong.

117.

P	Q	$P \vee Q$	$Q \vee P$	$P \& Q$	$Q \& P$
T	T	T	T	T	T
T	F	T	T	F	F
F	T	T	T	F	F
F	F	F	F	F	F

118. No.
119. Does not.

120. No.
121. Does not.
122. $P \lor Q$.
123. "But."
124. "And."
125. The same.
126. Ampersand.

Chapter 12 *Truth Tables*

1. $P \lor Q$.
   $-P$.
   So, Q.
2. Valid.
3. True.
4. Invalid.
5. Decision procedure.
6. Joe is at home and not in his office.
7. Possibility.
8. F.
9. T.
10. Joe is not at home, and he is in his office.
11. F.
12. F.
13. Joe is not at home, and he is not in his office.
14. T.
15. F.
16. No.
17. No.
18. Yes.
19. No.
20. Third.
21. F.
22. Yes.
23. Yes.
24. One.
25. T.
26. Yes.
27. T.
28. F.
29. Valid.

30.

P	Q	$P \lor Q$	$-Q$	P
T	T	T	F	T
T	F	T	T	T
F	T	T	F	F
F	F	F	T	F

31. Yes.
32. 1, 2.
33. No.
34. Yes.
35. No.
36. The argument form "$P \lor Q, -Q$, so P" is valid.
37. Yes.
38. Yes.
39. No.
40. No.
41.

P	Q	$P \lor Q$	Q	$-P$
T	T	T	T	F
T	F	T	F	F
F	T	T	T	T
F	F	F	F	T

42. No.
43. B.
44. The argument form "P or Q, P, so $-Q$" is not valid.
45. The connectives of the statement $-P \lor Q$ are: $-$, $\lor$.
46. P.
47. Q.
48. $-P$.
49. $-Q$.
50. $-P$.
51. $-Q$.
52. $-P$.
53. Q.
54. Both alternatives are false.
55. F.
56. T.
57. No.
58. T.
59. Both alternatives are false.
60. $-P$.
61. Q.
62. 2.
63. No.
64–66. 64 and 66 are correct. 65 is not, because in row 4, premises are T, but P is F.

P	Q	$-P$	$-P \lor Q$	P	Q	$-Q$	$P \lor -Q$	P	$-P$	$-Q$	$-P \lor -Q$	Q	$-P$
T	T	F	T	T	T	F	T	T	F	F	F	T	F
T	F	F	F	T	F	T	T	T	F	T	T	F	F
F	T	T	T	F	T	F	F	F	T	F	T	T	T
F	F	T	T	F	F	T	T	F	T	T	T	F	T

67. Yes.
68. No.
69. Different.
70. The same.
71. Bar.
72. $-P$.
73. $--P$.
74. No.
75. Yes.
76. No.
77. Yes.
78–83. Check as correct: 79, 80, 81.
84. Q.
85. $-Q$.
86. Q.
87. $P \lor Q$.
88–93. Check as correct: 88, 89, 90, 93.
94. Yes.
95. Cannot.
96. Invalid.

97.

P	Q	$P \lor Q$
T	T	T
T	F	T
F	T	T
F	F	F

Valid, because at every line where the premise Q is T, $P \lor Q$ is T too.

98.

P	Q	$P \lor Q$	Q
T	T	T	T
T	F	T	F
F	T	T	T
F	F	F	F

Invalid, for at row 2, premise $P \lor Q$ is T and conclusion Q is F.

99–101. Check as correct: 100, 101.

102.

P	Q	$P \lor Q$	$Q \lor P$
T	T	T	T
T	F	T	T
F	T	T	T
F	F	F	F

103. Yes.

104. No.

105. *P* & *Q* is stronger than *P* ∨ *Q* because the former is T at row 1 only. The latter is T there, too. So *P* & *Q* ⊢ *P* ∨ *Q*. But *P* ∨ *Q* is T in rows 2 and 3 as well so, *P* ∨ *Q* does not imply *P* & *Q*.

P	*Q*	*P* & *Q*	*P* ∨ *Q*
T	T	T	T
T	F	F	T
F	T	F	T
F	F	F	F

106. Yes.

107–126. Check as correct: 109, 110, 111, 114, 115, 116, 117, 120, 121, 122, 124, 125.

Chapter 13　*De Morgan's Laws*

1. −*P*.

2. *Q*.

3. *P*.

4. − *Q*.

5. *P*.

6. −(*P* & *Q*).

7. Something different.

8. *P* & − *Q*.

9. −(*P* & *Q*).

10. Yes.

11. No.

12. Yes.

13. Complete with:

	T
F	T

14. *P*.

15. − *Q*.

16. T.

17. *P*.

18. − *Q*.

19. T.

20. F.

21. No.

22. Are not.

23. No.

24. Yes.

25. (d).

26. (e).

27. (c).

28. (f).

29. (b).
30. (h).
31. (g).
32. (a).
33.

P	Q	$-P$	$-Q$	$P \& Q$	$-P \& Q$	$P \& -Q$	$-P \& -Q$
T	T	F	F	T	F	F	F
T	F	F	T	F	F	T	F
F	T	T	F	F	T	F	F
F	F	T	T	F	F	F	T

$-(P \& Q)$	$-(-P \& Q)$	$-(P \& -Q)$	$-(-P \& -Q)$
F	T	T	T
T	T	F	T
T	F	T	T
T	T	T	F

34. T.
35. T.
36. F.
37. $-P \& -Q$.
38. No.
39. B.
40. (m).
41. (l).
42. (k).
43. (o).
44. (j).
45. (p).
46. (n).
47. (i).
48. T.
49. F.
50. T.
51. F.
52. Equivalent.
53. Logically equivalent.
54. Yes.
55. Yes.
56. Yes.
57. Yes.
58. They both take the value T in row 4 only.
59. They both take the value T in row 2 only.
60. $-(-P \lor -Q)$.
61. $-P$.
62. Q.
63. $-P \lor Q$.

64. $--P \vee -Q$.
65. $-(--P \vee -Q)$.
66. $-(P \vee -Q)$.
67. $-(P \vee -Q)$.
68. $-(P \vee -Q)$.
69. $P \vee -Q$.
70. P.
71. $-Q$.
72. $-P \& --Q$.
73. $-(-P \& --Q)$.
74. $-(-P \& Q)$.
75. $P \vee -Q$.
76. $-(-P \& Q)$.
77. $-(-P \& Q)$.
78. $--(-P \& Q)$.
79. $-P \& Q$.
80. $-(P \vee -Q)$.
81. $-P \& Q$.
82. 26.
83. 25.
84. 28.
85. 27.
86. 31.
87. 32.
88. 29.
89. 30.
90. Equivalent.
91. Logically equivalent.
92.

P	Q	$-P$	$-Q$	$-P \& Q$	$-(P \vee -Q)$
T	T	F	F	F	F
T	F	F	T	F	F
F	T	T	F	T	T
F	F	T	T	F	F

93. $-(-F \& D)$.
94. $F \vee -D$.
95. He either failed the examination or was not detested by his teacher.
96. $-(-R \& -T)$.
97. $R \vee T$.
98. He is responsible or trustworthy (or both).
99. $-(-R \vee -E)$.
100. $R \& E$.
101. The glyptodon is an extinct reptile.
102. $-(P \vee -R)$.
103. $-P \& R$.
104. There is not a first point in time, and time is capable of running backwards.
105. The same.

106. T.
107. T.
108. Valid.
109. "Q, so P" is valid means that P is T wherever Q is T. This must occur if P and Q are logically equivalent, for if they are equivalent and Q is T, so is P.

Chapter 14 *Building Truth Tables*

1. The argument form "P, so Q" is valid.
2. No.
3. Yes.
4–14. Check: 4, 6, 10, 13.
15. 6, 13.
16. Either, or; and, and.
17. Chicago lost to Philadelphia.
18. $((M \& S) \lor (P \& H))$.
19. (Chicago beat Montreal) and {either (lost to St. Louis) or (beat Pittsburgh)} and (it also lost to Philadelphia).
20. $(M \& (S \lor P)) \& H$.
21. Either Chicago beat Montreal and lost to St. Louis, or, it beat Pittsburgh; also, it lost to Philadelphia.
22. (a).
23. (b).
24. (c).
25. (d).
26. $-P$.
27. $-(P \lor Q)$.
28. Alternations.
29. Alternation.
30. Conjunctions.
31. T.
32. F.
33. $P \lor Q$.
34. $R \lor S$.
35. T.
36. T.
37. T.
38. T.
39. T.
40. F.
41. F.
42. T.
43. F.
44. T.
45. Two.
46. One.
47. Two.
48. One.
49. Two.

50. Two.
51. F.
52. Two.
53. T.
54. F.
55. Two.
56. Twice as many.
57. Four.
58. Eight.
59. Eight.
60. 16.
61. Four areas.
62. Eight.
63. 16.
64. Conjunction.
65. $Q \vee -R$.
66. Alternation.
67. Q.
68. R.
69. The spaces should be filled in as follows:

$-R$	$Q \vee -R$	$P \& (Q \vee -R)$
F	F	F
T	T	T
F	T	F
T	T	F
F	F	F
T	T	F

70. T.
71. F.
72. Q.
73. $-R$.
74. T.
75. F.
76. T.
77. F.
78. P.
79. $Q \vee -R$.
80. T.
81. T.
82. T.
83. T.
84. F.
85. Alternation.
86. F.
87. F.

88. *Q.*
89. −*R.*
90. F.

Chapter 15 *Tests for Validity*

1–8. Cross out: 6.
9–16. Cross out: 10, 13, 14, 16.
17. "*P* ⊢ *Q*" means that the argument form "*P,* so *Q*" is valid.
18–21. Cross out: 19, 21.
22–26. Cross out: 23, 24, 25, 26.
27. T.
28. T.
29. T.
30. Invalid, because in row 4 the premises are T whereas the conclusion is F.

			Premise	Premise Conclusion
P	*R*	− *R*	*P* ∨ − *R*	*P*
T	T	F	T	T
T	F	T	T	T
F	T	F	F	F
F	F	T	T	F

31. Valid.   Both premises are T in row 1 only.   Conclusion is T there, too.

			Premise	Premise	Conclusion
P	*R*	− *R*	*P* ∨ − *R*	*R*	*P*
T	T	F	T	T	T
T	F	T	T	F	T
F	T	F	F	T	F
F	F	T	T	F	F

32. 1. Either (the faculty honored the dean's recommendation to nullify the penalties imposed on the five students) or (the dean resigned.)   In fact, (the students remained adamant), but (the faculty did not honor the dean's recommendation.)   Hence, (the dean resigned) while (the students remained adamant).

   2. *H* ∨ *D.*
       S & − *H.*
       So, *D* & *S.*

3.

H	D	S	−H	H ∨ D	S & −H	D & S
				Premise	Premise	Conclusion
T	T	T	F	T	F	T
T	T	F	F	T	F	F
T	F	T	F	T	F	F
T	F	F	F	T	F	F
F	T	T	T	T	T	T
F	T	F	T	T	F	F
F	F	T	T	F	T	F
F	F	F	T	F	F	F

4. Valid. Only in row 5 are both premises T and conclusion is T there.

33. 1. Either (the universe began at some moment in time) or (it has been going on forever.). (God created the universe) and (the universe has a definite beginning in time). So, either (God created the universe) or (the universe has been going on forever).

2. *B* ∨ *F*.
   G & *B*.
   So, *G* ∨ *F*.

3.

B	F	G	B ∨ F	G & B	G ∨ F
			Premise	Premise	Conclusion
T	T	T	T	T	T
T	T	F	T	F	T
T	F	T	T	T	T
T	F	F	T	F	F
F	T	T	T	F	T
F	T	F	T	F	T
F	F	T	F	F	T
F	F	F	F	F	F

4. Valid. Only in rows 1 and 3 are both premises T. In those rows, the conclusion is T also.

34. 1. Either (God created the universe), or (the universe has been going on forever). Either (the universe has been going on forever) or (the universe has a definite beginning in time).   (The universe has a definite beginning in time.)   Hence, (the universe has been created by God).

2. $G \vee F.$
    $F \vee B.$
    $B.$
    So $G.$

3.

G	F	B	$G \vee F$ (Premise)	$F \vee B$ (Premise)	G (Conclusion)
T	T	T	T	T	T
T	T	F	T	T	T
T	F	T	T	T	T
T	F	F	T	F	T
F	T	T	T	T	F
F	T	F	T	T	F
F	F	T	F	T	F
F	F	F	F	F	F

4.   Invalid.   At row 5 all premises are T but conclusion is F.

35. 1.   Abel: Either he did not enlist in the army, or (he did not, after all resolve to avoid combat).   Cain: In fact, (either (he enlisted in the army) and (at the same time either resolved to avoid combat,)) or else he simply did not think what he was doing.   Abel: Therefore he simply did not think what he was doing.

2. $-E \vee -R.$
    $(E \& R) \vee -T.$
    So, $-T.$

3.

E	R	T	$-E$	$-R$	$-T$	$E \& R$	$-E \vee -R$ (Premise)	$(E \& R) \vee -T$ (Premise)	$-T$ (Conclusion)
T	T	T	F	F	F	T	F	T	F
T	T	F	F	F	T	T	F	T	T
T	F	T	F	T	F	F	T	F	F
T	F	F	F	T	T	F	T	T	T
F	T	T	T	F	F	F	T	F	F
F	T	F	T	F	T	F	T	T	T
F	F	T	T	T	F	F	T	F	F
F	F	F	T	T	T	F	T	T	T

    4. Valid. All premises are T at rows 4, 6, 8. But conclusion is also T at those rows.

36. Contained in.

37. Correct.

38. Valid.

39. T.

40. F.

41. Four.

42. FF.

43. No.

44. No life on Mars, but life on Venus.

45. No life on Mars or Venus.

46. Do.

47. Interpretation.

48. F.

49. No.

50. F.

51. Valid.

52. Invalid.

53. 3.

54. 4.

55. F.

56. Invalid.

57. T.

58. F.

59. Interpretation.

60. F.

61. Yes.

62. False.

63. Yes.

64. The premise is T if $P = $ F, $Q = $ T. But the conclusion is false. So make a counterexample by setting P for a false proposition, Q for a true one. For example, let P: Mars is larger than earth; Q: Mars is smaller than earth.

65. The premise is T if both P and Q are T and the conclusion is F. For a counterexample, let P: Lincoln was American; Q: Churchill was English.

66. Any example where P is T and Q is F will be a counterexample.

67. Are.

68. Yes.

69. Weaker.

70. (c).

71. (b).

72. (a).

73. $P \& Q \vdash Q \vee P.$

74. $P \vee Q.$

75. Permutation.

76. Permutation.

77. De Morgan.

78. De Morgan applied to last alternative.

Chapter 16 *Truth Functional Connectives*

1. Conjunction.
2. He took her a present.
3. She did not thank him.
4. Denial.
5. She did thank him.
6. T.
7. T.
8. Yes.
9. Yes.
10. Yes.
11. Yes.
12. Because.
13. And.
14. Yes.
15. Components.
16. The truth value of the components connected.
17. She is kind.
18. Do not.
19. Is not.
20. No.
21. Yes.
22. T.
23. F.
24. Yes.
25. Yes.
26. T.
27. T.
28. F.
29. T.
30. T.
31. Uniquely.
32. Compound.
33. Two.
34. One.
35. *Story One:* Joseph is an idiot, but is passed because the teacher likes him, and for no other reason.

    Story Two: Joseph is a straight A student. The teacher likes him, but that is not why he passes.

    In both stories, the components are T, but the truth value of the compound is not thereby determined, for in Story One, the compound is T, whereas it is F in Story Two.

36. T.
37. T.
38. T.
39. T.

40. T.
41. T.
42. F.
43. T.
44. Determined.
45. Truth functional.
46. F.
47. T.
48. Antecedent: The present 7 percent investment tax credit is continued.
    Consequent: Racial harmony will be even more difficult to achieve than at
    present.
49. Arguments.
50. If, then statements.
51. Consequent.
52. Premise.
53. Conclusion.
54. No.
55. No.
56. Adam is very conscientious. He tries to stay on the job no matter what
    happens. He would go home only if he were *very* sick. So if Adam went
    home to bed, he was ill: H is T. But even if he was ill, he may not have
    gone home: G is F.
57. Could not.
58. Antecedent: Joseph smokes marijuana this January.
    Consequent: He will be a drug addict by Christmas.
59. F.
60. F.
61. Antecedent.
62. T.
63. Consequent.
64. F.
65. Compound statement.
66. F.
67. No.
68. F.
69. No.
70. Consequent.
71. Antecedent.
72. F.
73. F.
74. F.
75. Truth functional.
76. An election is held.
77. There will be civil disorder.
78. F.
79. F.
80. Yes.
81. F.
82. T.

83. Yes.
84. Yes.
85. F.
86. F.
87. F.
88. F.
89. T.
90. F.
91. F.
92. Truth functional.
93. Example. *Story One:* He has been dating the boss's daughter and has been warned that he will be fired if this continues. It is no idle threat, so he stops dating her and is not fired. So both components are F, and the compound is still T.

    Story Two: In contrast, the man is in no danger of losing his job. He simply gets bored with the girl and drops her. Here both components are F, but the compound is F too.
94. "If, then" is not truth functional because the truth value of the compound is not uniquely determined by the truth values F, F, of the components.
95. F.
96. Yes.
97. T.
98. F.
99. F.
100. T.
101. F.
102. Four.
103. Yes.
104. Yes.
105. $N \rightarrow M$.
106. $-N \lor M$.
107. Yes.
108. Is.
109. Is not.
110. T.
111. T.
112. T.
113. F.
114. T.
115. T.
116. T.
117. T.
118. F.
119. F.
120. F.
121. T.
122. F.
123. T.

Chapter 17 *The Conditional*

1. $D \to M$.
2. $A \to C$.
3. $(C \& P) \vee (-C \& R)$.
4. $A \to (E \vee M)$.
5. $(C \to B) \& (-C \to H)$.
6. If the plane crashed, then the rescue party found the pilot.
7. If the quarry was unmarked, then the rescue party found the pilot.
8. If the rescue party found the pilot, the quarry was unmarked.
9. If the rescue party did not find the pilot, then either the plane crashed or the quarry was unmarked.
10. If the rescue party did not find the pilot, then if the plane did not crash, the quarry was unmarked.
11. P is T and Q is F.
12. F, T.
13. T, T.

14–17. Check 14 and 16.

15 is invalid because when Q is T, P is F, the premise is true and conclusion is F.

17 is invalid (take $P = F$, $Q = F$).

18. $-H \vee A$.

So, $H \to A$.

H	A	$-H$	$-H \vee A$	$H \to A$
T	T	F	T	T
T	F	F	F	F
F	T	T	T	T
F	F	T	T	T

Valid.

19. $H \to A$.

So, $-H \vee A$.

Valid.   Same table as for 18.

20. $J \to S$.

$W \to S$.

So, $W \vee J$.

J	S	W	$J \to S$	$W \to S$	$W \vee J$
T	T	T	T	T	T
T	T	F	T	T	T
T	F	T	F	F	T
T	F	F	F	T	T
F	T	T	T	T	T
F	T	F	T	T	F
F	F	T	T	F	T
F	F	F	T	T	F

Invalid.

21. $-P \to -M$.
         $-P \to B$.
         So, $-P \to (-M \& B)$.

P	M	B	$-P$	$-M$	$-M \& B$	$-P \to -M$	$-P \to B$	$-P \to (-M \& B)$
T	T	T	F	F	F	T	T	T
T	T	F	F	F	F	T	T	T
T	F	T	F	T	T	T	T	T
T	F	F	F	T	F	T	T	T
F	T	T	T	F	F	F	T	F
F	T	F	T	F	F	F	F	F
F	F	T	T	T	T	T	T	T
F	F	F	T	T	F	T	F	F

Valid.

22. $B \to A$.
         So, $-(B \& -A)$.

B	A	$-A$	$(B \& -A)$	$B \to A$	$-(B \& -A)$
T	T	F	F	T	T
T	F	T	T	F	F
F	T	F	F	T	T
F	F	T	F	T	T

Valid.

23. A.
24. B.
25. A.
26. B.
27. The same.
28. $P \to Q$.
29. Antecedent.

30.

P	Q	$P \leftrightarrow Q$
T	T	T
T	F	F
F	T	F
F	F	T

31. No.
32. The same.
33. Yes.

34. F.
35. $R \leftrightarrow P$.
36. No.
37. $P \rightarrow R$.
38. If and only if.
39. If.
40. $P \rightarrow R$.
41. $R \rightarrow P$.
42. (e), (f).
43. (d), (g).
44. "If P then Q."
45. "Only if Q, P."
46. "Only G are F."
47. $R \rightarrow C$.
48. $B \rightarrow C$.
49. $E \rightarrow P$.
50. Joseph did work harder than he did last year.
51. Eve is rich.
52. "$-P$ unless Q."
53. (a), (e).
54. (b), (d).
55. (c), (f).
56. $-F \rightarrow R$.
57. $-N \rightarrow M$.
58. $R \rightarrow D$.
59. $-A \rightarrow J$.
60. (e).
61. (j).
62. (c).
63. (a).
64. (m).
65. (f).
66. (d).
67. (k).
68. (g).
69. (i).
70. (h).

Chapter 18 *Deduction*

1. Interchangeable.
2. P.
3. Equivalence.
4. $-(-P \& -Q)$.
5. $P \vee -Q$.
6. $Q \& P$.
7. $Q \vee P$.

8. $P \vdash P \lor Q,\ Q \vdash P \lor Q.$

9. $P,\ Q \vdash P \& Q.$
   $P \& Q \vdash P.$
   $P \& Q \vdash Q.$

10–15. Incorrect: 11, 12, 14.

16–23. Incorrect: 16, 17, 21, 22.

24. (b).

25. (a).

26. (d).

27. (f).

28. (g).

29. (e).

30. (c).

31. T.

32. F.

33. P is T, Q is F.

34. Equivalent.

35. Q.

36. Q.

37. $P \rightarrow Q.$

38. $-P \lor Q.$

39. $-(P \& -Q).$

40. $-(P \& -Q).$

41. T.

42. F.

43. $-(-P \& -Q).$

44. $Q \& -P.$

45. $-P \& -Q.$

46. No.

47.

P	Q	$P \rightarrow Q$	$-Q \rightarrow -P$
T	T	T	T
T	F	F	F
F	T	T	T
F	F	T	T

48. $P \rightarrow -Q.$

49. $Q \rightarrow P.$

50. $-(R \lor P) \rightarrow Q.$

51. 1. $-P \rightarrow -Q \vdash --P \lor -Q.$ Wedge-arrow.
    2.   „ $\vdash P \lor -Q.$ Double denial.
    3.   „ $\vdash -Q \lor P.$ Permutation.
    4.   „ $\vdash Q \rightarrow P.$ Wedge-arrow.

52. Second.

53. De Morgan.

54. Contraposition.

55. Detachment.

56. De Morgan.
57. Conjunction.
58. Weakening.
59. Wedge-arrow.
60. Conjunction.
61. De Morgan.
62. Detachment.
63. P.
64. $P \rightarrow Q$.
65. R.
66. $Q \rightarrow R$.
67. Contraposition.
68. Detachment.
69. Detachment.
70. $-(P \lor Q) \rightarrow -R, R \vdash R \rightarrow (P \lor Q)$.
            ,, $\vdash P \lor Q$.

Supply the *reasons* for each step yourself.

71. $-(P \lor Q) \rightarrow -R, R \vdash -(-P \,\&\, -Q)$.
72. $-P \rightarrow -Q, P \rightarrow R, Q \vdash Q \rightarrow P$.
         ,, $\vdash P$.
         ,, $\vdash R$.
73. $(P \lor Q) \rightarrow -R \vdash R \rightarrow -(P \lor Q)$.
         ,, $\vdash R \rightarrow (-P \,\&\, -Q)$.
74. $P \rightarrow Q \vdash -P \lor Q$.
      ,, $\vdash Q \lor -P$.
      ,, $\vdash -(-Q \,\&\, P)$.
75. $(-P \lor -Q) \lor R, P \,\&\, Q \vdash -(-P \lor -Q)$.
         ,, $\vdash R$.
76–89. 76, 77, 79, 84, 85, 88.

Chapter 19 *Conditional Proof*

1. The argument form "P, Q, so R" is valid.
2. F.
3. Yes.
4. Yes.
5. No.
6. Yes.
7. Q.
8. If P, then Q.
9. Q.
10. $P \rightarrow Q$.
11. Valid.
12. P.
13. $P \rightarrow Q$.
14. $Q \rightarrow R$.

15. $Q \to R$.

16. $Q \to R$.

17. $P \to R$.

18. Conditional proof.

19–23. Cross out 20, 22.

24. Q.

25. $P \to Q$.

26. Are not.

27. Premise, detachment.

28. Conditional proof.

29. Yes.

30. No.

31. The argument form "$P, P \to (P \to Q)$, so $P \to Q$" is valid.

32. The argument form "$P \to (P \to Q)$, so $P \to Q$" is valid.

33. No.

34. Conditional proof.

35. Conditional proof.

36. $Q \to R$.

37. $(P \to Q) \to (P \to R)$.

38. P.

39. $(P \to Q) \to R$.

40. Detachment from $P, P \to R$.

41. Detachment from $P, P \to Q$.

42. Conditional proof.

43. If he is ill, he will go to the hospital and he needs a doctor.

44. $Q \vee P$.

45. $Q \& P$.

46. See Joseph.

47. Alternative.

48–52. Cross out 51.

53. Conjunction on the premise $P \& Q$.

54. 1, weakening.

55. 2, premise, detachment.

56. Conditional proof.

57. No. (The row $P = T$, $Q = F$, $R = F$, shows it is invalid.)

58. $(P \to Q) \to (P \to R)$.

59. Arrow.

60. Conditional proof.

61. Above.

62. $P \to R$.

63. $\to$ (the arrow).

64. Conditional proof.

65. $Q \to R$.

66. Q.

67. Detachment.

68. Detachment.

69. 3. $P \to (Q \to R)$, $P \to Q$, $P \vdash R$. Detachment.

70. 4. $P \to (Q \to R)$, $P \to Q \vdash P \to R$. Conditional proof.

71. 5. $P \to (Q \to R) \vdash (P \to Q) \to (P \to R)$. Conditional proof.

72–79.   Correct: 72, 73, 75, 76, 77, 78, 79.
80.   Conjunction.

Chapter 20   *Tautologies*

1.   If we have deduced that $P, Q \vdash R$, then $P \vdash Q \to R$.
2.   F.
3.   T.
4.

P	$P \to P$
T	T
F	T

5.   No.
6.   F.
7.   Valid.
8.   F.
9.   F.
10.   Wedge-arrow equivalence.
11.

P	$-P$	$P \lor -P$
T	F	T
F	T	T

12.   No.
13–16.   13 and 16 are tautologies.
17.   Identity.
18.   Conditional proof.
19.   Conjunction.
20.   Conditional proof.
21.   De Morgan.
22.   Wedge-arrow.
23.   Wedge-arrow.
24.   1. $P \& (-Q \to -P) \vdash P.$ Conjunction.
    2.   „ $\vdash -Q \to -P.$ Conjunction.
    3.   „ $\vdash P \to Q.$ Contraposition.
    4.   „ $\vdash Q.$ Detachment using 1,3.
    5.   „ $\vdash (P \& (-Q \to -P)) \to Q.$
                                                Conditional proof.
25.   "Q, so P" is valid unless there is a row where Q is T and P is F.   There is no such row where P is F, so long as P is a tautology.
26.   Two.
27.   T.
28.   F.
29.   F.
30.   T.
31.   Tautology.

32. T.
33. F.
34. Valid.
35. If P, Q, R, so S is valid, there is no row where P, Q, and R all take T and S takes F. Hence $((P \ \& \ Q) \ \& \ R) \rightarrow S$ never takes F and is a tautology.

    On the other hand, if $((P \ \& \ Q) \ \& \ R) \rightarrow S$ is a tautology, there is no row at which S takes F, and $(P \ \& \ Q) \ \& \ R$ takes T. Hence, there is no row at which P, Q, and R all take T while S takes F. So, P, Q, $R \vdash S$.
36. T.
37. The same.
38. If P and Q are logically equivalent, they take the same truth values at each row. Hence, $P \leftrightarrow Q$ never takes F at any row, and $P \leftrightarrow Q$ is thus a tautology.

    On the other hand, if $P \leftrightarrow Q$ is a tautology, it never takes F at any row. Hence, P and Q never differ in truth value at any row, so P and Q are logically equivalent.

39.

P	$-P$	$P \ \& -P$
T	F	F
F	T	F

40. Yes.
41. No.
42–44. 42 and 43 are contradictions.
45. A tautology takes T at every row. So its denial takes F at every row and is thus a contradiction. Likewise the denial of a contradiction takes T at every row and is thus a tautology.
46. Contradiction.
47. Is.
48. $-P$ is not a contradiction.
49. $P \rightarrow Q$.
50. Ask Oscar if $-(P \rightarrow Q)$ is a contradiction, where P is the premise, and Q the conclusion of the argument form.
51. $P \leftrightarrow Q$.
52. Tautology.
53. Ask if their biconditional is a tautology.
54. Tautology.
55. T.
56. The same.
57. T.
58. Tautology.
59. If you want to know whether Q is a tautology, ask Pard whether $Q \leftrightarrow (-P \lor P)$ is a tautology.
60. Can.
61. No.
62. Yes.
63. Ask whether $-Q \leftrightarrow (-P \lor P)$ is a tautology. Or: Ask whether $Q \leftrightarrow (P \ \& -P)$ is a tautology.

64. No.
65. No.
66. A.
67. T.
68. T.
69. The same.
70. The same.
71. Equivalent.
72. F.
73. T.
74. Contradiction.
75. True.
76. Tautology.
77. No.
78. Yes, biconditional is true.
79. No, biconditional is not true.
80. F.
81. Roger.   (He can tell you *anything* you want to know!)
82. T.
83. F.
84. T.
85. T.
86. F.
87. T.
88. T.
89. F.
90. T.
91. T.
92. T.
93. F.
94. F.
95. T.
96. T.
97. F (because Q could be a contradiction, too).
98. F.
99. T.
100. No.
101. Consistent.
102. T.

103.

P	Q	$P \lor Q$	$-P \& -Q$
T	T	T	F
T	F	T	F
F	T	T	F
F	F	F	T

Inconsistent.

104.

P	Q	R	P → Q	Q → R	R	
T	T	T	T	T	T	←
T	T	F	T	F	F	
T	F	T	F	T	T	
T	F	F	F	T	F	
F	T	T	T	T	T	←
F	T	F	T	F	F	
F	F	T	T	T	T	←
F	F	F	T	T	F	

Consistent.   In rows 1, 5, and 7 all three statements take the value T.

105.

P	Q	R	Q → R	P → R	P & − R
T	T	T	T	T	F
T	T	F	F	F	T
T	F	T	T	T	F
T	F	F	T	F	T
F	T	T	T	T	F
F	T	F	F	T	F
F	F	T	T	T	F
F	F	F	T	T	F

Inconsistent.   There is no row where all three take the value T.

106.

P	Q	R	− P ∨ Q	− Q ∨ R	− R ∨ P	
T	T	T	T	T	T	←
T	T	F	T	F	T	
T	F	T	F	T	T	
T	F	F	F	T	T	
F	T	T	T	T	F	
F	T	F	T	F	T	
F	F	T	T	T	F	
F	F	F	T	T	T	←

Consistent.   In rows 1 and 8 all three statements take the value T.

107. $W → M.$
        $M → N.$
        $W → − N.$

W	M	N	W → M	M → N	W → −N	
T	T	T	T	T	F	
T	T	F	T	F	T	
T	F	T	F	T	F	
T	F	F	F	T	T	
F	T	T	T	T	T	←
F	T	F	T	F	T	
F	F	T	T	T	T	
F	F	F	T	T	T	←

Consistent.   In rows 5 and 8 all three statements take the value T.

108. *P* → *A*.
A → *S*.
−*S*.

P	A	S	P → A	A → S	−S	
T	T	T	T	T	F	
T	T	F	T	F	T	
T	F	T	F	T	F	
T	F	F	F	T	T	
F	T	T	T	T	F	
F	T	F	T	F	T	
F	F	T	T	T	F	
F	F	F	T	T	T	←

Consistent.   In row 8 all three statements take the value T.

109. *B* ∨ −*C*.
C → *G*.
−*G* → −*B*.
G → −*B*.

B	C	G	B ∨ −C	C → G	−G → −B	G → −B	
T	T	T	T	T	T	F	
T	T	F	T	F	F	T	
T	F	T	T	T	T	F	
T	F	F	T	T	F	T	
F	T	T	F	T	T	T	
F	T	F	F	F	T	T	
F	F	T	T	T	T	T	←
F	F	F	T	T	T	T	←

Consistent.   In rows 7 and 8 all three statements take the value T.

110. $-S.$
$-S \rightarrow G.$ Inconsistent, since even S and $-S$ are inconsistent.
$S.$
$G.$
111. Inconsistent.
112. Consistent.
113. Nothing.
114. No.
115. Yes.
116. Are not.
117. No.
118. Change "premises" to "statements."
119. No.
120. Consequent.
121. Antecedent.

Chapter 21 *Reduction to Absurdity*

1. The argument form "P, so Q" is valid.
2. T.
3. No.
4. No.
5. F.
6. Convicted murderers must be executed in order to deter other would-be murderers.
7. F.
8. F.
9. F.
10. Conclusion.
11. Premises.
12. T.
13. F.
14. T.
15. F.
16. T.
17. T.
18. Valid.
19. Contraposition.
20. Detachment.
21. The earth is not round.
22. Yes.
23. Yes.
24. There is a false premise that people would fall off.
25. Physics.
26. Is not.
27. Tautology.
28. Contradiction.
29. F.

30. T.

31. Absurdity.

32. Lying.

33. F.

34. $Q \vee -Q$.

35. Contraposition of $P \to Q$.

36. Contraposition of $P \to -Q$.

37. Double denial, 3.

38. Alternatives, 2, 4.

39. Detachment, 1, 5.

40. F.

41.

P	$-P$	$P \to -P$	$-P$
T	F	F	F
F	T	T	T

42. A truth functional connective is a statement connective such that the truth value of the compound formed using the connective is uniquely determined by the truth values of the components connected by the connective.

43. And; or; neither, nor; not; it is not the case that.

44. A premise is a statement from which one derives conclusions in an argument; an antecedent is the first component in a conditional or "if, then" statement.

45. A tautology takes T at every row in its truth table.

46. A contradiction takes F at every row in its truth table.

47. No.

48. If P always takes the value F, then $P \to Q$ always takes the value T.

49. Likewise, if Q always takes the value T, so does $P \to Q$.

50. When they cannot all be T at once.

51. If the premises always take the value F, the argument can never have T premises and F conclusion, and so is valid.

52. The premises cannot all be T simultaneously.

53. An interpretation in which the premises are seen to be T, whereas the conclusion is seen to be F.

54. If R always takes the value T, there can be no row in the truth table with premises P, Q being T while conclusion R is F.

55. You must construct an example in which the truth values of the components do not uniquely determine the truth values of the conclusion. Consult Chapter 16.

56. To change an alternation to conjunction: replace wedge by ampersand, write bars in front of components and in front of the compound; then delete double bars. Likewise in changing conjunction to alternation, replace ampersand by wedge and carry on as above.

57. If P and Q never differ in truth value, $P \leftrightarrow Q$ always takes the value T.

58. If $P \vdash Q$, then, if P is T, Q is also T. If $Q \vdash P$, then if Q is T, P is also T. Hence, P is T if and only if Q is T. Hence, they never differ in truth value and are logically equivalent.

59. Make sure your example has a false premise. Example: All dogs are cats; all dogs talk; so, all cats talk.

60. Example: Some women are people. Some people talk. So, some women talk.

61. *P* and *Q* take the value T at all rows in their truth tables, and hence never differ in truth value, and hence are logically equivalent.

62. Similarly, when *P* and *Q* both take the value F at every row in their truth tables, they never differ in truth value so $P \leftrightarrow Q$ always takes the value T.

63. (h).
64. (j).
65. (a).
66. (e).
67. (b).
68. (k).
69. (e).
70. (i).
71. (c).
72. (g).
73. (k).
74. (j).
75. (f).
76. (b).
77. (d).
78. (c).

79–90. Cross out: 79, 81, 85, 87, 89, 90.

91. (o).
92. (m).
93. (v)
94. (u).
95. (s).
96. (t).
97. (r).
98. (o).
99. (v).
100. (r).

101–105. Cross out: 102, 105.

106. Consistent, as shown by rows where $P = $ T and $R = $ T.

107. Consistent, as shown by rows where *R* is F, and *P* is T, *Q* is F or *P* is F, *Q* is T.

108. Consistent, as shown by the rows where *P*, *Q*, and *R* are F.

109. Consistent, as shown by the row where *P*, *Q*, and *R* are F.

Chapter 22 *The Existential Quantifier*

1. $C \vee I$. $-C$. So, *I*.
2. Either, or.
3. Not.
4. Statement connectives.
5. Syllogisms.

6. Some *C* are *D*.
   No *D* is *A*.
   So, some *C* are not *A*.

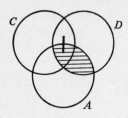

7. All *A* are *H*.
   All *H* are *F*.
   So, all *A* are *F*.

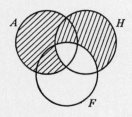

8. 6 and 7.
9. All, Some, No.
10. Valid.
11. Any, everybody, some, none.
12. Venn diagrams.
13. Gandhi.
14. One.
15. Predicate.
16. Washington.
17. Predicate.
18. Lake Superior.
19. Is navigable.
20. The world's largest lake.
21. Lake Superior.
22. The St. Lawrence, the Pacific Ocean, the Mississippi, etc.
23. Rio de Janeiro.
24. The world's most beautiful city.
25. Mendel.
26. The great pioneer of genetics.
27. Is rich in copper.
28. Is windy.
29. Is windy.
30. Practically never needs more than four minutes to run a mile.
31. *a, d, e.*

32. Predicate.
33. Gandhi.
34. Gandhi.
35. No.
36. *Gb.*
37. *Fa & Gb.*
38. Abraham is a father or Boaz is a great lover.
39. *Fa → Gb.*
40. If Abraham is a father and Abraham is a great lover, then Boaz is a father or Boaz is a great lover.
41. Antecedent.
42. *Pk.*
43. *Pk & Pg.*
44. *Cg ∨ Ck.*
45. *(Ck & Pk) & − Ik.*
46. *Ig → Ck.*
47. (c).
48. (e).
49. (a).
50. (b).
51. (d).
52. *(((Dc & Dd) & Md) ∨ − Dc) & (− Dc → − Md).*
53. Do.
54. No.
55. The statements about Russell, Sartre, and Plato's teacher (Socrates) are true.
56. For example,
    1. Heidegger.
    2. Aristotle.
    3. Leibniz.
57. Choose your own nonphilosophers.
58. No.
59. Is not.
60. _____ is the highest mountain.
61. _____ was the first president.
62. There is vegetation on _____.
63. Mars, Venus.
64. Three.
65. _____ of .... nearly conquered _____.
66. _____ gave us law, ... gave us philosophy, but _____ gave us no philosophy.
67. A person, a country, a document, and a university:
    Thomas Jefferson, United States, Declaration of Independence, University of Virginia.
68. Change second dots to a long dash.
69. _____ was president of .... during _____, and _____ was assassinated by **********.
70. A.
71. For example, Russell.
72. For example, Sartre.

73. x is a dictator.

74. True statement.

75. There is some way of filling in the blank x in "x is a unicorn" to get a true statement.

76. There are some baseball stars.

77. Sb.

78. $(\exists x)(Sx)$.

79. x is a baseball star.

80. Cross out: $(\exists x)(Sy)$, $(\exists b)(Sb)$.

81. x made a million and x retired.

82. Mx & Rx.

83. $(\exists x)(Mx$ & $Rx)$.

84. (c), (f).

85. (b), (e).

86. (b), (e).

87. (c), (f).

88. (a), (d).

89. (a), (d).

90. Insert "&."

91. Add final ")."

92. Capitalize "p."

93. Change "x" to "y."   (Or, change "y" to "x.")

94. Change "X" to "x."

95. Put brackets around "$\exists y$."

96. Put brackets around "Pz & Wz."

97. Insert missing "(."

98. A.

99. B.

100. B.

101. A.

102. (c).

103. Needs a closing ")."

104. (b).

105. Needs brackets for the second "$\exists z$."

106. (a).

107. (d).

108. $(\exists y)(Py$ & $-Ay)$.

109–112. Cross out: 109, 112.

113. 106, 111.

114. $(\exists x)(Ax$ & $-(Px$ & $Tx))$.   (Other letters, such as "y" or "z" could have been used consistently in this and subsequent answers.)

115. $(\exists x)(Tx$ & $-(Px$ & $Ax))$.

116. $(\exists x)(Px$ & $-(Tx$ & $Ax))$ & $(\exists x)(Ax$ & $-(Tx$ & $Px))$.

117–122. Cross out: 119, 122. There are often several ways of expressing the rest in good English.

117. Some generous policemen are not louts.

118. Some policemen are sadistic and some policemen are not sadistic.

120. There are generous policemen who are louts, but who are not sadistic.

121. Some policemen are not louts and some generous things are not policemen.

Chapter 23 *The Universal Quantifier*

1. $(\exists x)(Bx)$.
2. Isn't.
3. F.
4. Everything is beautiful.
5. $(\exists x)$.
6. $(\forall x)(Wx)$. (Many books use $(x)(Wx)$, but that is not our convention. Use the upside down "A.")
7. $(\forall x)(-Wx)$ or $(\forall x)-(Wx)$.
8. $(\exists x)-(Wx)$.
9. $-(\forall x)(Wx)$.
10. B.
11. No.
12. No.
13. No.
14. No.
15. Everything is not stupid.
16. C.
17. A and C.
18. B.
19. Everything is ungenerous.
    It is false that something is generous.
20. $-(\exists x)(Sx)$.
21. $(\forall x)-(Sx)$.
22. $(\exists x)-(Sx)$.
23. $-(\forall x)(Sx)$.
24. Double denial.
25. (b).
26. (d).
27. Needs "(" and ")" around "$\exists x$."
28. (d).
29. (c).
30. (c).
31. Needs "(" and ")" around "Ox."
32. (a).
33. (b).
34. (a).
35. Everything is created by God.
36. Something is not created by God.
37. It is not true that everything is not created by God = Something is created by God.
38. It is not true that something is created by God = Nothing is created by God.
39. $(\exists x)(Cx \ \& \ Bx)$.
40. You, for example, are not a planet in the solar system that goes around the sun.
41. Incorrect.
42. $(\forall x)(Px \rightarrow Sx)$.
43. $(\exists x)(Px \ \& \ Cx)$.

44. $(\exists x)(Wx \ \& \ Jx)$.
45. $(\forall x)(Wx \rightarrow Jx)$.
46. $(\forall x)(Mx \rightarrow Bx)$.
47. $(\exists x)(Mx \ \& \ Fx)$.
48. $(\forall x)(Ax \rightarrow Lx)$.
49. $(\exists x)(Ax \ \& \ -Px)$.
50. Arrow.
51. Ampersand.
52.

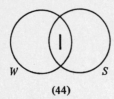

(44)

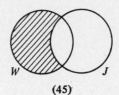

(45)

53. Putting in a bar.
54. Scratching out an area.
55. Arrow.
56. Ampersand.
57. $-(-P \lor -Q)$.
58. $-(P \lor -Q)$.
59. $-(P \lor Q)$.
60. $-P \lor -Q$.
61. $P \lor -Q$.
62. $-(-P \rightarrow Q)$.
63. $P \rightarrow -Q$.
64. $-P \rightarrow -Q$.
65. $-(P \rightarrow -Q)$.
66. $-(-P \lor -Q); -(P \rightarrow -Q)$.
67. $-P \lor Q; P \rightarrow Q$.
68. $-(P \lor Q); -(-P \rightarrow Q)$.
69. $P \lor -Q; -P \rightarrow -Q$.
70. $-(\forall x)-(Fx)$.
71. $-(\forall x)(Fx)$.
72. $(\forall x)(Fx)$.
73. $(\forall x)-(Fx)$.
74. $-(\exists x)(Ax \ \& \ -Lx)$.
75. $(\forall x)-(Ax \ \& \ -Lx)$.
76. $(\forall x)--(-Ax \lor Lx)$.
77. $(\forall x)(Ax \rightarrow Lx)$.
78. $(\forall x)(Ax \rightarrow Lx)$.
79. $(\forall x)(Ax \rightarrow Lx)$.
80. Arrow.
81. Ampersand.
82. No actors are lecherous.
83. Some actors are lecherous (or, for example, There are lecherous actors).

84. All actors are lecherous.
85. Everything is a lecherous actor.
86. All nonactors are not lecherous.
87. Some actors are not lecherous.
88. Everything is both not lecherous and an actor.
89. Everything not lecherous is an actor.
90. It is not true that everything not lecherous is an actor.
91. $(\forall x)(Ax \rightarrow Lx)$.
92. $(\exists x)(-Ax \lor Lx)$.

Chapter 24 *Monadic Predicate Logic*

1. Arrow.
2. Ampersand.
3. $(\forall x)(Sx \rightarrow Hx)$.
4. $(\exists x)(Sx \,\&\, Hx)$.
5. $-(\exists x)(Sx \,\&\, Hx)$, or $(\forall x)(Sx \rightarrow -Hx)$.
6. $-(\exists x)(Sx \,\&\, Hx)$.
7. $(\forall x)(Sx \rightarrow -Hx)$.
8. Logically equivalent.
9. Not some F are G.
10. $-(\exists x)(Rx \,\&\, Gx)$.
11. $(\forall x)(Cx \rightarrow Ex)$.
12. $-(\exists x)(Ix \,\&\, Tx)$.
13. $(\exists x)(Mx \,\&\, Ix)$.
14. $(\exists x)((Sx \,\&\, Tx) \,\&\, Ix)$.
15. $(\forall x)((Sx \,\&\, Tx) \rightarrow Ix)$.
16. Something different.
17. $(\forall x)(Sx \rightarrow (Tx \,\&\, Ix))$.
18. If something is a speech, then, if it is tedious, it is ignored.
19. Does not.
20. Everything is a tedious speech that is ignored.
21. $(\forall x)(Sx \rightarrow Tx)$.
22. $(\forall x)(Sx \rightarrow Tx)$.
23. All biased witnesses are untrustworthy.
24. Some biased witnesses are trustworthy.
25. Everything is a biased witness that is trustworthy.
26. Cross out.
27. All witnesses are unbiased or untrustworthy.
28. There are no biased witnesses that are trustworthy.
29. Cross out.
30. Cross out.
31. Cross out.
32. Cross out.
33. $(\forall x)((Rx \,\&\, Gx) \rightarrow Tx)$.
34. $-(\exists x)(Ex \,\&\, Kx)$.
35. $(\forall x)(Sx \rightarrow (Mx \,\&\, Ax))$.
36. $(\exists x)((Dx \,\&\, Cx) \,\&\, Mx)$.

37. $(\forall x)(Vx \rightarrow (Mx \lor Ix))$.
38. $(\exists x)((Mx \& Px) \& (Ix \& -Vx))$.   (Other bracketings are permissible in 35 and 38.)
39. All G are F.
40. All F are G.
41. $(\forall x)(Lx \rightarrow (-Rx \& Cx))$.
42. $(\forall x)((Cx \& Lx) \rightarrow -Rx)$.
43. $(\forall x)(Cx \rightarrow (Px \& Ox)) \& (\exists x)((Px \& Ox) \& -Cx)$.
44. $(\forall x)((Px \& Dx) \rightarrow (Mx \& (-Yx \& -Ox)))$.
45. Conditional.
46. Antecedent.
47. All voters are misinformed.
48. Consequent.
49. None should vote.
50. $(\forall x)(Vx \rightarrow Mx)$.
51. $-(\exists x)(Vx \& Sx)$.
52. $(\forall x)(Vx \rightarrow Mx) \rightarrow -(\exists x)(Vx \& Sx)$.
53. $(\exists x)(Vx \& Mx) \lor (\exists x)(Vx \& Ix)$.
54. $(\exists x)((Px \& Ox) \& Mx) \rightarrow ((\forall x)((Px \& Ox) \rightarrow Vx) \rightarrow (\exists x)(Vx \& Mx))$.
55. $-(\exists x)-(Fx \rightarrow Gx)$.
56. $-(\exists x)-(Fx) \rightarrow -(\forall x)-(Gx)$.
57. $(\exists x)-(Fx) \lor -(\forall x)-(Gx)$.
58. Needs brackets for "Fx".
59. $(\forall x)(Fx) \& (-(\exists x)-(Gx) \rightarrow -(\exists x)-(Hx))$.
60. $-(-Fx \& Gx)$.
61. No.
62. $(\exists x)-(-Fx \lor -Gx)$.
63. Yes.
64. $(\exists x)(Fx)$, $(\forall x)(Gx)$.
65. Not equivalent.
66. Equivalent.
67. Not equivalent.
68. Ungrammatical.
69. Not equivalent.
70. Not equivalent.
71. $(\exists x)-(-Fx \lor -Gx)$.
72. $(\exists x)(Fx \& Gx)$.
73. $(\exists x)(Fx \lor Gx)$.
74. $(\forall x)(Fx \& Gx)$.
75. $(\exists x)(Fx) \lor (\forall x)(Gx)$.
76. (c).
77. (a).
78. (j).
79. (f).
80. (d).
81. (b).
82. (g).
83. (h).
84. (e).

85. (i).
86. √.
87. × (Correct. $-(\forall x)(-Fx \lor -Gx)$.)
88. Needs brackets.
89. √.
90. Needs ")" after last quantifier.
91. √.

Chapter 25 *Deductions and Counterexamples*

1. Is.
2. Diagrams.
3. Invalid.
4. Interpretation.
5. T.
6. F.
7. No.
8. For example,
   Some cars are Fords.
   Some Fords go.
   So, some cars go.
9. Is not.
10. Valid.
11. Invalid.
12. Valid.
13. Yes.
14. Tables.
15. Invalid.
16. Negative.
17. T.
18. F.
19. Positive.
20. Procedures.
21. Negative.
22. Invalid.
23. No.
24. Valid.
25. Valid.
26. No.
27. Valid.
28. Positive.
29. No.
30. Positive.
31. Negative.
32. Deduction.
33. Counterexample.
34. No.
35. No.

36. Both positive and negative.

37. No.

38. Procedures.

39. Venn diagrams.

40. Truth tables.

41. Cannot.

42. Is no.

43. Valid.

44. Counterexample.

45. Capital letters.

46. Lower case letters from the end of the alphabet.

47. Lower case letters from the beginning of the alphabet.

48. "Blank."

49. Name.

50. There are some philosophers.

51. Valid.

52. *Fb.*
So, $(\exists x)(Fx)$.

53–62. Correct: 53, 61.

63. Philosopher.

64. Valid.

65. $(\forall x)(Lx \rightarrow Px)$.
So, $Lg \rightarrow Pg$.

66. Everything is ferocious, so, Abraham is ferocious.

67. ×. Because of G in premises, while F in conclusion.

68. ×. Needs brackets.

69. ×. For instantiation, should be $(\forall x)$. Note that $Gc \vdash (\exists x)(Gx)$ is correct existential conclusion.

70. ×. "x" and "y" are different. $(\forall x)(Hx) \vdash Ha$ is correct instantiation.

71. ×. Should be, for example, $Fc \vdash (\exists x)(Fx)$ for existential conclusion.

72. ×. For existential conclusion we require an existential quantifier.

73. ×.

74. ×.

75. Wrong way around. Interchange premise and conclusion.

76–78. Correct.

79. No name "a" or "b" has been changed to "x," in the conclusion.

80. Both "a" *and* "b" have been changed to "x" in the conclusion.

81–83. Correct.

84. "b" should be "a."

85. Correct.

86. "b" should be "a," or "a" should be "b."

87. In the conclusion, "x" should be "a" for example.

88. In the conclusion, "z" should be "c."

89. Conclusion should be: $(\forall x)(Fx \rightarrow Ga)$.

90. Instantiation.

91. Existential conclusion.

92. $(\forall x)(Fx) \vdash Fa$.
   „ $\vdash (\exists y)(Fy)$.

93. No.

94. Invalid.
95. Counterexample.
96. Interpretation.
97. T.
98. F.
99. Something.
100. Everything.
101. Yes.
102. No.
103. Counterexample.
104. Invalid.
105. For example, *F*: is a female.
106. *Fa* ⊢ (∃*x*)(*Fx*)   Existential conclusion.
    „   ⊢ −(∀*x*)−(*Fx*)   Quantifier interchange.
107. −(∃*x*)−(*Fx*) ⊢ (∀*x*)(*Fx*)   Quantifier interchange.
    „   ⊢ *Fb*   Instantiation.
108. Invalid.   Use, for example, *F*: is president of the United States, *c*: Bertrand Russell.
109. −(∃*x*)(*Fx* ∨ *Gx*) ⊢ (∀*x*)−(*Fx* ∨ *Gx*).   Quantifier interchange.
    „   ⊢ (∀*x*)(−*Fx* & −*Gx*).   De Morgan.
110. „   ⊢ −*Fb* & −*Gb*.   Instantiation.
111. *F*: Women; *G*: men; *a*: Mrs. Nixon; *b*: Mr. Nixon.
    Premise:
       Nothing is both a woman and a man.
       So Mrs. Nixon is not a woman, or
       Mr. Nixon is not a man.

Chapter 26   *More Deductions*

1. Antecedent: *Q*.
   Premise: the first *P*.
2. Antecedent: (∃*x*)(*Gx*).
   Premise: the first (∀*x*)(*Fx*).
3. Correct.
4. Incorrect.
5. Incorrect.
6. Correct.
7. Correct.
8. Correct.
9. *Fa* → *Ga*.
10. Contraposition.
11. Good to eat.
12. (∀*x*)(*Hx*).
13. (∀*y*)(*Hy*).
14. Instantiation of 2nd premise.
15. Instantiation of 1st premise.
16. Detachment.
17. (∀*x*)(*Gx*).

18. No.
19. *Ga.*
20. *G*: is President of the United States.
    a: Richard Nixon.
21. *Ga.*
22. $(\forall x)(Gx).$
23. $(\forall x)(Fx \rightarrow Gx), (\forall x)(Fx) \vdash Fe.$
         ,, $\vdash Fe \rightarrow Ge.$
         ,, $\vdash Ge.$
24. *Ga.*
25. Does not.
26. No.
27. No.
28. Yes.
29. $(\forall x)(Fx)$ or $(\forall y)(Fy)$, etc.
30. $(\forall x)(Gx)$, etc.
31. "*a*" is in the premise.
32. $(\forall x)(Gx)$, etc.
33. $(\forall x)(Gx \rightarrow Fx).$
34. "*a*" is in the third premise.
35. Is correct.
36. Is incorrect, for "*a*" is in the third premise.
37. Instantiation.
38. Instantiation.
39. Generalization.
40. Generalization.
41. Instantiation.
42. Instantiation.
43. Detachment.
44. Generalization.
45. Conditional proof.
46. Conditional proof.
47. No.
48. For example,
    $(\forall x)(Fx) \vdash -(\exists x)-(Fx).$
49. For example, $Fa \vdash (\exists x)(Fx).$
50. For example, $(\forall x)(Fx) \vdash Fa.$
51. Correct.
52. Incorrect.
53. Correct.
54. Incorrect.
55. Four.
56. Instantiation.
57. ×. Existential conclusion is $Fa \vdash (\exists x)(Fx)$. Existential premise says, if we have derived "$Fa \vdash$ conclusion", we conclude "$(\exists x)(Fx)$ conclusion."
58. *Cross out.* Conclusion lacks a ")." Otherwise correct instantiation.
59. Instantiation.
60. *Cross out.* Change "*x*" throughout conclusion to, say, "*a*," (or "*b*," etc.).
61. ×.

62. Existential conclusion.
63. ×.
64. *Cross out.* Quantifier lacks brackets.
65. Existential conclusion.
66. ×. For instantiation, reverse premise and conclusion.
67. Existential premise.
68. ×. "*a*" in conclusion.
69. ×. "*a*" in premises.
70. Generalization.
71. $(\forall x)(Fx) \vdash Fa$ Instantiation.
    „ $\vdash (\forall y)(Fy)$ Generalization.
72. $Fa \vdash (\exists y)(Fy)$ Existential conclusion.
    $(\exists x)(Fx) \vdash (\exists y)(Fy)$ Existential premise.
73. $(\forall x)(\forall y)(Fx \,\&\, Gy) \vdash (\forall y)(Fa \,\&\, Gy)$ Instantiation.
    „ $\vdash Fa \,\&\, Gb$ Instantiation.
    „ $\vdash (\forall x)(Fx \,\&\, Gb)$ Generalization.
    „ $\vdash (\forall y)(\forall x)(Fx \,\&\, Gy)$ Generalization.
74. $Fa \,\&\, Gb \vdash (\exists x)(Fx \,\&\, Gb)$ Existential conclusion.
    $Fa \,\&\, Gb \vdash (\exists y)(\exists x)(Fx \,\&\, Gy)$ Existential conclusion.
    $(\exists y)(Fa \,\&\, Gy) \vdash (\exists y)(\exists x)(Fx \,\&\, Gy)$ Existential premise.
    $(\exists x)(\exists y)(Fx \,\&\, Gy) \vdash (\exists y)(\exists x)(Fx \,\&\, Gy)$ Existential premise.

Chapter 27 *Relations*

1. Anne.
2. Is lovely.
3. Anne ⟨is a woman .⟩
4. If *x* is a woman, then *x* is lovely.
5. All women are lovely.
6. Two.
7. *x* is the mother of *y*.
8. *x* is a sister.
9. *x* is a brother.
10. *x* is the sister of *y*.
11. Adam, Cain.
12. Is the father of.
13. *aFc*.
14. *bFa*.
15. (b).
16. (d).
17. (a).
18. (e).
19. (c).
20. No.
21. Paul is Timothy's father.
22. $(\exists x)(xFd)$.
23. $(\exists x)(dFx)$.
24. No.

25. (e).
26. (b).
27. (g).
28. (f).
29. (d).
30. (c).
31. (a).
32. (h).
33. Jupiter is larger than earth.
34. *eLj*.
35. Something is larger than earth.
36. Jupiter is larger than something.
37. *x* is larger than *y*.
38. $(\exists x)(\exists y)(xLy)$.
39. $(\exists x)(\exists y)(xFy)$.
40. The only *correct* answers are: $(\exists z)(\exists w)(zMw)$ and $(\exists y)(\exists x)(yMx)$.
41. $(\forall x)(xLj)$.
42. $(\forall x)(jLx)$.
43. $(\forall x)(xLe)$.
44. $(\forall x)(eLx)$.
45. $(\forall z)(\forall w)(zLw)$, $(\forall x)(\forall y)(xLy)$.
46. (d).
47. (l).
48. ×.
49. (c).
50. ×.
51. (k).
52. (b).
53. ×.
54. (f).
55. (a).
56. ×.
57. (e).
58. (j).
59. (g).
60. ×.
61. (i).
62. (h).
63. *jSe*.
64. $(\exists x)(xSj)$.
65. $(\exists x)(\exists y)(xSy)$.
66. *jSj*.
67. *jSj*.
68. $(\exists x)(xSx)$.
69. $(\forall x)(xSx)$.
70. Everything, something.
71. Everything.
72. Cross out $(\forall x)$(something is larger than *x*).
73. $(\exists x)(jLx)$.

74. Cross out $(\exists y)(\forall x)(x$ is larger than $y)$.
75. Cross out $(\forall x)(\exists y)(yLx)$.
76. Cross out $(\exists x)($everything is larger than $x)$.
77. Cross out $(\forall y)(\exists x)(x$ is larger than $y)$.
78. Cross out $(\exists x)(\forall y)(yLx)$.
79. No.
80. H, I.
81. F, I.
82. G, H.
83. Purtill, Riley, and O'Neill hit Sugar and no-one else.
84. For example: Riley hits all three; the other two policemen do nothing.
85. For example: Purtill hits Peter only.   Riley hits Rachel only.   O'Neill hits Sugar only.
86. For example: Purtill hits Peter only, Riley and O'Neill hit Sugar only.
87. Riley hits Rachel and Sugar only, and Purtill hits Peter only.
88. No.
89. No.
90. Yes.
91. (87) and (86).
92. Outside.
93. There is a.
94. Conjunction.
95. No.
96. Every.
97. Universal.
98. Arrow.
99. x shouts at every policeman.
100. $(\forall y)(y$ is a policeman $\rightarrow x$ shouts at $y)$.
101. Second.
102. First is correct.
103. First is correct.
104. First is correct.
105. Third is correct.
106. Third is correct.
107. Third is correct.
108. Third is correct.
109. Second is correct.
110. First is correct.
111. Third is correct.
112. Third is correct.
113. Second is correct.
114. $(\exists x)(Sx \& (\forall y)(Py \rightarrow xOy))$.
115. $(\exists x)(Px \& (\forall y)(Sy \rightarrow xHy))$.
116. Yes.
117. H.
118. There is a policeman who hits every student.
119. $(\exists x)(Px \& (\forall y)(Sy \rightarrow yOx))$.
120. $(\exists x)(Sx \& (\forall y)(Py \rightarrow yHx))$.
121. $(\forall x)(Sx \rightarrow (\exists y)(Py \& xOy))$.

122. $(\forall x)(Px \rightarrow (\exists y)(Sy \;\&\; xHy))$.
123. $(\forall x)(Px \rightarrow (\exists y)(Sy \;\&\; yOx))$.
124. $(\forall x)(Sx \rightarrow (\exists y)(Py \;\&\; yHx))$.
125. (d).
126. (a).
127. (f).
128. (i).
129. (j).
130. (e).
131. (g).
132. (c).
133. (b).
134. (h).
135. Every newspaper supports some candidate or other.
136. Every candidate is supported by some newspaper or other.
137. There is a candidate not supported by any newspaper.
138. No newspaper supports every candidate.
139. $(\exists x)(Nx \;\&\; (\forall y)(Cy \rightarrow xSy))$.
140. $(\exists x)(Vx \;\&\; -(\exists y)(Cy \;\&\; xSy))$.
141. $(\exists x)(Vx \;\&\; (\forall y)((Cy \;\&\; (\exists z)(Nz \;\&\; zSy)) \rightarrow xSy))$.

Chapter 28 *Kinds of Relation*

1. Yes.
2. Truth tables.
3. No.
4. Invalid.
5. Valid.
6. Valid.
7. No.
8. T.
9. F.
10. Everything is smaller than something or other.
11. No.
12. Yes.
13. Yes.
14. Yes.
15. Yes.
16. Yes.
17. No.
18. No.
19. Yes.
20. No.
21. No.
22. Yes.
23. Every human is older than himself.
24. Every human is exactly as old as himself.
25. (24).

26–37. R: 27, 29, 30, 32, 37.

38. It is hard even to express a simple thing like (38) in English. The following might do:

Given any two humans (possibly but not necessarily different people) if one is older than the other, then the latter is older than the former.

39. Given any two humans, if one is exactly as old as the other, the latter is exactly as old as the former.

40. (39).

41. Does not.

42. S: 27, 29, 35.

43. For any three (not necessarily different) people you choose, if the first is older than the second, and the second is older than the third, then the first is older than the third.

44. The same as 43, but with "exactly as old as" instead of "older than."

45. Yes.

46. T: 26, 27, 30, 31, 32, 33.

47. No.

48. The father of a father of x is grandfather of x not father of x.

49. Yes.

50. (Pasteur is different from Curie, and Curie is different from Pasteur) → (Pasteur is different from Pasteur).

51. Yes.

52. No.

53. No.

54. No.

55. 28. Loves, in the domain of people. Also 34 and 36.

56. 37. Knowing the name of, in the domain of people who know their own names.

57. 35. Different from, in any domain with two or more things in it.

58. 26, 31, and 33 all provide examples.

59. 29. Born within five days of the birthday of, in the domain of people.

60. 30 and 32 both provide examples.

61. 27. Equals, in the domain of whole numbers.

62. T.

63. F.

64. Transitive.

65. Not reflexive.

66. Use 29. Interpretation. R: Born within five days of.
Domain: people.

67. Use 30 or 32. Interpretation. R: No richer than (or, taller than or equal in height to).
Domain: people.

68. Abel is the brother of Abel.

69. No.

70. No.

71. $(xRy \ \& \ yRz) \rightarrow xRz$.

72. $xRy \ \& \ yRz$.

73. xRz.

74. No.

75. No.

76. T.

77. No.

78. Yes.

79. Symmetry requires that for any way of filling in the blanks in

$$xRy \rightarrow yRx$$

in the domain, we get a true statement. In the domain of only sons, the antecedent xRy can never be filled in truly, so the conditional is true and symmetry is satisfied.

80. No.

81. R: Brother of.

82. Domain: Only sons.

83. R: Brother of.

84. Only sons.

85. Sons of Adam.

86. Brother of.

87. Only sons.

Chapter 29 *Prenex Forms*

1–4. Correct: 1, 3.

5. For example: Interpretation: F: President of U.S.A.

a: Bertrand Russell.

Domain: people.

6. For example: Interpretation: F: President of U.S.A.

a: Richard Nixon.

Domain: people.

7–10. Valid: 7, 9.

11. a does not occur in the premises.

12. Generalization.

13. a does not occur in the other premises or in the conclusion.

14. Existential premise.

15. $(\forall x)(x$ is a pacifist $\rightarrow x$ despises every general).

$(\forall x)(x$ is a pacifist $\rightarrow (\forall y)(y$ is a general $\rightarrow x$ despises $y))$.

$(\forall x)(Px \rightarrow (\forall y)(Gy \rightarrow xDy))$.

16. $(\forall x)(Gx \rightarrow (\exists y)(Py \,\&\, xDy))$.

17. Weakening.

18. Existential conclusion.

19. Conditional proof.

20. Weakening.

21. Existential conclusion.

22. Existential premise.

23. Conditional proof.

24. Wedge-arrow.

25. Wedge-arrow.

26. Weakening.

27. Existential conclusion.

28. Conditional proof.
29. Weakening.
30. Existential conclusion.
31. Existential premise.
32. Conditional proof.
33. Instantiation.
34. Wedge-arrow.
35. Generalization.
36. Wedge-arrow.
37. Note that 17–25 is the same as 26–36 aside from the two extra operations 33 and 35.
38. 5.   For *b* occurs in the premise "*Fb*."
    6.   Is not authorized by our rules.
39. No.
40. Deduction.
41. Counterexample.
42. Instantiation.
43. Weakening.
44. Generalization.
45. Yes, both assertions labeled "6" are the same.
46. Logically equivalent.
47. Existential conclusion.
48. Weakening.
49. Conditional Proof.
50. Weakening.
51. Conditional Proof.
52. Alternatives.
53. Wedge-arrow.
54. Detachment, using (6) and (7).
55. Existential premise.
56. Wedge-arrow.
57. Q.
58. Equivalent.
59. $(\exists y)(Q \rightarrow Fy)$.
60. Consequent.
61. $(\forall y)(Q \rightarrow Fy)$.
62. $(\forall x)(Px \rightarrow Sx) \rightarrow Q$.
63. Antecedent.
64. Interpretation.
65. Premise.
66. T.
67. Conclusion.
68. F.
69. False.
70. Antecedent.
71. True.
72. It is true of anything whatsoever, that if it is a fish, the oceans cannot support life.
73. No.

74. The premise is true because the antecedent is false. (It is false that all numbers are smaller than 15). But the conclusion is false. (It is false, for example, of the number 4 that if it is less than 15, then $2 + 2 = 6$.)
75. Yes.
76. Yes.
77. No.
78. $-Q \rightarrow -(\forall x)(Fx)$.
79. $-Q \rightarrow (\exists x)-(Fx)$.
80. $-(Fx)$.
81. $(\exists x)(-Q \rightarrow -Fx)$.
82. Quantifier equivalence.
83. Instantiation.
84. Weakening.
85. Conditional Proof.
86. Weakening.
87. Conditional Proof.
88. Alternatives.
89. Wedge-arrow.
90. Detachment, using 7 and 8.
91. Generalization.
92. Wedge-arrow.
93. Left.
94. No.
95. $(\exists x)(Gx \rightarrow P)$.
96. $(\forall x)(Gx \rightarrow (P \vee Q))$.
97. $(\exists x)(P \rightarrow Fx)$.
98. $(\forall x)((P \ \& \ Q) \rightarrow Gx)$.
99. $(\forall x)(\forall y)(Fx \rightarrow Gy)$ or $(\forall y)(\forall x)(Fx \rightarrow Gy)$.
100. $(\exists y)(Gy)$.
101. $(\forall x)(\forall y)(Fx \rightarrow Gy)$.
102. $(\exists x)(\exists y)(\forall z)((Fx \rightarrow Gx) \rightarrow (Fy \rightarrow Gz))$.

Chapter 30 *Arranging Quantifiers*

1. No.
2. C.
3. Yes.
4. No.
5. B implies A, but A does not imply B.
6. Invalid.
7. Valid.
8. Instantiation.
9. Existential conclusion.
10. Generalization.
11. Existential premise.
12. Step 2 is incorrect. The universal quantifier $(\forall x)$ should have gone outside, yielding $(\forall x)(\exists y)(xVy)$.
13. Generalization at step 1 is incorrect, for "a" is in the premise.

14. No.
15. Counterexample.
16. T.
17. False.
18. Invalid.
19. False.
20. Yes.
21. Yes.
22. Would not.
23. They both took the value T at some row in the truth table.
24. Both are true.
25. Interpretation: V: equals.   Domain: the number 2.
26. We need a relation that is symmetric and reflexive.   We can use, for example, 29 of Chapter 28.   Interpretation: R: born within five days of the birthday of.   Domain: people.
27. We need a relation that is neither reflexive nor transitive.   We can use, for example, 28 of Chapter 28.   Interpretation: R: loves.   Domain: people.
28. We need a relation that is transitive, reflexive, but not symmetric.   We can use 30 of Chapter 28.   Interpretation: R: no richer than.   Domain: people.
29. Consistent.
30. No.
31. Deduction.
32. Counterexample.
33. Inconsistent.
34. Deduction.
35. Counterexample.
36. True.
37. Deduction.   (Deducing a contradiction.)
38. P, Q.
39. T.
40. F.
41. T.
42. T.

Index

Index of Rules of Deduction

Rules About Truth Functional Connectives

Rules About Quantifiers

A summary appears on pages 213–214; *see also*:

About the Author

Ian Hacking has been University Lecturer, Faculty of Philosophy, Cambridge University, since 1969. He received his Ph.D. from Cambridge in 1962. He has also taught at the University of British Columbia; Makerere University College, Kampala, Uganda; and the University of Illinois, Chicago Circle. Dr. Hacking has contributed to numerous professional journals, including the *Journal of Symbolic Logic* and the *Philosophical Review*, and is the author of *Logic of Statistical Inference*.